South Africa

South Africa

Volume One

Anthony Trollope

NONSUCH

First published 1878

Nonsuch Publishing Limited
The Mill, Brimscombe Port, Stroud, Gloucestershire, GL5 2QG
www.nonsuch-publishing.com

British Library Cataloguing in Publication Data.
A catalogue record for this book is available from the British Library.

ISBN 1-84588-047-1
Typesetting and origination by Nonsuch Publishing Limited
Printed in Great Britain by Oaklands Book Services Limited

CONTENTS

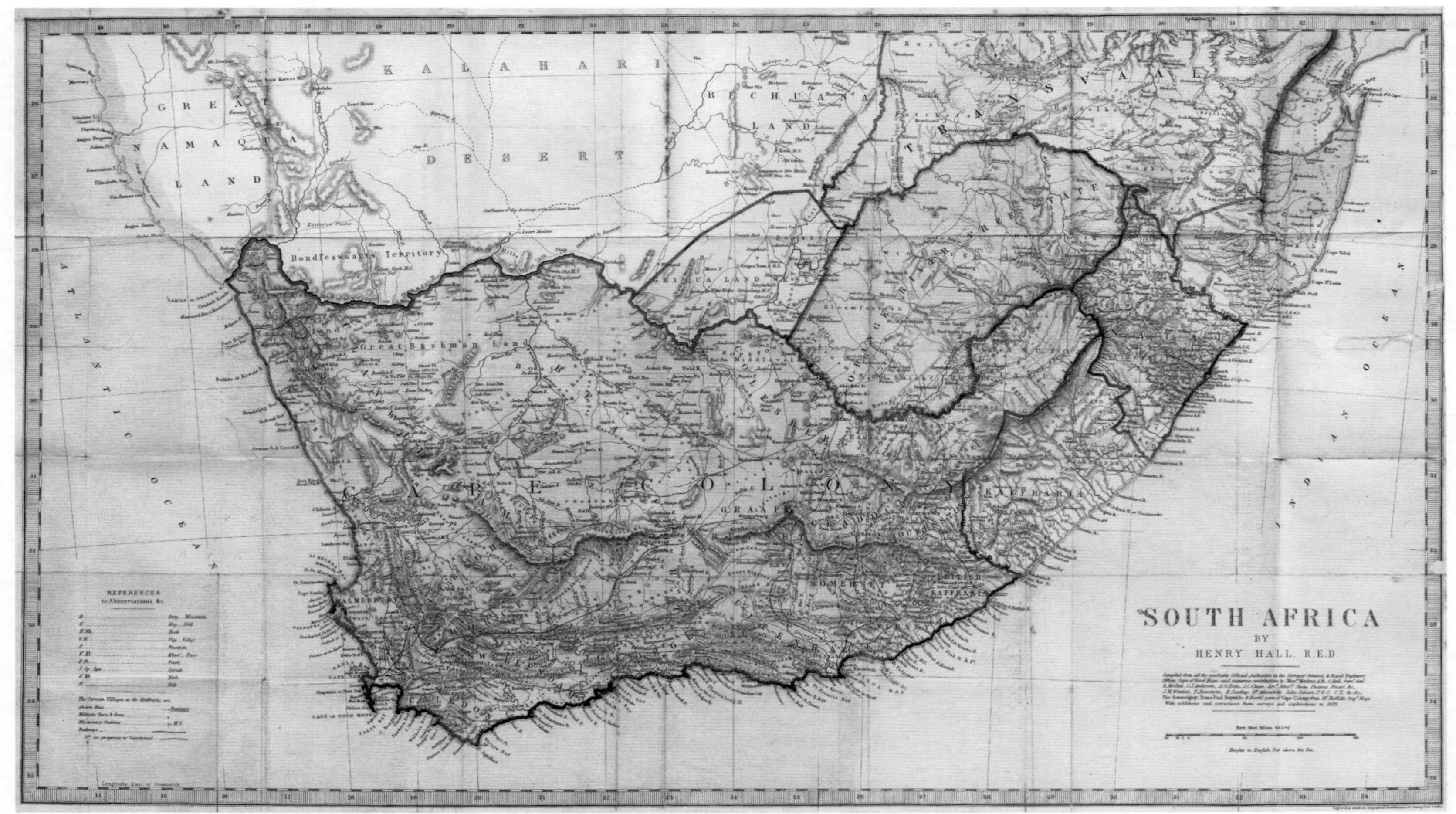
SOUTH AFRICA
BY
HENRY HALL, R.E.D.
REFERENCES
to Abbreviations &c.
KALAHARI
DESERT
GREAT NAMAQUA LAND
BECHUANA LAND
TRANSVAAL
ORANGE FREE STATE
GRIQUA LAND
Bondfezwaart's Territory
Great Bushman Land
CAPE COLONY
KAFFRARIA
BRITISH KAFFRARIA
SOMERSET
GRAAFF
NATAL
ATLANTIC OCEAN
INDIAN OCEAN
CAPE of GOOD HOPE
Longitude East of Greenwich

Introduction to the Modern Edition

ANTHONY TROLLOPE, WAS BORN IN 1815, the son of Thomas Anthony Trollope, a failed barrister, and Frances Trollope, a successful writer. His father's inability to provide for the family meant that his mother was forced to do so, initially by moving to America to sell English goods. The young Trollope was left in England with his father, but his mother's project failed and she returned home, beginning her successful career as an author with *Domestic Manners of the Americans*, published in 1832.

Whether or not Trollope's literary ambition stemmed from his mother's success, he wrote his first book, *The Macdermots of Ballycloran*, a melodramatic tale of seduction and murder in an impoverished Irish family during the Famine, in 1843, although it was not published until 1847, and did not meet with great acclaim. It was not until 'The Warden', the first of his 'Barchester' novels, published in 1855, that Trollope met with the success which he had been hoping for with his earlier works. The final 'Barchester' novel, *The Last Chronicle of Barset*, was published in 1867.

Trollope also had considerable success with a later, more political series, the 'Palliser' novels. Beginning with *Can You Forgive Her?* in 1864 and ending with *The Duke's Children* in 1880, the series is interesting for its sympathetic portrayal of female characters and the restrictions imposed upon them by Victorian society, a theme which he was to revisit in other novels. Trollope combined both comedy and social comment in his novels, although as he got older the latter became more prevalent. Although most of his fictional writings are a critique of nineteenth-century, middle-class English society specifically, they still have relevance today, even to the extent of being adapted for a television audience, most recently *He Knew He Was Right* (1869) and *The Way We Live Now* (1875).

Best known for his forty-seven novels, Trollope also published forty short stories, three biographies and five travel books. He died in 1882.

The South Africa which Anthony Trollope visited in 1877 was a very different place to the Republic which is today one of the largest and most powerful countries in

Africa. Indeed, 'South Africa' did not exist as a single entity: the country which now bears that name was then made up of British colonies, such as Cape Colony and Natal, and the Boer republics of Transvaal and the Orange Free State. Diamonds had been discovered at Kinberley in 1869, but gold would not be found in the Witwatersrand until 1886. The Boer Wars were still to come and Cecil Rhodes and the de Beers Company did not yet run southern Africa as their own private fiefdom. Through Trollope's account of his visit to this area, we are able to see the land as it was before its exploitation for natural resources began in earnest.

When Trollope arrived in South Africa Transvaal, one of the Boer republics, had recently been annexed by the British, although they were to restore its independence four years later. He begins his account of his visit to the country with the history of colonial South Africa, under both the Dutch and the English, before describing his impressions of this breathtaking land. As would have been natural for an Englishman visiting at this time, he begins his journey in Cape Town, the capital of Cape Colony and the gateway to southern Africa. He is not especially impressed with Cape Town itself, but he gives a detailed account of it, including all the most important buildings, before turning his attention to the colony's legislature and executive, of which he is generally approving. He goes on to describe his tour of Western Province of the colony, telling the reader about both the grandeur and beauty of the scenery as well as the towns and villages through which he passed. He visited Fort Elizabeth, Grahamstown and King Williamstown, all of which pleased him far more than Cape Town did, and East London, which he descibes as 'not a nice place.' Before recounting his travels in Natal, he gives a description of education for aboriginal South Africans, of which he has a mixed opinion, and reflects on the general condition of Cape Colony, in particular its economy. In Natal he visited Durban, Pieter Maritzburg and Newcastle, giving the history of the colony and spending some time describing the native inhabitants, the Zulus.

Anthony Trollope's description of his visit to South Africa in 1877 is a comprehensive and extremely well-written account of the country, its history, its people and its landscape. His skill as a writer is as apparent in this travel journal as it is in his novels, and his opinions on this fascinating place are perceptive and penetrating. Although ostensibly visiting South Africa for his own enjoyment, he took great care with his observations and recorded them in meticulous detail. *South Africa* is a book which will appeal to a wide audience, to those with an interest in British colonial history, to those who enjoy reading about distant lands and to fans of Trollope's novels who want to know more about the man himself.

SOUTH AFRICA

CHAPTER I

INTRODUCTION

IT WAS IN APRIL OF last year, 1877, that I first formed a plan of paying an immediate visit to South Africa. The idea that I would one day do so had long loomed in the distance before me. Except the South African group I had seen all our great groups of Colonies,—among which in my own mind I always include the United States, for to my thinking, our colonies are the lands in which our cousins, the descendants of our forefathers, are living and still speaking our language. I had become more or less acquainted I may say with all these offshoots from Great Britain, and had written books about them all,—except South Africa. To "do" South Africa had for some years past been on my mind, till at last there was growing on me the consciousness that I was becoming too old for any more such "doing." Then, suddenly, the newspapers became full of the Transvaal Republic. There was a country not indeed belonging to Great Britain but which once had been almost British, a country, with which Britain was much too closely concerned to ignore it,—a country, which had been occupied by British subjects, and established as a Republic under British authority,—now in danger of being reconquered by the native tribes which had once peopled it. In this country, for the existence of which in its then condition we were in a measure responsible, the white man there would not fight, nor pay taxes, nor make himself conformable to any of these rules by which property and life are made secure. Then we were told that English interference and English interference only could save the country from internecine quarrels between black men and white men. While this was going on I made up my mind that now if ever must I visit South Africa. The question of the Confederation of the States was being mooted at the same time, a Confederation which was to include not only this

Republic which was so very much out of elbows, but also another quiet little Republic of which I think that many of us did not know much at home,—but as to which we had lately heard that it was to receive £90,000 out of the revenue of the Mother Country, not in compensation for any acknowledged wrong, but as a general plaster for what ever little scratches the smaller community, namely the Republic of the Orange Free States, might have received in its encounters with the greater majesty of the British Empire. If a tour to South Africa would ever be interesting, it certainly would be so now. Therefore I made up my mind and began to make enquiries as to steamers, cost, mode of travelling, and letters of introduction. It was while I was doing this that the tidings came upon us like a chip of thunder of the great deed done by Sir Theophilus Shepstone. The Transvaal had already been annexed! The thing which we were dreaming of as just possible,—as an awful task which we might perhaps be forced to undertake in the course of some indefinite number of months to come, had already been effected. A sturdy Englishman had walked into the Republic with five and twenty policemen and a Union Jack and had taken possession of it. "Would the inhabitants of the Republic like to ask me to take it?" So much enquiry he seems to have made. No; the people by the voice of their parliament declined even to consider so monstrous a proposition. "Then I shall take it without being asked," said Sir Theophilus. And he took it.

That was what had just been done in the Transvaal when my idea of going to South Africa had ripened itself into a resolution. Clearly there was an additional reason for going. Here had been done a very high-handed thing as to which it might be the duty of a Briton travelling with a pen in his hand to make a strong remonstrance. Or again it might be his duty to pat that sturdy Briton on the back,—with pen and ink,—and hold his name up to honour as having been sturdy in a righteous cause. If I had premeditated a journey to South Africa a year or two since, when South Africa was certainly not very much in men's mouths, there was much more to reconcile me to the idea now that Confederation and the Transvaal were in every man's mouth.

But when my enquiries which had at first been general came down to minute details, when I was warned by one South African friend that the time I had chosen for my journey was so altogether wrong that I should be sure to find myself in some improvisioned region between two rivers of which I should be as unable to repass the one as to pass the other, and by another that the means of transit through the country were so rough as to be unfit for any except the very strong,—or very slow; when I was assured that the time I had allowed myself was insufficient even to get up to Pretoria and back, I confess that I became alarmed. I shall never forget the portentous shaking of the head of one young man who evidently thought that my friends were neglecting me in that I was allowed to think of such a job of work. Between them all they nearly scared me. Had I not been ashamed to abandon my plan I think I should have gone into the city and begged Mr. Donald Currie to absolve me from responsibility in regard to that comfortable berth which he had promised to secure for me on board the Caldera.

I have usually found warnings to be of no avail, and often to be ill founded. The Bay of Biscay as I have felt it is not much rougher than other seas. No one ever attempted to gouge me in Kentucky or drew a revolver on me in California. I have lived in Paris as cheaply as elsewhere; and have invariably found Jews to be more liberal than other men. Such has been the case with the South African lions which it was presumed that I should find in my path. I have never been stopped by a river and have never been starved; and am now, that the work is done, heartily glad that I made the attempt. Whether my doing so can be of any use in giving information to others will be answered by the fate of my little book which is thus sent upon the waves within twelve months of the time when I first thought of making the journey; but I am sure that I have added something worth having to my own stock of knowledge respecting the Colonies generally.

As I have written the following chapters I think that I have named the various works, antecedent to my own, from which I have made quotations or taken information as to any detail of South African history. I will, however, acknowledge here what I owe to Messrs. Wilmot and Chase's "History of the Colony of the Cape of Good Hope,"—to the "Compendium of South African History and Geography," by George M. Theal, as to which the reader may be interested to know that the entire work in two volumes was printed, and very well printed, by native printers, at Lovedale,—to Mr. John Noble's work, entitled "South Africa, Past and Present,"—to Messrs. Silver and Co.'s "Handbook to South Africa," which of all such works that have ever come into my hands is the most complete; and to the reprints of two courses of lectures, one given by Judge Watermeyer on the Cape Colony, and the other by Judge Cloëte "On the Emigration of the Dutch Farmers." I must also name the "Compendium of Kafir Laws and Customs" collected and published by Col. Maclean, who was at one time Lieut.-Governor of British Kafraria. Were I to continue the list so as to include all the works that I have read or consulted I should have to name almanacks, pamphlets, lectures, letters and blue books to a very great number indeed.

I have a great deal of gratitude to own to gentlemen holding official positions in the different Colonies and districts I have visited, without whose aid my task would have been hopeless. Chief among these have been Captain Mills the Colonial Secretary at Capetown, without whom I cannot presume it possible that the Cape Colony should continue to exist. There is however happily no reason why for many years to come it should be driven to the necessity of even contemplating such an attempt. At Pieter Maritzburg in Natal I found my old friend Napier Broome, and from him and from the Governor's staff generally I received all the assistance that they could give me. At Pretoria Colonel Brooke and Mr. Osborn, who were ruling the Dutchmen in the absence of Sir Theophilus Shepstone, were equally kind to me. At Bloemfontein Mr. Höhne, who is the Government Secretary, was as cordial and communicative as though the Orange Free States were an English Colony and he an English Minister. I must also say that Mr. Brand, the President of the Free States, though he is Dutch to the back bone, and has in his time had some little tussles with what he has thought to be British high-handedness,—in every one of which by-the-bye he has succeeded in achieving something good for his country,—was with me as open and unreserved as though I had been a Dutch Boer, or he a member of the same political club with myself in England. But how shall I mention the full-handed friendship of Major Lanyon, whom I found administering the entangled affairs of Griqualand West,—by which perhaps hitherto unknown names my readers will find, if they go on far enough with the task before them, that the well-known South African Diamond Fields are signified? When last I had seen him, and it seems but a short time ago, he was a pretty little boy with a pretty little frock in Belfast. And there he was among the diamonds carrying on his government in a capital which certainly is not lovely to look at,—which of itself is perhaps the most unlovely city that I know,—but which his kindness succeeded in making agreeable, though not even his kindness could make it other than hideous.

These names I mention because of the information which I have received from their owners. What I owe to the hospitality of the friends I have made in South Africa is a matter private between me and them. I may however perhaps acknowledge the great courtesy which I have received from Sir Bartle Frere and Sir Henry Bulwer, the Governors of the Cape Colony and Natal. As to the former it was a matter of much regret to me that I should not have seen him on my return to Capetown after my travels, when he was still detained at the frontier by the disturbances with Kreli and the Galekas. It was my misfortune not to become personally acquainted with Sir Theophilus Shepstone, who unhappily for me was absent inspecting his new dominion when I was at Pretoria.

I must express my hearty thanks to Sir Henry Barkly, the late Governor of the Cape Colony, who had returned home just before I started from London, and who was kind enough to prepare for me with great minuteness a sketch of my journey, as, in his opinion, it ought to be made, giving me not only a list of the places which I should visit but an estimate of the time which should be allotted to each, so as to turn to the best advantage the months which I had at my disposal.

I have not quite done all which his energy would have exacted from me. I did not get to the Gold-fields of the Transvaal or into Basutoland. But I have followed his guidance throughout, and can certainly testify to the exactness of his knowledge of the country.

My readers will find that in speaking of the three races I found in South Africa, the native tribes namely, the Dutch and the English, I have attributed by far the greater importance to the former because of their numbers. But I fear that I have done so in such a way as not to have conciliated the friends of the aborigines at home, while I shall certainly have insured the hostility,—or at any rate opposition,—of the normal white men in the Colonies. The white man in the South African Colonies feels that the colony ought to be his and kept up for him, because he, perhaps, with his life in his hand, went forth as a pioneer to spread the civilization of Europe and to cultivate the wilds of the world's surface. If he has not done so himself, his father did it before him, and he thinks that the gratitude of the Mother Country should maintain for him the complete ascendency which his superiority to the black man has given him. I feel confident that he will maintain his own ascendency, and think that the Mother Country should take care that that ascendency be not too complete. The colonist will therefore hardly agree with me. The friend of the aborigines, on the other hand, seems to me to ignore the fact,—a fact as it presents itself to my eyes,—that the white man has to be master and the black man servant; and that the best friendship will be shown to the black man by seeing that the terms on which the master and servant shall be brought together are just. In the first place we have to take care that the native shall not be subjected to slavery on any pretence or in any of its forms; and in doing this we shall have to own that compulsory labour, the wages for which are to be settled by the employer without the consent of the employed, is a form of slavery. After that,—after acknowledging so much, and providing against any infraction of the great law so laid down,—the more we do to promote the working of the coloured man, the more successful we are in bringing him into his harness, the better for himself, and for the colony at large. A little garden, a wretched hut, and a great many hymns do not seem to me to bring the man any nearer to civilization. Work alone will civilize him, and his incentive to work should be, and is, the desire to procure those good things which he sees to be in the enjoyment of white men around him. He is quite alive to this desire, and is led into new habits by good eating, good clothes, even by finery and luxuries, much quicker than by hymns and gardens supposed to be just sufficient to maintain an innocent existence. The friend of the aboriginal would, I fear, fain keep his aboriginal separated from the white man; whereas I would wish to see their connexion as close as possible. In this way I fear that I may have fallen between two stools.

In regard to Kreli and his rebellious Galekas,—in regard also to the unsettled state of the Zulus and their borders, I have to ask my readers to remember that my book has been written while these disturbances were in existence. In respect to them I can not do more than express an opinion of my own,—more or less crude as it must necessarily be.

CHAPTER II

EARLY DUTCH HISTORY

OUR POSSESSIONS IN SOUTH AFRICA, like many of our other Colonial territories, were taken by us from others who did the first rough work of discovering and occupying the land. As we got Canada from the French, Jamaica from the Spaniards, and Ceylon from the Dutch, so did we take the Cape of Good Hope from the latter people. In Australia and New Zealand we were the pioneers, and very hard work we found it. So also was it in Massachusetts and Virginia, which have now, happily, passed away from us. But in South Africa the Dutch were the first to deal with the Hottentots and Bushmen; and their task was nearly as hard as that which fell to the lot of Englishmen when they first landed on the coast of Australia with a cargo of convicts.

The Portuguese indeed came before the Dutch, but they only came, and did not stay. The Cape, as far as we know, was first doubled by Bartholomew Diaz in 1486. He, and some of the mariners with him, called it the Cape of Torments, or Capo Tormentoso, from the miseries they endured The more comfortable name which it now bears was given to it by King John of Portugal, as being the new way discovered by his subjects to the glorious Indies. Diaz, it seems, never in truth saw the Cape but was carried past it to Algoa Bay where he merely landed on an island and put up a cross. But he certainly was one of the great naval heroes of the world and deserves to be ranked with Columbus. Vasco da Gama, another sailor hero, said to have been of royal Portuguese descent, followed him in 1497. He landed to the west of the Cape. There the meeting between Savage and Christian was as it has almost always been. At first there was love and friendship, a bartering of goods in which the Christian of course had the advantage, and a general interchange of amenities. Then arose mistakes, so natural among strangers who could not speak to each other, suspicion, violence, and very quickly an internecine quarrel in which the poor Savage was sure to go to the wall. Vasco da Gama did not stay long at the Cape, but proceeding on went up the East Coast as far as our second South African colony, which bears the name which he then gave to it. He called the land Tierra de Natal, because he reached it on the, day of our Lord's Nativity. The name has stuck to it ever since and no doubt will now be preserved. From thence Da Gama went on to India, and we who are interested in the Cape will lose sight of him. But he also was one of the world's mighty mariners,—a man born to endure much, having to deal not only with Savages who mistook him and his purposes, but with frequent mutinies among his own men,—a hero who had ever to do his work with his life in his hand, and to undergo hardships of which our sailors in these happier days know nothing.

The Portuguese seem to have made no settlement at the Cape intended even to be permanent; but they did use the place during the sixteenth and first half of the next century as a port at which they could call for supplies and assistance on their way out to the East Indies.

The East had then become the great goal of commerce to others besides the Portuguese. In 1600 our own East India Company was formed, and in 1602 that of the Dutch. Previous to those dates, in 1591, an English sailor, Captain Lancaster, visited the Cape, and in 1620 Englishmen landed and took possession of it in the name of James I. But nothing came of these visitings and declarations, although an attempt was made by Great Britain to establish a house of call for her trade out to the East. For this purpose a small gang of convicts was deposited on Robben Island, which is just off Capetown, but as a matter of course the convicts quarrelled with themselves and the Natives, and came to a speedy end. In 1595 the Dutch came, but did not then remain. It was not till 1652 that the first Europeans who were destined to be the pioneer occupants of the new land were put on shore at the Cape of Good Hope, and thus made the first Dutch settlement. Previous to that the Cape had in fact been a place of call for vessels of all nations going and coming to and from the East. But from this date, 1652, it was to be used for the Dutch exclusively. The Hollanders of that day were stanch Protestants and sound Christians, but they hardly understood their duty to their neighbours. They had two ideas in forming their establishment at the Cape;—firstly that of aiding their own commerce with the East, and secondly that of debarring the commerce of all other nations from the aid which they sought for themselves. It is on record that when a French merchant-vessel was once treated with hospitality by the authorities at the Cape, the authorities at home brought their colonial dependents very severely to task for such forgetfulness of their duty. The Governor at the time was dismissed for not allowing the Frenchman to "float on his own fins." It was then decided that water should be given to Europeans in want of it, but as little other refreshment as possible.

The home Authority at this time was not the Dutch Government, but the Council of Seventeen at Amsterdam, who were the Directors of the Dutch East India Company. For, as with us, the commercial enterprise with the East was a monopoly given over to a great Company, and this Company for the furtherance of its own business established a depôt at the Cape of Good Hope. When therefore we read of the Dutch Governors we are reading of the servants not of the nation but of a commercial firm. And yet these Governors, with the aid of their burgher council, had full power over life and limb.

Jan van Riebeek was the first Governor, a man who seems to have had a profound sense of the difficulties and responsibilities of his melancholy position, and to have done his duty well amidst great suffering, till at last, after many petitions for his own recall, he was released. He was there for ten sad years, and seems to have ruled,—no doubt necessarily,—with a stern hand. The records of the little corn at this time are both touching and amusing, the tragedy being interspersed with much comedy. In the first year Volunteer Van Vogelaar was sentenced to receive a hundred blows from the butt of his own musket for "wishing the purser at the devil for serving out penguins instead of pork." Whether the despatch devilwards of the purser or of Van Vogelaar was most expedited by this occurrence we are not told. Then the chaplain's wife had a child, and we learn that all the other married ladies hurried on to follow so good an example. But the ladies generally did not escape the malice of evil tongues. Early in the days of the establishment one Woüters was sentenced to have his tongue bored, to be banished for three years, and to beg pardon on his bare knees for speaking ill of the Commander's wife and of other females. It is added that he would not have been let off so lightly but that his wife was just then about to prove herself a good citizen by adding to the population of the little community. In 1653, the second year of Van Riebeek's government, we are told that the lions seemed as though they were going to take the fort by storm, and that a wolf seized a sheep within sight of the herds. We afterwards hear that a dreadful ourang-outang was found, as big as a calf.

From 1658, when the place was but six years old, then comes a very sad record indeed. The first cargo of slave was landed at the Cape from the Guinea Coast. In this year, out of an entire population of 360, more than a half were slaves. The total number of these was 187. To control them and to defend the place there were but 113 European men capable of bearing arms. This slave element at once became antagonistic to any system of real colonization, and from that day to this has done more than any other evil to retard the progress of the people. It was extinguished, much to the disgust of the old Dutch inhabitants, under Mr. Buxton's Emancipation Act in 1834;—but its effects are still felt.

In 1666 two men were flogged and sentenced to work in irons for three years for stealing cabbages. Terrible severity seems to have been the only idea of government. Those who were able to produce more than they consumed were allowed to sell to no purchaser except the Company. Even the free men, the so-called burghers, were little better than slaves, and were bound to perform their military duties with almost more than Dutch accuracy. Time was kept by the turning of an official hour glass, for which purpose two soldiers called Rondegangers were kept on duty, one to relieve the other through the day and night. And everything was done vigorously by clockwork,—or hour-glass work rather; the Senate sitting punctually at nine for their executive and political duties. A soldier, if he was found sleeping at his post, was tied to a triangle and beaten by relays of flagellators. Everything was done in accordance with the ideas of a military despotism, in which, however, the Commander-in-chief was assisted by a Council or Senate.

And there was need for despotism. Food often ran short, so that penguins had to be supplied in lieu of pork,—to the infinite disgust we should imagine of others besides poor Van Vogelaar. It often became a serious question whether the garrison,—for then it was little more than a garrison,—would produce food sufficient for their need. But this was not the only or the worse trouble to which the Governor was subjected. The new land of which he had taken possession was by no means unoccupied or unpossessed. There was a race of savages in possession, to whom the Dutch soon gave the name of Hottentots[1], and who were friendly enough as long as they thought that they were getting more than they gave; but, as has always been the case in the growing relations between Christians and Savages, the Savages quickly began to understand they were made to have the worst in every bargain. Soon after the settlement was established the burghers were forbidden to trade with these people at all, and then hostilities commenced. The Hottentots found that much, in the way of land, had been taken from them and that nothing was to be got. They too, Savages though they were, became logical, and asked whether they would be allowed to enter Holland and do there as the Dutch were doing with them. "You come," they said, "quite into the interior, selecting our best land, and never asking whether we like it;"—thus showing that they had made themselves accustomed to the calling of strangers at their point of land, and that they had not objected to such mere calling, because something had always been left behind; but that this going into the interior and taking from them their best land was quite a different thing. They understood the nature of pasture land very well, and argued that if the Dutchmen had many cattle there would be but little grass left for themselves. And so there arose a war.

The Hottentots themselves have not received, as Savages, a bad character. They are said to have possessed fidelity, attachment, and intelligence; to have been generally good to their children; to have believed in the immortality of the soul, and to have worshipped a god. The Hottentot possessed property and appreciated its value. He was not naturally cruel, and was prone rather to submit than to fight. The Bosjesman, or Bushman, was of a lower order, smaller in stature, more degraded in appearance, filthier in his habits, occasionally a cannibal eating his own children when driven by hunger, cruel, and useless. Even he was something better than the Australian aboriginal, but was very inferior to his near relative the Hottentot.

But the Hottentot, with all his virtues, was driven into rebellion. There was some fighting in which the natives of course were beaten, and rewards were offered, so much for a live Hottentot, and so much for a dead one. This went on till, in 1672, it was found expedient to purchase land from the natives. A contract was made in that year to prevent future cavilling, as was then alleged, between the Governor and one of the native princes, by which the district of the Cape of Good Hope was ceded to the Dutch for a certain nominal price. The deed is signed with the marks of two Hottentot chiefs and with the names of two Dutchmen. The purchase was made simply as an easy way out of the difficulty. But after a very early period—1684—there was no further buying of land. "There was no longer affectation of a desire on the part of the Dutch authority as we are told by Judge Watermeyer, "that native claims to land should be respected." The land was then annexed by Europeans as convenience required.

In all this the Dutch of those days did very much as the English have done since. Of all the questions which a conscientious man has ever had to decide, this is one of the most difficult. The land clearly belongs to the habitants of it,—by as good a title as England belongs to the English or Holland to the Dutch. But the advantage of spreading population is so manifest, and the necessity of doing so has so clearly been indicated to by nature, that no man, let him be ever so conscientious, will say that throngs of human beings from the over-populated civilized countries should refrain from spreading themselves over unoccupied countries or countries partially occupied by savage races. Such a doctrine would be monstrous, and could be held only by a fanatic in morality. And yet there always comes a crisis in which the stronger, the more civilized, and the Christian race is called upon to inflict a terrible injustice on the unoffending owner of the land. Attempts have been made to purchase every acre needed by the new comers,—very conspicuously in New Zealand. But such attempts never can do justice to the Savage. The savage man from his nature can understand nothing of the real value of the article to be sold. The price must be settled by the purchaser, and he on the other side has no means of ascertaining who in truth has the right to sell, and cannot know to whom the purchase money should be paid. But he does know that he must have the land. He feels that in spreading himself over the earth he is carrying out God's purpose, and has no idea of giving way before this difficulty. He tries to harden his heart against the Savage, and gradually does so in spite of is own conscience. The man is a nuisance and must be made to go. Generally he has gone rapidly enough. The contact with civilization does not suit his nature. We are told that he takes the white man's vices and ignores the white man's virtues. In truth vices are always more attractive than virtues. To drink is easy and pleasant. To love your neighbour as yourself is very difficult, and sometimes unpleasant. So the Savage has taken to drink, and has worn his very clothes unwholesomely, and has generally perished during the process of civilization. The North American Indian, the Australian Aboriginal, the Maori of New Zealand are either going or gone,—and so in these lands there has come, or is coming, an end of trouble from that source.

The Hottentot too of whom we have been speaking is said to be nearly gone, and, being a yellow man, to have lacked strength to endure European seductions. But as to the Hottentot and his fate there are varied opinions. I have been told by some that I have never seen a pure Hottentot. Using my own eyes and my own idea of what Hottentot is, I should have said that the bulk of the population of the Western Province of the Cape Colony is Hottentot. The truth probably is that they have become so mingled with other races as to have lost much of their identity; but that the race has not perished, as have the Indians of North America and the Maoris. The difficulty as to the Savage has at any rate not been solved, in South Africa as in other countries in which our Colonies have settled themselves. The Kafir with his numerous varieties of race is still here, and is by no means inclined, to go. And for this reason South Africa at present differs altogether from the other lands from which white Colonists have driven the native inhabitants. Of these races I shall have to speak further as I go on with my task.

In 1687 and 1689 there arrived at the Cape a body of emigrants whose presence has no doubt had much effect creating the race which now occupies the land, and without whom probably the settlers could not have made such progress as they did effect. These were Protestant Frenchmen who in consequence of the revocation of the Edict of Nantes were in want of a home in which they could exercise their religion in freedom. These arrived to the number of about 300, and the names of most of them have been duly recorded. Very many of the same names are now to be found through the Colony—to such an extent as to make the stranger ask why the infant settlement should have been held to exclusively Dutch. These Frenchmen, who were placed out round the Cape as agriculturists, were useful, industrious religious people. But though they grew and multiplied they also had their troubles, and hardly enjoyed all the freedom which they had expected. The Dutch, indeed appear to have had no idea of freedom either as to private life, political life, or religious life. Gradually they succeeded in imposing their own language upon the new corners. In 1709 the use of French was forbidden in all public matters, and in 1724 the services of the French Church were for the last time performed in the French language. Before the end of the last century the language was gone. Thus the French corners with their descendants were forced by an iron hand into Dutch moulds, and now nothing is left to them of their old country but their names. When one meets a Du Plessis or a De Villiers it is impossible to escape the memory of the French immigration.

The last half of the seventeenth and the whole of the eighteenth century saw the gradual progress of the Dutch depôt,—a colony it could hardly be called,—going on in the same slow determined way, and always with the same purpose. It was no colony because those who managed it at home in Holland, and they who at the Cape served with admirable fidelity their Dutch masters, never entertained an idea as to the colonization of the country. A half-way house to India was erected by the Dutch East India Company for the purpose of commerce, and it was necessary that a community should be maintained at the Cape for this purpose. The less of trouble, the less of expense, the less of anything beyond mechanical service with which the work could be carried on, the better. It was not for the good of the Dutchmen who were sent out or of the Frenchmen who joined them, that the Council of 17 at Amsterdam troubled with the matter; but because by doing so they could assist their own trade and add to their own gains. Judge Watermeyer in one of three lectures which he gave on the state of the Colony under the Dutch quotes the following opinion on colonization from a Dutch Attorney General of the time. "The object of paramount importance in legislation for Colonies should be the welfare of the parent State of which the Colony is but a subordinate part and to which it owes its existence!" I need hardly point out that the present British theory of colonization is exactly the reverse of this. Some of those prosperous but by no means benevolent looking old gentlemen with gold chains, as we see them painted by Rembrandt and other Dutch Masters, were no doubt the owners of the Cape and its inhabitants. Slave labour was the readiest labour, and therefore slave labour was procured. The native races were not to be oppressed beyond endurance, because they would rise and fight. The community itself was not to grow rich, because if rich it would no longer be subservient to its masters. In the midst of all this there were fine qualities. The Governors were brave, stanch, and faithful. The people were brave and industrious,—and were not self-indulgent except with occasional festivities in which drunkenness was permissible. The wonder is that for so long a time they should have been so submissive, so serviceable, and yet have had so little of the sweets of life to enjoy.

There were some to whom the austerities of Dutch rule proved too hard for endurance, and these men moved away without permission into further districts in which they might live a free though hard life. In other words they "trekked," as the practice has been called to this day. This system has been the mode of escape from the thraldom of government which has been open to all inhabitants of South Africa. Men when they have been dissatisfied have gone away, always intending to get beyond the arm of the existing law; but as they have gone, the law has of necessity followed at their heels. An outlawed crew on the borders of any colony or settlement must be ruinous to it. And therefore far as white men have trekked, government has trekked after them, as we shall find when we come by and bye to speak of Natal, the Orange Free State, and the Transvaal.

In 1795 came the English. In that year the French Republican troops had taken possession of Holland, and the Prince of Orange, after the manner of dethroned potentates, took refuge in England. He gave an authority, which was dated from Kew, to the Governor of the Cape to deliver up all and everything in his hands to the English forces. On the arrival of the English fleet there was found to be, at the same time, a colonist rebellion. Certain distant burghers,—for the territory had of course grown,—refused to obey the officers of the Company or to contribute to the taxes. In this double emergency the poor Dutch Governor, who does not seem to have regarded the Prince's order as an authority, was sorely puzzled. He fought a little, but only a little, and then the English were in possession. The castle was given up to General Craig, and in 1797 Lord Macartney came out as the first British Governor.

Great Britain at this time took possession of the Cape to prevent the French from doing so. No doubt it was a most desirable possession, as being a half-way house for us to India as it had been for the Dutch. But we should not, at any rate then, have touched the place had it not been that Holland, or rather the Dutch, were manifestly unable to retain it. We spent a great deal of money at the settlement, built military works, and maintained a large garrison. But it was but for a short time, and during that short time our rule over the Dutchmen was uneasy and unprofitable. Something of rebellion seems to have been going on during the whole time,—not so much against English authority as against Dutch law, and this rebellion was complicated by continual quarrels between the distant Boers, or Dutch farmers, and the Hottentots. It was an uncomfortable possession, and when at the peace of Amiens in 1802 it was arranged that the Cape of Good Hope should be restored to Holland, English Ministers of State did not probably grieve much at the loss. At this time the population of the Colony is supposed to have been 61,947, which was divided as follows:—

Europeans	21,746
Slaves	25,754
Hottentots	14, 447

But the peace of Amiens was delusive, and there was soon war between England and France. Then again Great Britain felt the necessity of taking the Cape, and proceeded to do so on this occasion without any semblance of Dutch authority. At that time whatever belonged to Holland was almost certain to fall into the hands of France. In 1805 while the battle of Austerlitz was making Napoleon a hero on land, and Trafalgar was proving the heroism of England on the seas, Sir David Baird was sent with half a dozen regiments to expel, not the Dutch, but the Dutch Governor and the Dutch soldiers from the Cape. This he did easily, having encountered some slender resistance; and thus in 1806, on the 19th January, after a century and a half of Dutch rule, the Cape of Good Hope became a British Colony.

It should perhaps be stated that on the restoration of the Cape to Holland the dominion was not given back to the Dutch East India Company, but was maintained by the Government at the Hague. The immediate consequence of this was a great improvement in the laws, and considerable relaxation of tyranny. Of this we of course had the full benefit, as we entered in upon our work with the idea of maintaining in most things the Dutch system.

1. The name was probably taken from some sound in their language which was of frequent occurrence. They seem to have been called "Ottentoos," "Hotnots," "Hottentotes," "Hodmodods," and "Hadmandods" promiscuously.

CHAPTER III

ENGLISH HISTORY

I HAVE TO SAY THAT I feel almost ashamed of the headings given to these initiatory chapters of my book as I certainly am not qualified to write a history of South Africa. Nor, were I able to do so, could it be done in a few pages. And, again, it has already been done and that so recently that there is not as yet need for further work of the kind. But it is not possible to make intelligible the present condition of any land without some reference to its antecedents. And as it is my object to give my reader an idea of the country as I saw it I am obliged to tell something of what I myself found it necessary to learn before I could understand that which I heard and saw. When I left England I had some notion more or less correct as to Hottentots, Bushmen, Kafirs, and Zulus. Since that my mind has gradually become permeated with Basutos, Griquas, Bechuanas, Amapondos, Suazies, Gaikas, Galekas, and various other native races,—who are supposed to have disturbed our serenity in South Africa, but whose serenity we must also have disturbed very much,—till it has become impossible to look at the picture without realizing something of the identity of those people. I do not expect to bring any readers to do that. I perhaps have been filling my mind with the subject for as many months as the ordinary reader will take hours in turning over these pages. But still I must ask him to go back a little with me, or, as I go on, I shall find myself writing as though I presumed that things were known to him, as to which if he have learned much, it may be unnecessary that he should look at my book at all.

The English began their work with considerable success. The Dutch laws were retained, but were executed with mitigated severity; a large military force was maintained in the Colony, numbering from four to five thousand men, which of course created a ready market for the produce of the country; and there was a Governor with almost royal appanages and a salary of £12,000 a year,—as much probably, when the change in the value of money is considered, as the Governor-General of India has now. Men might sell and buy as they pleased, and the intolerable strictness of Dutch colonial rule was abated. Whatever Dutch patriotism might say, the English with their money were no doubt very welcome at first, and especially at or in the neighbourhood of Capetown. We are told that Lord Caledon, who was the first regular Governor after the return of the English, was very popular. But troubles soon came, and we at once hear the dreaded name of Kafir.[1]

In 1811 the Dutch Boers had stretched themselves as far east as the country round Graff Reynet,—for which I must refer my reader to the map. Between the Dutch and the Kafirs a neutral district had been established in the vain hope of maintaining limits. Over this district the Kafirs came plundering,—no doubt thinking that they were exercising themselves in the legitimate and patriotic defence of their own land. The Dutch inhabitants of course called for Government aid, and such aid was forthcoming. An officer sent to report on the matter recommended that all the Kafirs should be expelled from the Colony, and that the district called the Zuurveld,—a district which by treaty had been left to the Kafirs,—should be divided among white farmers. "This," says the chronicler, "was hardly in accordance with the agreement with Ngquika, but necessity has no law." The man whose name has thus been imperfectly reduced to letters was the Kafir chieftain of that ilk, and is the same as the word Gaika now used for a tribe of British subjects. Necessity we all know has no law. But what is necessity? A man must die. A man, generally, must work or go to the wall. But need a man establish himself as a farmer on another man's land? The reader will understand that I do not deny the necessity;—but that I feel myself to be arrested when I hear it asserted as sufficient excuse.

The Dutch never raised a question as to the necessity. The English have in latter days continually raised the question, but have so acted that they have been able to argue as sufferers while they have been the aggressors. On this occasion the necessity was allowed. A force was sent, and a gallant Dutch magistrate, one Stockenstroom, who trusted himself among the Kafirs, was, with his followers, murdered by them. Then came the first Kafir war. We are told that no quarter was given by the white men, no prisoners taken;—that all were slaughtered, till the people were driven backwards and eastwards across the Great Fish River. This, the first Kafir war, took place in 1811.

The next and quickly succeeding trouble was of another kind. There have been the two great troubles;—the contests between the white men and the savages, and then the contests between the settled colonists and those who have ever been seceding or "trekking" backwards from the settlements. These latter have been generally, though by no means exclusively, Dutchmen; and it is of them we speak when we talk of the South African up-country Boers. These men, among other habits of their time, had of course been used to slavery;—and though the slavery of the Colony had never been of its nature cruel, it had of course been open to cruelty. Laws were made for the protection of slaves, and these laws were unpalatable to the Boer who wished to live in what he called freedom,—"to do what he liked with his own," according to the Duke of Newcastle,—"to do what he dam pleased," as the American of the South used to say. A certain Dutchman named Bezuidenhout refused to obey the law, and hence there arose a fight between a party of Dutch who swore that they would die to a man rather than submit, and the armed British authorities. The originator of the rebellion was shot down. The Dutch invited the Kafirs to join them; but the Kafir chief declared that as sparks were flying about, he would like to wait and see which way the wind blew. But the battle went on, and of course the rebels were beaten. There then followed an act of justice combined with vengeance. The leaders were tried and six men were condemned to be hanged. That may have been right;—but their friends and relatives were condemned to see them executed. That must have been wrong, and in the result was most unfortunate. Five of the six were hanged,—while thirty others had to stand by and see. The place of execution was called Slagter's Nek, a name long remembered by the retreating Dutch Boers. But they were hanged,—not simply once, but twice over. The apparatus, overweighted with the number, broke down when the poor wretches dropped from the platform. They were half killed by the ropes, but gradually struggled back to life. Then there arose prayers that they might now at least be spared;—and force was attempted, but in vain. The British officer had to see that they were hanged, and hanged they were a second time, after the interval of man hours spent in constructing a second gallows. They were all Dutchmen, and the Dutch implacable Boer has said ever since that he cannot forget Slagter's Nek. It was the followers and friends of these men who trekked away northwards and eastwards till after many a bloody battle with the natives they at last came to Natal.

From this time the Colony went on with a repetition of those two troubles,—war with the Kafirs and disturbances with other native races, and an ever-increasing disposition on the part of the European Colonists to go backwards so that they might live after their own fashion and not be forced to treat either slaves or natives according to humanitarian laws. While this was going on the customary attempts were made to civilize and improve both the colonists and the natives. Schools, libraries, and public gardens were founded, and missionaries settled themselves among the Kafirs and other coloured people. The public institutions were not very good, nor were the missionaries very wise;—but some good was done. The Governors who were sent out were of course various in calibre. Lord Charles Somerset, who reigned for nearly twelve consecutive years, is said to have been very arbitrary; but the Colony prospered in spite of Kafir wars. From time to time further additions were made to our territories, always of course at the expense of the native races. In 1819 the Kafirs were driven back behind the Keiskamma River; where is the region now called British Kafraria,—which was then allowed to be Kafirs' land. Since that they have been compressed behind the Kei River, where lies what is now called Kafraria Proper. Whether it will continue "proper" to the Kafirs is hardly now matter of doubt. I may say that a considerable portion of it has been already annexed.

In 1820 it was determined to people the districts from which the natives had last been driven by English emigrants. The fertility of the land and the salubrity of the climate had been so loudly praised that there was no difficulty in procuring volunteers for the purpose. The applications from intending emigrants were numerous, and from these four thousand were selected, and sent out at the expense of Government to Algoa Bay;—where is Port Elizabeth, about four hundred miles west of Capetown. Hence have sprung the inhabitants of the Eastern Province, which is as English as the Western Province is Dutch. And hence has come that desire for separation,—for division into an Eastern and a Western Colony, which for a long time distracted the Colonial Authorities both at home and abroad. The English there have prospered better than their old Dutch neighbours,—at any rate as far as commerce is concerned. The business done in Algoa Bay is of a more lively and prosperous kind than that transacted at Capetown. Hence have arisen jealousies, and it may easily be understood that when the question of Colonial Parliaments arose, the English at Algoa Bay thought it beneath them to be carried off, for the purpose of making laws, to Capetown.

It was from the coming of these people that the English language began to prevail in the Colony. Until 1825 all public business was done in Dutch. Proceedings in the law courts were carried on in that language even later than that,—and it was not till 1828 that the despatches of Government were sent out in English. The language of social and commercial life can never be altered by edicts, but gradually, from this time the English began to be found the most convenient. Now it is general everywhere in the Colony, though of course Dutch is still spoken by the descendants of the Dutch among themselves: and church services in the Lutheran churches are performed in Dutch. It will probably take another century to expel the language. In 1825 the despotism of the Governors was lessened by the appointment of a Council of seven, which may be regarded as the first infant step towards Parliamentary institutions; and in 1828 the old Dutch courts of Landdrosts and Neemraden were abolished, and resident magistrates and justices were appointed.

But in the same year a much greater measure was accomplished. A very minority of liberal-minded men in the Colony, headed by Dr. Philip, the missionary, bestirred them on behalf of the Hottentots, who were in a condition very little superior to that of absolute slavery. The question was stirred in England, and was taken up by Mr. Buxton, who gave notice of a motion in the House of Commons on the subject. But the Secretary of State for the Colonies was beforehand with Mr. Buxton, and declared in the House that the Government would grant all that was demanded. The Hottentots were put on precisely the same footing as the Europeans, much to the disgust of the Colonists in general and of the rulers of the Colony. So much was this understood at home, and so determined was the Home Government that the colonial feeling on the matter should not prevail, that a clause was added to the enactment declaring that it should not be competent for any future Colonial Government to rescind its provisions.

To argue as to the wisdom and humanity of such a measure now would be futile. The question has so far settled itself that no one dreams of supposing that a man's social rights should be influenced by colour or race. But these Dutchmen and English knew very well that a lot could not be made to be equal in intelligence or moral sense to a European, and they should I think be pardoned for the ill will with which they accepted the change. And this becomes the more clear to us when we remember that slavery was at the time still an institution of the country, and that the slaves, who were an imported people from the Straits and the Guinea Coast, were at any rate equal in intelligence to the Hottentots.

Six years afterwards, in 1834, slavery itself was abolished in all lands subject to the British flag,—and this created even a greater animosity among the Dutch than the enactments in favour of the Hottentots. Perhaps no one thing has so strongly tended to alienate the Boer from us as this measure and the way in which it was carried out. In the first place the institution of slavery recommended itself entirely to the Dutch mind. Taking him altogether we shall own that he was not a cruel slave owner; but he was one to whom slavery of itself was in no way repugnant. That he as the master should have a command of labour seemed to him to be only natural. To throw away this command for the sake of putting the slave into a condition which,—as the Dutchman thought,—would be worse for the slave himself was to him an absurdity. He regarded the matter as we regard the doctrine of equality. The very humanitarianism of it was to him a disgusting pretence. The same feeling exists still. It strikes one at every corner in the Colony. A ready mode to comfort, wealth, and general prosperity was, as the Dutch man thinks,—and also some who are not Dutch,—absolutely thrown away. Then came the question of compensation. Some of us are old enough to remember the difficulty in distributing the twenty millions which were voted for the slave owners. The slaves of the Cape Colony were numbered at 35,745, and were valued at £3,000,000. The amount of money which was allowed for them was £1,200,000. But even this was paid in such a manner that much of it fell into the hands of fraudulent agents before it reached the Boer. There was delay and the orders for the money were negotiated at a great discount. The sum expected dwindled down to so paltry a sum that some of the farmers refused to accept what was due to them. Then there was further trekking away from a land which in the minds of the emigrants was so abominably mismanaged. But the slaves fell into the body of the coloured population without any distinction, and were added of course to the free labour of the country. The ordinary labourer in all countries earns so little more than board lodging and clothes for himself and his children, and it is so indispensable a necessity on the slave owner to provide board lodgings and clothes for his slaves, that the loss of slaves, when all owners lose them together, ought not to impoverish any one. There may be local circumstances, as there were in Jamaica, which upset the working of this rule. In the Cape Colony there were no such circumstances; and it seems that those who remained and accepted the law were not impoverished. There can be no doubt, however, that the inhabitants of the Colony generally were disgusted. The measure was brought into effect in 1838, an apprenticeship of four years having been allowed.

But we must go back for a moment to the Kafir war of l835,—third Kafir war, for there was a second, of which as being less material I have spared the reader any special mention. Of all our Kafir wars this was probably the most bitter. There had been continual contests, in all of which the Kafirs had undoubtedly thought themselves to be ill used, but in all of which the evils inflicted upon them had been perpetrated in punishment and reprisal for thefts of cattle. The Kafir thefts were in comparison small but were often repeated. Then the Europeans sent out what were called "Commandos,"—which consisted of an armed levy of mounted men intent upon seizing cattle by way of restitution. The reader of the histories of the period is compelled to think that the unfortunate cattle were always being driven backwards and forwards over the borders. During the period, however, more than once cattle were restored by the colonists to the Kafirs which were supposed to have been taken from them in excess of just demands. In December 1834 this state of things was brought to a crisis by an attempt which was made by a party of Europeans to recover some stolen horses. Some cattle were seized, and others were voluntarily surrendered, but the result was that in December a large body of Kafirs invaded the European lands, and massacred the farmers, to their hearts' content. They overran the border country to the number of ten or twelve thousand, and then returned, carrying with them an immense booty. It all reads as a story out of Livy, in which the Volsci will devastate the Roman pastures and then return with their prey to one of their own cities. The reader is sure that the Romans are going to get the best of it at last;—but in the meantime the Roman people are nearly ruined.

Sir Benjamin D'Urban was then Governor, and he took strong and ultimately successful steps to punish the Kafirs. I have not space here to tell how Hintsa, the Kafir chief, was shot down as he was attempting to escape from the British whom he had undertaken to guide through his country, or how the Kafirs were at last driven to sue for peace and to surrender the sovereignty of their country. The war was not only bloody, but ruinous to thousands. The cattle were of course destroyed, so that no one was enriched. Ill blood, of which the effects still remain, was engendered. Three hundred thousand pounds were spent by the British. But at last the Kafirs were supposed to have been conquered, and Sir Benjamin D'Urban supposed to be triumphant.

The triumph, however, to Sir Benjamin D'Urban was not long-lived. At this time Lord Glenelg was Secretary of State for the Colonies in England, and Lord Glenelg was a man subject to what I may perhaps not improperly call the influences of Exeter Hall. When the full report of the Kafir war reached him a certain party at home had been loud in expressions of pity and perhaps of admiration for the South African races. Hottentots and Kafirs had been taken home,—or at any rate a Hottentot and a Kafir,—and had been much admired. No doubt Lord Glenelg gave his best attention to the reports sent to him;—no doubt he consulted those around him;—certainly without doubt he acted in accordance with his conscience and with a full appreciation of the greatness of the responsibility resting upon him;—but I think he acted with very bad judgment. He utterly repudiated what Sir Benjamin D'Urban had done, and asserted that the Kafirs had had "ample justification" for the late war. He declared in his despatch that "they had a perfect right to hazard the experiment of extorting by force that redress which they could not expect otherwise to obtain," and he caused to be returned to the Kafirs the land from which they had been driven,—which land has since that again become a part of the British Colony. There was a correspondence in which Sir B. D'Urban supported his own views,—but this ended in the withdrawal of the Governor in 1838, Lord Glenelg declaring that he was willing to take upon himself the full responsibility of what he had done, and of all that might come from it.

I think I am justified in saying that since that time public opinion has decided against Lord Glenelg, and has attributed to his mistake the further Kafir wars of 1846 and 1850. It is often very difficult in the beginning of such quarrels to say who is in the right, the Savage or the civilized invader of the country. The Savage does not understand the laws as to promises, treaties, and mutual compacts which we endeavour to impose upon him, and we on the other hand are deter mined to live upon his land whether our doing so be just or unjust. In such a condition of things we,—meaning the civilized intruders,—are obliged to defend our position. We cannot consent to have our throats cut when we have taken the land, because our title to possession is faulty. If ever a Governor was bound to interfere for the military defence of his people, Sir Benjamin D'Urban was so bound. If ever a Savage was taken red-handed in treachery, Hintsa was so taken, and was so shot down. The full carrying out of Lord Glenelg's views would have required us to give back all the country to the Hottentots, to compensate the Dutch for our interference, and to go back to Europe. Surely no man was ever so sorely punished for the adequate performance of a most painful public duty as Sir Benjamin D'Urban.

In 1838 slavery was abolished;—and as one of the consequences of that abolition, the Dutch farmers again receded. Their lands were occupied by the English and Scotch who followed them, and in the hands of these men the growth of wool began to prevail. Merino sheep were introduced, and wool became the most important production of the colony.

During the whole of this period the practice was continued by the old-fashioned farmers of receding from their farms in quest of new lands in which they might live without interference. The Colony in spite of Kafirs had prospered under English rule, whilst the Dutch farmers had no doubt enjoyed the progress as well as their English neighbours. Their condition was infinitely more free than it had ever been under Dutch rule, and very much more comfortable. But still they were dissatisfied. British ideas as to Hottentots and Kafirs and British ideas as to slavery were in their eyes absurd, unmanly and disagreeable. And therefore they went away across the Orange River; but we shall be able to deal better with their further journeyings when we come to speak of the colony of Natal, of the Orange Free State, and of the Transvaal Republic.

In 1846 came another Kafir war, called the war of the axe,[2] which lasted to the end of 1847. This too grew out of a small incident. A Kafir prisoner was rescued and taken into Kafir land, and the Kafirs would not give him up when he was demanded by the Authorities. It seems that whenever any slight act of rebellion on their parts was successful, the whole tribe and the neighbouring tribes would be so elated as to think that, now had come the time for absolutely subduing the white strangers. They were at last beaten and starved into submission, but at a terrible cost; and it seems to have been acknowledged at home that Lord Glenelg had been wrong. Sir Harry Smith was sent out, and he again extended the Colony to the Kei River, leaving the district between that and the Keiskamma as a British home for Kafirs, under the name of British Kafraria.

In 1849, when Earl Grey was at the Colonial Office, an attempt was made to induce the Cape Colony to receive convicts, and a ship laden with such a freight was sent to Table Bay. But they were never landed. With an indomitable resolution which had about it much that was heroic the inhabitants resolved that the convicts should not be allowed to set foot on the soil of South Africa. The Governor, acting under orders from home, no doubt was all powerful, and there was a military force at hand quite sufficient to enforce the Governor's orders. Nothing could have prevented the landing of the men had the Governor persevered. But the inhabitants of the place agreed among themselves that if the convicts were landed they should not be fed? No stores of any kind were to be sold to any one concerned should the convicts once be put on shore. The remedy then seemed to be rebellious and has since been called ridiculous;—but it was successful, and the convicts were taken away. For four wretched months the ship with its miserable freight lay in the bay, but not a man was landed. No such freight had ever been brought to the Cape before since the coming of a party of criminals from the Dutch East India possessions, who were sold as slaves,—and no such attempt has been made since. Those who know anything of the history of our Australian Colonies are aware that there is nothing to which the British Colonist has so strong an objection as the presence of a convict from the mother country. Whatever the mother country may send let it not send her declared rascaldom. The use of a Colony as a prison is no doubt in accordance with the Dutch theory that the paramount object of the outlying settlement is the welfare of the parent state,—but it is not at all compatible with the existing British idea that the paramount object is the well-being of the Colonists themselves. It seems hard upon England that with all her territories she can find no spot of ground for the reception of her thieves and outcasts,—that she, with all her population, sending out her honest folks over the whole world, should be obliged to keep her too numerous rascals at home. But it seems that where the population is which creates' the crime, there the criminals must remain. The Colonies certainly will not receive them.

Then came the fifth Kafir war, which of all these wars was the bloodiest. It began in 1850, and seems to have been instigated by a Kafir prophet. It would be impossible in a short sketch such as this to give any individual interest to these struggles of the natives against their invaders. Through them all we see an attempt, made at any rate by the British rulers of the land, to bind these people by the joint strength of treaties and good offices. "If you will only do as we bid you, you shall be better off than ever you were. We will not hurt you, and the land will be enough for both of us." That is what we have said all along with a clear intention of keeping our word. But it has been necessary, if we were to live in the land at all, that we should bind them to keep their word whether they did or did not understand what it was to which they pledged themselves. Lord Glenelg's theory required that the British holders of the land should recognise and respect the weakness of the Savage without using the strength of his own civilization. Colonization in such a country on such terms is impossible. He may have had abstract justice on his side. On that point I say nothing here. But if so, and if Great Britain is bound to reconcile her conduct to the rules which such justice requires, then she must abandon the peculiar task which seems to have been allotted to her, of peopling the world with a civilized race. In 1850 the fifth Kafir war arose, and the inhabitants of one advanced military village after another were murdered. This went on for nearly two years and a half, but was at last suppressed by dint of hard fighting. It cost Great Britain upwards of two millions of money, with the lives of about four hundred fighting men. This was the last of the Kafir wars,—up to that of 1877, if that is to be called a Kafir war.

After that, in 1857, occurred what seems to be the most remarkable and most unintelligible of all the events known to us in Kafir history. At this time Sir George Grey was Governor of the Colony,—a most remarkable man, who had been Governor of South Australia and of New Zealand, who had been once recalled from his office of Governor at the Cape and then restored, who was sent back to New Zealand as Governor in the hottest of the Maori warfare, and who now lives in that Colony and is at this moment,—the beginning of 1878,—singularly enough Prime Minister in the dependency in which he has twice been the Queen's vicegerent. Whatever he may be, or may have been, in New Zealand, he certainly left behind him at the Cape of Good Hope a very great reputation. There can be no doubt that of all our South African Governors he was the most popular,—and probably the most high-handed. In his time there came up a prophecy among the Kafirs that they were to be restored to all their pristine glories and possessions not by living aid, but by the dead. Their old warriors would return to them from the distant world, and they themselves would all become young, beautiful, and invincible. But great faith was needed. They would find fat cattle in large caves numerous as their hearts might desire; and rich fields of flowing corn would spring up for them as food was required. Only they must kill all their own cattle, and destroy all their own grain, and must refrain from sowing a seed. This they did with perfect faith, and all Kafirdom was well nigh starved to death. The English and Dutch around them did what they could for their relief;—had indeed done what they could to prevent self-immolation; but the more that the white men interfered the more confirmed were the black men in their faith. It is said that

50,000 of them perished of hunger. Since that day there has been no considerable Kafir war, and the spirit of the race has been broken.

Whence came the prophecy? There is a maxim among lawyers that the criminal is to be looked for among those who have profited by the crime. That we the British holders of the South African soil, and we only, were helped on in our work by this catastrophe is certain. No such prophecy,—nothing like to it,—ever came up among the Kafirs before. They have ever been a superstitious people, given to witchcraft and much afraid of witches. But till this fatal day they were never tempted to believe that the dead would come back to them, or to look for other food than what the earth gave them by its natural increase. It is more than probable that the prophecy ripened in the brain of an imaginative and strong-minded Anglo-Saxon. This occurred in 1857 when the terrible exigences of the Indian Mutiny had taken almost every redcoat from the Cape to the Peninsula. Had the Kafirs tried their old method of warfare at such a period it might have gone very hard indeed with the Dutch and English farmers of the Eastern Province.

During the last twenty years of our government there have been but two incidents in Colonial life to which I need refer to in this summary,—and both of them will receive their own share of separate attention in the following chapters. These two are the finding of the Diamond Fields, and the commencement of responsible government at the Cape Colony.

In 1867 a diamond was found in the hands of a child at the south side of the Orange River. Near to this place the Vaal runs into the Orange, and it is in the angle between the two that the diamonds have been found. This particular diamond went through various hands and was at last sold to Sir Philip Wodehouse, the Governor, for £500. As was natural, a stream of seekers after precious stones soon flowed in upon the country, some to enrich themselves, and many to become utterly ruined in the struggle. The most manifest effect on the Colony, as it has always been in regions in which gold has been found, has been the great increase in consumption. It is not the diamonds or the gold which enrich the country in which the workings of Nature have placed her hidden treasures, but the food which the diggers eat, and the clothes which the diggers wear, and, I fear, the brandy which the diggers drink. Houses are built; and a population which flows in for a temporary purpose gradually becomes permanent.

In 1872 responsible government was commenced at Capetown with a Legislative Council and House of Assembly, with full powers of passing laws and ruling the country by its majorities;—or at any rate with as full powers as belong any other Colony. In all Colonies the Secretary of State at home has a veto; but such as is the nature of the constitution in Canada or Victoria, such is it now in the Cape Colony. For twenty years previous to this there bad been a Parliament in which the sucking legislators of the country were learning how to perform their duties. But during those twenty years the Ministers were responsible to the Governors. Now they are responsible to Parliament.

1. The first record we have of the Kafirs refers to the years 1683-84, when we are told the Dutch were attacked by the Kafirs, who, however, quickly ran away before the firearms of the strangers.

2. A Kafir thief who had stolen an axe was rescued by a band of Kafirs on his way to jail.

CHAPTER IV

POPULATION AND FEDERATION

IN A FORMER CHAPTER I endeavoured to give a rough idea of the geographical districts into which has been divided that portion of South Africa which Europeans have as yet made their own. I will now attempt to explain how they are at present ruled and will indulge in some speculations as to their future condition.

How the Cape Colony became a Colony I have already described. The Dutch came and gradually spread themselves, and then the English becoming owners of the Dutch possessions spread themselves further. With the natives,—Hottentots as they came to be called,—there was some trouble but not very much. They were easily subjected,—very easily as compared with the Kafirs,—and then gradually dispersed. As a race they are no longer troublesome;—nor are they very profitable to the Cape Colony. The labour of the Colony is chiefly done by coloured people, but by people who have mainly been immigrants,—the descendants of those whom the Dutch brought, and bastard Hottentots as they are called, with a sprinkling of Kafirs and Fingos who have come from the East in quest of wages. The Colony is divided into a Western and Eastern Province, and these remarks refer to the whole of the former and to the western portion of the latter district. In this large portion of the Colony there is not now nor has there been for many years anything to be feared from pugnacious natives. It is in the eastern half of the Eastern Province that Kafirs have been and still are troublesome.

The division into Provinces is imaginary rather than real. There are indeed at this moment twenty-one members of the Legislative Council of which eleven are supposed to have been sent to Parliament by the Western District, and ten by the Eastern;—but even this has now been altered, and the members of the next Council will be elected for separate districts that no such demarcation will remain. I think that I am justified in saying that the constitution knows no division. In men's minds, however, the division is sharp enough, and the political feeling thus engendered is very keen. The Eastern Province desires to be separated and formed into a distinct Colony, as Victoria was separated from New South Wales, and afterwards Queensland. The reasons for separation which it puts forward are as follows. Capetown, the capital, is in a corner and out of the way. Members from the East have to make long and disagreeable journeys to Parliament, and, when there, are always in a minority. Capetown and the West with its mongrel population is perfectly safe, whereas a large portion of the Eastern Province is always subject to Kafir "scares" and possibly to Kafir wars. And yet the Ministry in power is, and has been, and must be a Western Ministry, spending the public money for Western objects and ruling the East according to its pleasure. It was by arguments such as these that the British Government was induced to sanction the happy separation of Queensland from New South Wales. Then why not separate the Eastern from the Western Province in the Cape Colony But the western people, as a matter of course, do not wish to see a diminution of their own authority. Capetown would lose half its glory and more than half its importance if it were put simply on a par with Grahamstown, which is the capital of the East. And the western politicians have their arguments which have hitherto prevailed. As to the expenditure of public money they point to the fact that two railway enterprises have been initiated in the East,—one up the country from Port Elizabeth, and the other from East London,—whereas there is but the one in the West which starts from Capetown. Of course it must be understood that in the Colonies railways are always or very nearly always made by Government money. The western people also say that the feeling produced by Kafir aggression in the Eastern Province is still too bitter to admit of calm legislation. The prosperity of South Africa must depend on the manner in which the Kafir and cognate races, Fingos and Basutos, Pondos, Zulus and others are amalgamated and brought together as subjects of the British Crown; and if every unnecessary scare is to produce a mixture of fear and oppression then the doing of the work will be much protracted. If the Eastern Province were left alone to arrange its affairs with the natives the chances of continual Kafir wars would be very much increased.

Arguments and feelings such as these have hitherto availed to prevent a separation of the Provinces; but though a belief in this measure is still the eastern political creed, action in that direction is no longer taken. No eastern politician thinks that he will see simple separation by a division of the Colony into two Colonies. But another action has taken place in lieu of simple separation which, if successful, would imply something like separation, and which is called Federation. Here there has been ample ground for hope because it has been understood that Federation is popular with the authorities of the Colonial Office at home.

It will hardly be necessary for me to explain here what Federation means. We have various Groups of Colonies and the question has arisen whether it may not be well that each group should be bound together under one chief or Federal Government, as the different States of the American Union are bound. It has been tried, as we all believe successfully, with British North America. It has been recommended in regard to the Australian Colonies. It has been attempted, not as yet successfully, in the West Indies. It has been talked of and become the cause of very hot feeling in reference to Her Majesty's possessions in South Africa.

I myself have been in favour of such Federation since I have known anything of our colonial possessions. The one fact that at present the produce of a Colony, going into an adjacent district as closely connected with it as Yorkshire is with Lancashire, should be subjected to Custom duties as though it came from a foreign land, is a strong reason for a union. And then the mind foresees that there will at some future time be a great Australia, and. probably a great South Africa, in which a division into different governments will, if continued, be as would be a Heptarchy restored in England. But it is this very feeling,—the feeling which experience and, foresight produce among us in England,—which renders the idea of Federation unpalatable in the Colonies generally. The binding together of a colonial group into one great whole is regarded as a preparation for separation from the mother country. It is as though we at home in England were saying to our children about the world;—"We have paid for your infantine bread and butter; we have educated you and given you good trades; now you must go and do for yourselves." There is perhaps no such feeling in the bosom of the special Colonial Minister at home who may at this or the other time be advocating this measure; but there must be an idea that some preparation for such a possible future event is expedient. We do not want to see such another colonial crisis as the American war of last century between ourselves and an English-speaking people. But in the Colonies there is a sort of loyalty of which we at home know nothing. It may be exemplified to any man's mind by thinking of the feeling as to home which is engendered by absence. The boy or girl who lives always on the paternal homestead does not care very much for the kitchen with its dressers, or for the farmyard with its ricks or the parlour with its neat array. But let the boy or girl be banished for a year or two and every little detail becomes matter for a fond regret. Hence I think has sprung colonial anger which has been, entertained against Ministers at home who have seemed to prepare the way for final separation from the mother country.

Federation, though generally unpopular in the Colonies, has been welcomed in the Eastern Province of South Africa, because it would be a means of giving if not entire at any rate partial independence from Capetown domination. If Federation were once sanctioned and carried out, the Eastern Province thinks that it would enter the union as a separate state, and that it would have such dominion as to its own affairs as New York and Massachusetts have in the United States.

But there would be various other States in such a Federation besides the two into which the Cape Colony might be divided, and in order that my readers may have some idea of what would or might be the component parts of such a union, I will endeavour to describe the different territories which would be included, with some regard to their population.

At present that South African district of which the South African politician speaks when he discusses the question of South African Federation, contains by a rough but fairly accurate computations,[1] 2,276,000 souls, of whom 340,000 may be classed as white men and 1,936,000 as coloured men. There is not therefore one white to five coloured men. And these coloured people are a strong and increasing people,—no means prone to die out and cease to be either useless or useful, as are the Maoris in New Zealand and the Indians in North America. Such as they are we have got to bring them into order, and to rule them and teach them to earn their bread,—a duty which has not fallen upon us in any other Colony. The population above stated may be divided as follows:—

Estimated Population of European South Africa

Names of Districts	White Persons	Coloured Persons	Total
Orange Free State	30,000	15,000	45,000
Transkeian Districts		501,000	501,000
The Cape Colony	235,000	485,000	720,000
Native districts belonging to the cape colony		335,000	335,000
The Diamond Fields	15,000	30,000	45,000
Natal	20,000	320,000	340,000
Transvaal	40,000	250,000	290,000
Total	340,000	1,936,000	2,276,000

I must first remark in reference to this table that the district named first,—the one containing by far the smallest number of native inhabitants, called the Orange Free State—is not a British possession nor, as far as I am aware, is it subject to British influences. It is a Dutch Republic, well ruled as regards its white inhabitants, untroubled by the native question and content with its own position. It is manifest, however, that it has succeeded in making the natives understand that they can live better outside its borders, and it has continued by its practice to banish the black man and to rid itself of trouble on that score. My reader if he will refer to the map will see that now, since the annexation of the Transvaal by Great Britain, the Free State is surrounded by British territory,—for Basuto land, which lies to the west of the Free State between the Cape Colony and Natal, is a portion of the Cape Colony. This being so I cannot understand how the Orange Free State can be comprised in any political Confederation. The nature of such a Confederation seems to require one Head, one flag, and one common nationality. I cannot conceive that the Savoyards should confederate with the Swiss,—let their interests be ever so identical,—unless Savoy were to become a Swiss Canton. The Dutch Republic is no doubt free to do as she pleases, which Savoy is not; but the idea of Confederation presumes that she would give herself up to the English flag. There may no doubt be a Confederation without the Orange Free State, and that Confederation might offer advantages so great that the Dutchmen of the Free State should ultimately feel disposed to give themselves up to Great Britain; but the question for the present must be considered as subject to considerable disturbance from the existence of the Republic. The roads from the Cape Colony to the Transvaal and the Diamond Fields lie through the Free State, and there would necessarily arise questions of transit and of Custom duties which would make it expedient that the districts should be united under one flag; but I can foresee no pretext for compulsion. In the annexation of the Transvaal there was at any rate an assignable cause,—of which we were not slow to take advantage. In regard to the Orange Free State nothing of the kind is to be expected. The population is chiefly Dutch. The political influence is altogether Dutch. A reference to the above table will show how the Dutchman succeeds, whether for good or ill,—in ridding himself of the coloured man. The Free State is a large district; but it contains altogether only 45,000 inhabitants,—and there are on the soil no more than 15,000 natives.

I will next say a word as to the Transkeian districts, which also have been supposed to be outside the dominion of the British Crown and which therefore it would seem to be just to exclude were we to effect a Confederation of our British South African Colonies.[2] But all these districts would certainly be included in any Confederation, with great advantage to the British Colonies, and with greater advantages to the Kafirs themselves who live beyond the Kei. I must again refer my readers to the map. They will see on the South Eastern Coast of the continent a district called Kafraria,—as distinct from British Kafraria further west,—the independence of which is signified by its name. Here they will find the river Kei, which till lately was supposed to be the boundary of the British territories,—beyond which the Kafir was supposed to live according to his own customs, and in undisturbed possession of independent rule. But this, even before the late Kafir outbreak, was by no means the case. A good deal of British annexation goes on in different parts of the world of which but little mention is made in the British Parliament, and but little notice taken even by the British press. It will be seen that in this territory there live 501,000 natives, and it is here, no doubt, that Kafir habits are to be found in their fullest perfection. The red Kafir is here,—the man who dyes himself and his blanket and his wives with red clay, who eschews breeches and Christianity, and meditates on the coming happy day in which the pestilent interfering European may be driven at length into the sea. It is here that Kreli till lately reigned the acknowledged king of Kafirdom as being the chief of the Galekas. Kreli had fought and been conquered and been punished by the loss of much of his territory;—but still was allowed to rule over a curtailed empire. His population is now not above 66,000. Among even these,—among the Pondos, who are much more numerous than the Galekas, our influence is maintained by European magistrates, and the Kafirs, though allowed to do much according to their pleasures, are not allowed to do everything. The Pondos number, I believe, as many as 200,000. In the remainder of Kafraria British rule is nearly as dominant to the east as to the west of the Kei. Adam Kok's land,—or no man's land, as it has been called,—running up north into Natal, we have already annexed to the Cape Colony, and no parliamentary critic at home is at all the wiser. The Fingos hold much of the remainder, and wherever there is a Fingo there is a British subject. There would now be no difficulty in sweeping Kafraria into a general South African Confederation.

I will now deal with those enumerated in the above table who are at present undoubtedly subjects of Her Majesty, and who are bound to comply with British laws. The Cape Colony contains nearly three-quarters of a million of people, and is the only portion of South Africa which has what may be called a large white population; but that population, though comparatively large,—something over a quarter of a million,—is less in number than the inhabitants of the single city of Melbourne. One colonial town in Australia, and that a town not more than a quarter of a century old, gives a home to more white people than the whole of the Cape Colony, which was colonized with white people two hundred years before Melbourne was founded. And on looking at the white population of the Cape Colony a further division must be made in order to give the English reader a true idea of the Colony in reference to England. A British colony to the British mind is a land away from home to which the swarming multitudes of Great Britain may go and earn a comfortable sustenance, denied to them in the land of their birth by the narrowness of its limits and the greatness of its population, and may do so with the use of their own language, and in subjection to their own laws. We have other senses of the word Colony,—for we call military garrisons Colonies,—such as Malta, and Gibraltar, and Bermuda. But the true Colony has, I think, above been truly described; and thus the United States of America have answered to us the purpose of a Colony as well as though they had remained under British rule. We should, therefore, endeavour to see how far the Cape Colony has answered the desired purpose.

The settlement was Dutch in its origin, and was peopled by Dutchmen,—with a salutary sprinkling of Protestant French who assimilated themselves after a time to the Dutch in language and religion. It is only by their religion that we can now divide the Dutch and the English; and on enquiry I find that about 150,000 souls belong to the Dutch Reformed and Lutheran Churches,—leaving 85,000 of English descent in the Colony. If to these we add the 20,000 white persons inhabiting Natal, and 15,000 at the Diamond Fields, we shall have the total English population of South Africa;—for the Europeans of the Transvaal, as of the Orange Free State, are a Dutch people. There are therefore about 120,000 persons of British descent in these South African districts,—the number being little more than that of the people of the small unobtrusive Colony which we call Tasmania.

I hope that nobody will suppose from this that I regard a Dutch subject of the British Crown as being less worthy of regard than an English subject. My remarks are not intended to point in that direction, but to show what is the nature of our duties in South Africa. Thus are there about 220,000[3] persons of Dutch descent, though the emigrants from Holland to that land during the present century have been but few;—so few that I have found no trace of any batch of such emigrants; and there are but 120,000 of English descent although the country has belonged to England for three-quarters of a century! The enquirer is thus driven to the conclusion that South Africa has hardly answered the purpose of a British Colony.

And I hope that nobody will suppose from this that I regard the coloured population of Africa as being unworthy of consideration. My remarks, on the other hand, are made with the object of showing that in dealing with South Africa the British Parliament and the British Ministers should think,—not indeed exclusively,—but chiefly of the coloured people. When we speak of Confederation among these Colonies and districts we should enquire whether such Confederation will be good for those races whom at home we lump under the name of Kafirs. As a Colony, in the proper sense of the word, the Cape

Colony has not been successful. Englishmen have not flocked there in proportion to its area or to its capabilities for producing the things necessary for life. The working Englishman,—and it is he who populates the new lands,—prefers a country in which he shall not have to compete with a black man or a red man. He learns from some only partially correct source that in one country the natives will interfere with him and that in another they will not; and he prefers the country in which their presence will not annoy him.

But then neither have Englishmen flocked to India, which of all our possessions is the most important,—or to Ceylon which as being called a Colony and governed from the Colonial Office at home may afford us the nearest parallel we can find to South Africa. No doubt they are in many things unlike. No English workman takes his family to Ceylon because the tropical sun is too hot for a European to work beneath it. South Africa is often hot, but it is not tropical, and an Englishman can work there. And again in Ceylon the coloured population have from the first British occupation of the island been recognised as "the people,"—an interesting and submissive but still foreign and coloured people, whom she should not dream of inviting to govern themselves. It is a matter of course that Ceylon should be governed as a Crown Colony,—with edicts and laws from Downing Street, administered by the hand of a Governor. A Cingaleee Parliament would be an absurdity in our eyes. But in the Cape Colony we have, as I shall explain in another chapter, all the circumstances of parliamentary government. The real Governor is the Colonial Prime Minister for the time, with just such restraints as control our Prime Minister at home. Therefore Ceylon and the Cape Colony are very unlike in their circumstances.

But the likeness is much more potential than the unlikeness. In each country there is a vast coloured population subject to British rule,—and a population which is menaced by no danger of coming extermination. It must always be remembered that the Kafirs are not as the Maoris. They are increasing now more quickly than ever because, under our rule, they do not kill each other off in tribal wars. No doubt the white men are increasing too,—but very slowly; so that it is impossible not to accept the fact a few white men have to rule a great number of coloured men, and that that proportion must remain.

A coloured subject of the Queen in the Cape Colony has all the privileges possessed by a white subject,—all the political privileges. The elective franchise under which the constituencies elect their members of Parliament is given under a certain low property qualification. A labourer who for a year shall have earned £25 in wages and his diet may be registered as a voter, or if a man shall have held year a house, or land, or land and house conjointly, worth £50, he may be registered. It is certainly the case that even at present a very large number of Kafirs might he registered. It has already been threatened in more than one case that a crowd of Kafirs should be taken to the poll to carry an election in this or that direction. The Kafirs themselves understand but little about it,—as yet; but they will come to understand. The franchise is one which easily admits of a simulated qualification. It depends on the value of land,—and who is to value it? If one Kafir were now to swear that he paid another Kafir 10s. a week and fed him; no registrar would perhaps believe the oath. But it will not be long before such oath might probably be true, or at any rate impossible of rejection. The Registrar may himself be a Kafir,—as may also be the member of Parliament. We have only to look at the Southern States of the American Union to see how quickly the thing may run when once it shall have begun to move. With two million and a quarter of coloured people as against 340,000 white, all endowed with equal political privileges, why should we not have a Kafir Prime Minister at Capetown, and a Kafir Parliament refusing to pay salary to any but a Kafir Governor?

There may be those who think that a Kafir Parliament and a Kafir Governor would be very good for a Kafir country. I own that I am not one of them. I look to the civilization of these people, and think that I see it now being effected by the creation of those wants the desire for supplying which has since the creation of the world been the one undeviating path towards material and intellectual progress. I see them habituating their shoulders to the yoke of daily labour,—as we have all habituated ours in Europe, and I do not doubt the happiness of the result. Nor do I care at present to go into the question of a far distant future. I will not say but that in coming ages a Kafir may make as good a Prime Minister as Lord Beaconsfield. But he cannot do so now, in this age,—nor for ages to come. It will be sufficient for us if we can make up our minds that at least for the next hundred years we shall not choose to be ruled by him. But if so, seeing how greatly preponderating is his number, how are we to deal with him when he shall have come to understand the meaning of his electoral privileges, but shall not yet have reached that intellectual equality with the white man which the more ardent of his friends anticipate for him? Such are the perils and such the political quagmire among which the Southern States of the Union are now floundering. In arranging for the future government of South Africa, whether with, or without, a Confederation, we should I think on the alert to guard against similar perils and a similar quagmire there.

I have now spoken of the Queen's subjects in the Cape Colony. Then come on my list as given above the inhabitants of native districts which are subject to the Cape Colony, either by conquest or by annexation in accordance with their own wishes. These are so various and scattered that I can hardly hope to interest my reader in the tribes individually. The Basutos are probably the most prominent.

They are governed by British magistrates, pay direct and indirect taxes,—are a quiet orderly people, not given to fighting since the days of their great King Moshesh, and are about 127,000 in number. Then there are the Damaras and Namaquas of the Western coast, people allied to the Hottentots, races of whom no great notice is taken because their land has not yet been good enough to tempt colonists. But a small proportion of these people as yet live within electoral districts and therefore at present they have no votes for members of Parliament. But were any scheme of Confederation carried out their position would have to be assimilated to that of the other natives.

The Diamond Fields are in a condition very little like that of South Africa generally. They are now, so to say, in the act of being made a portion of the Cape Colony, the bill for this purpose having been passed only during the last Session. They were annexed to the British Dominions in 1871, and have been governed since that time by a resident Sub-Governor under the Governor and High Commissioner of the Cape Colony. The district will now have a certain allotment of members of Parliament, but it has not any strong bearing on the question we are considering. The population of the district is of a shifting nature, the greater portion of even the coloured people having been drawn there by the wages offered by capitalists in search of diamonds. The English have got into the way of calling this territory the Diamond Fields, but its present proper geographical name is Griqualand West.

We then come to Natal with its little handful of white people,—20,000 Europeans among 320,000 Kafirs and Zulus. Natal at present is under a separate Governor of its own and a separate form of government. There is not a Parliament in our sense of the word, but a Legislative Council. The Executive Officers are responsible to the Governor and not to the Council. Natal is therefore a Crown Colony, and is not yet afflicted with any danger from voting natives. I can understand that it should be brought into a Confederation with other colonies or Territories under the same flag without any alteration in its own Constitution,—but in doing so it must consent to take a very subordinate part. Where there is a Parliament, and the clamour and energy and strife of parliamentary life, there will be the power. If there be a Confederation with a central Congress,—and I presume that such an arrangement is always intended when Confederation is mentioned,—Natal would demand the right to elect members. It would choose its own franchise, and might perhaps continue to shut out the coloured man; but it would be subjected to and dominated by the Institutions of the Cape Colony, which, as I have endeavoured to show, are altogether different from its own. The smaller States are generally most unwilling to confederate, fearing that they will be driven to the wall. The founders of the American Constitution had to give Rhode Island as many Senators as New York before she would consent to Federation.

There remains the Transvaal, which we have just annexed with its 40,000 Dutchmen and its quarter of a million of native population,—a number which can only be taken as a rough average and one which will certainly be greatly exceeded as our borders stretch themselves in their accustomed fashion. Here again we have for the moment a Crown Colony, and one which can hardly get itself into working order for Confederation within the period allowed by the Permissive Bill of last Session. The other day there was a Dutch Parliament,—or Volksraad,—in which the Dutchman had protected himself altogether from any voting interference on the part of the native. Downing Street can make the Transvaal confederate if she so please, but can hardly do so without causing Dutch members to be sent up to the general Parliament. Now these Dutchmen do not talk English, and are supposed to be unwilling to mix with Englishmen. I fear that many years must pass by before the Transvaal can become an operative part of an Anglo-South African Confederation.

I have here simply endeavoured to point at the condition of things as they may affect the question of Confederation;—not as intending to express an opinion against Confederation generally. I am in doubt whether a Confederation of the South African States can be carried in the manner proposed by the Bill. But I feel sure that if such a measure be carried the chief object in view should be the amelioration of the coloured races, and that that object cannot be effected by inviting the coloured races to come to the polls. Voting under a low suffrage would be quite as appropriate to the people of the Indian Provinces and of Ceylon as it is the present moment to the people of South Africa. The same evil arose in Jamaica and we know what came from it there.

1. This is so far accurate that it certainly does not overstate the coloured population. No doubt the coloured people are more numerous. I have seen 800,000 stated as the black population of the Transvaal. But as the limits of the territory are not settled, any estimate must be vague.

2. It must at least have seemed so when the Permissive Bill for South African Confederation was passed. The present disturbance will no doubt lead to the annexation of these districts.

3.

Cape Colony	150,000
Orange Free State	30,000
The Transvaal	40,000
	220,000

The Cape Colony

CHAPTER V

Capetown: The Capital

I HAD ALWAYS HEARD THAT the entrance into Capetown, which is the capital of the Cape Colony, was one of the most picturesque things to be seen on the face of the earth. It is a town lying close down on the seashore, within the circumference of Table Bay so that it has the advantage of an opposite shore which is always necessary to the beauty of a seashore town; and it is backed by the Table Mountain with its grand upright cliffs and the Lion with its head and rump, as a certain hill is called which runs from the Table Mountain round with a semicircular curve back towards the sea. The "Lion" certainly put me in mind of Landseer's lions, only that Landseer's lions lie straight. All this has given to Capetown a character for landscape beauty, which I had been told was to be seen at its best as you enter the harbour. But as we entered it early on one Sunday morning neither could the Table Mountain nor the Lion be seen because of the mist, and the opposite shore, with its hills towards The Paarl and Stellenbosch, was equally invisible. Seen as I first saw it Capetown was not an attractive port, and when I found myself standing at the gate of the dockyard for an hour and a quarter waiting for a Custom House officer to tell me that my things did not need examination,—waiting because it was Sunday morning,—I began to think that it was a very disagreeable place indeed. Twelve days afterwards I steamed out of the docks on my way eastward on a clear day, and then I could see what was then to be seen; and I am bound to say that the amphitheatre behind the place is very grand. But by that time the hospitality of the citizens had put me in good humour with the city and had enabled me to forget the iniquity of that sabbatical Custom House official.

But Capetown in truth is not of itself a prepossessing town. It is hard to say what is the combination which gives to some cities their peculiar attraction, and the absence of which makes others unattractive. Neither cleanliness, nor fine buildings, nor scenery, nor even a look of prosperity will effect this—nor will all of them combined always do so. Capetown is not specially dirty,—but it is somewhat ragged. The buildings are not grand, but there is no special deficiency in that respect. The scenery around is really fine, and the multiplicity of Banks and of Members of Parliament,—which may be regarded as the two important institutions the Colonies produce,—seemed to argue prosperity. But the town is not pleasing to a stranger. It is as I have said ragged, the roadways are uneven and the pavements are so little continuous that the walker by night had better even keep the road. I did not make special enquiry as to the municipality, but it appeared to me that the officers of that body were not alert. I saw a market out in the open street which seemed to be rather more amusing than serviceable. To this criticism I do not doubt but that my friends at the Cape will object;—but when they do so I would ask whether their own opinion of their own town is not the same as mine. "It is a beastly place you know," one Capetown gentleman said to me.

"Oh no!" said I in that tone which a guest is obliged to use when the mistress of a house speaks ill of anything at her own table. "No, no; not that."

But he persisted. "A beastly place,"—he repeated. "But we have plenty to eat and plenty to drink, and manage to make out life very well. The girls are as pretty as they are any where else, and as kind;—and the brandy and water as plentiful." To the truth of all these praises I bear my willing testimony,—always setting aside the kindness of the young ladies of which it becomes no man to boast.

The same thing may be said of so many colonial towns. There seems to be a keener relish of life than among our steadier and more fastidious folk at home, with much less to give the relish. So that one is driven to ask oneself whether advanced Art, mechanical ingenuity and luxurious modes of living do after all add to the happiness of mankind. He who has once possessed them wants to return to them,—and if unable to do so is in a far worse position than his neighbours. I am therefore disposed to say that though Capetown as a city is not lovely, the Capetowners have as good a time of it as the inhabitants of more beautiful capitals.

The population is something over 30,000—which when we remember that the place is more than two centuries old and that it is the capital of an enormous country, and the seat of the colonial legislature, is not great. Melbourne which is just two hundred years younger than Capetown contains above a quarter of a million of inhabitants. Melbourne was of course made what it is by gold;—but then so have there been diamonds to enhance the growth of Capetown. But the truth, I take it, is that a white working population will not settle itself at any place where it will have to measure itself against coloured labour. A walk through the streets of Capetown is sufficient to show the stranger that he has reached a place not inhabited by white men,—and a very little conversation will show him further that he is not speaking with an English-speaking population. The gentry no doubt are white and speak English. At any rate the members of Parliament do so, and the clergymen, and the editors—for the most part, and the good-looking young ladies;—but they are not the population. He will find that everything about him is done by coloured persons of various races, who among themselves speak a language which I am told the Dutch in Holland will hardly condescend to recognise as their own. Perhaps, as regards labour, the most valuable race is that of the Malays, and these are the descendants of slaves whom the early Dutch settlers introduced from Java. The Malays are so-called Mahommidans, and some are to be seen flaunting about the town in turbans and flowing robes. These, I understand, are allowed so to dress themselves as a privilege in reward for some pious work done,—a journey to Mecca probably. Then there is a Hottentot admixture, a sprinkling of the Guinea-coast negro, and a small but no doubt increasing Kafir element. But all this is leavened and brought into some agreement with European modes of action and thought by the preponderating influence of Dutch blood. So that the people, though idle, are not apathetic as savages, nor quite so indifferent as Orientals. But yet there is so much of the savage and so much of the oriental that the ordinary Englishman does not come out and work among them. Wages are high and living, though the prices of provisions are apt to vary, is not costly. Nor is the climate averse to European labourers, who can generally work without detriment in regions outside the tropics. But forty years ago slave labour was the labour of the country, and the stains, the apathy, the unprofitableness of slave labour still remain. It had a curse about it which fifty years have not been able to remove.

The most striking building in Capetown is the Castle, which lies down close to the sea and which was built by the Dutch,—in mud when they first landed, and in stone afterwards, though not probably as we see it now. It is a low edifice, surrounded by a wall and a ditch, and divided within into two courts in which are kept a small number of British troops. The barracks are without, at a small distance from the walls. In architecture it has nothing to be remarked, and as a defence would be now of no avail whatever. It belongs to the imperial Government, who thus still keep a foot on the soil as though to show that as long as British troops are sent to the Cape whether for colonial or imperial purposes, the place is not to be considered free from imperial interference. Round the coast at Simon's Bay, which is at the back or eastern side of the little promontory which constitutes the Cape of Good Hope, Great Britain possesses a naval station, and this is another imperial possession and supposed to need imperial troops for its defence. And from this possession of a naval station there arises the fiction that for its need the British troops are retained in South Africa when they have been withdrawn from all our other self-governing Colonies. But we have also a station for ships of war at Sydney, and generally a larger floating force there than at Simon's Bay. But the protection of our ships at Sydney has not been made an excuse for having British troops in New South Wales. I will, however, recur again to this subject of soldiers in the Colony,—which is one that has to be treated with great delicacy in the presence of South African Colonists.

There was lately a question of selling the Castle to the Colony,—the price named having been, I was told, something over £60,000. If purchased by the municipality it would I think be pulled down. Thus would be lost the conspicuous relic of the Dutch Government;—but an almost useless building would be made to give way to better purposes.

About thirty years ago Dr. Gray was appointed the first bishop of Capetown and remained there as bishop till he died,—serving in his Episcopacy over a quarter of a century. He has been succeeded by Bishop Jones, who is now Metropolitan of South Africa to the entire satisfaction of all the members of the Church. Bishop Gray inaugurated the building of a Cathedral, which is a large and serviceable church, containing a proper ecclesiastical throne for the Bishop and a stall for the Dean; but it is not otherwise an imposing building and certainly is anything but beautiful. That erected for the use of the Roman Catholics has been built with better taste. Near to the Cathedral,—behind it, and to be reached by a shady walk which is one of the greatest charms of Capetown, is the Museum, a handsome building standing on your right as you go up from the Cathedral. This is under the care of Mr. Trimen who is well known to the zoologically scientific world as a man especially competent for such work and whose services and society are in high esteem at Capetown. But I did not think much of his African wild beasts. There was a lion and there were two lionesses,—stuffed of course. The stuffing no doubt was all there; but the hair had disappeared, and with the hair all that look of martial ardour which makes such animals agreeable to us. There was, too, a hippopotamus who seemed to be moulting,—if a hippopotamus can moult,—very sad to look at, and a long since deceased elephant, with a ricketty giraffe whose neck was sadly out of joint. I must however do Mr. Trimen the justice to say that when 1 remarked that his animals seemed to have needed Macassar oil, he acknowledged that they were a "poor lot," and that it was not by their merits that the Capetown Museum could hope to be remembered. His South African birds and South African butterflies, with a snake or two here and there, were his strong points. I am but a bad sightseer in a museum, being able to detect the deficiencies of a mangy lion, but unable from want of sight and want of education to recognise the wonders of a humming bird. But I saw a hideous vulture, and an eagle, and some buzzards, with a grand albatross or two, all of which were as glossy and natural as glass eyes and well brushed feathers could make them. A skeleton of a boa-constrictor with another skeleton of a little animal just going to be swallowed interested me perhaps more than anything else.

Under the same roof with the Museum is the public library which is of its nature very peculiar and valuable. It would be invidious to say that there are volumes there so rare that one begrudges them to a distant Colony which might be served as well by ordinary editions as by scarce and perhaps unreadable specimens. But such is the feeling which comes up first in the mind of a lover of books when he takes out and handles some of the treasures of Sir George Grey's gift. For it has to be told that a considerable portion of the Capetown library,—or rather a small separate library itself numbering about 5,000 volumes,—was given to the Colony by that eccentric but most popular and munificent Governor. But why a MS. of Livy, or of Dante, should not be as serviceable at Capetown as in some gentleman's country house in England it would be hard to say; and the Shakespeare folio of 1623 of which the library possesses a copy,—with a singularly close cut margin,—is no doubt as often looked at, and as much petted and loved and cherished in the capital of South Africa, as it is when in the possession of a British Duke. There is also a wonderful collection in these shelves of the native literature of Africa and New Zealand. Perhaps libraries of greater value have been left by individuals to their country or to special institutions, but I do not remember another instance of a man giving away such a treasure in his lifetime and leaving it where in all human probability he could never see it again.

The remaining, or outer library, contains over thirty thousand volumes, of which about 5,000 were left by a Mr. Dessin more than a hundred years ago to the Dutch Reformed Church in Capetown. These seem to have been buried for many years, and to have been disinterred and brought into use when the present public library was established in 1818. The public are admitted free and ample comforts are supplied for reading,—such as warmth, seats, tables and a handsome reading-room. A subscription of £1 per annum enables the subscriber to take a set of books home. This seems to us to be a munificent arrangement; but it should always be remembered that at Boston in the United States any inhabitant of the city may take books home from the public library without any deposit and without paying any thing. Among all the philanthropical marvels of public libraries that is the most marvellous. I was told that the readers in Capetown are not very numerous. When I visited the place there were but two or three.

A little further up along the same shady avenue, and still on the right hand side is the entrance to the Botanic Gardens. These, I was told, were valuable in a scientific point of view, were, as regards beauty and arrangement, somewhat deficient, because funds were lacking. There is a Government grant and there are subscriptions, but the Government is stingy?—what Good Government ever was not stingy?—and the subscriptions are slender. I walked round the garden and can imagine that if I were an inhabitant of Capetown and if, as would probably be the case, I made frequent use of that avenue, I might prolong my exercise by a little turn round the garden. But this could only be three times a week unless my means enabled me to subscribe, for on three days the place is shut against the world at large. As a public pleasure ground the Capetown gardens are not remarkable. As I walked up and down this somewhat dreary length I thought of the glory and the beauty and the perfect grace of the gardens at Sydney.

Opposite to the Museum and the Gardens is the Government House in which Sir Bartle Frere with his family had lately come to reside. In many Colonies, nay in most that I have visited, I have heard complaints that Government Houses have been too small. Seeing such hospitality as I have seen in them I could have fancied that Governors, unless with long private purses, must have found them too large. They are always full. At Melbourne, in Victoria, an evil-natured Government has lately built an enormous palace which must ruin any Governor who uses the rooms placed at his disposal. When I was there the pleasant house at Tourac sufficed, and Lord Canterbury, who has now gone from us, was the most genial of hosts and the most sage of potentates. At Capetown the house was larger than Tourac, and yet not palatial. It seemed to me to be all that such a house should be;—but I heard regrets that there were not more rooms. I know no office in which it can be less possible for a man to make money than in administering the government of a constitutional Colony. In a Colony that has no constitution of its own,—in which the Governor really governs,—the thing is very different. In the one there is the salary and the house, and that is all. In a Crown Colony there is no House of Commons to interfere when this and the other little addition is made. We all know what coals and candles mean at home. The constitutional Governor has no coals and candles.

Wherever I go I visit the post-office, feeling certain that I may be able to give a little good advice. Having looked after post-offices for thirty years at home I fancy that I could do very good service among the Colonies if I could have arbitrary power given to me to make what changes I pleased. My advice is always received with attention and respect, and I have generally been able to flatter myself that I have convinced my auditors. But I never knew an instance yet in which any improvement recommended by me was carried out. I have come back a year or two after my first visit and have seen that the things have been just as they were before. I did not therefore say much at Capetown;—but I thought it would have been well if they had not driven the public to buy stamps at a store opposite, seeing that as the Colony pays salaries the persons taking the salaries ought to do the work;—and that it would be well also if they could bring themselves to cease to look at the public as enemies from whom it is necessary that the officials inside should be protected by fortifications in the shape of barred windows and closed walls. Bankers do their work over open counters, knowing that no one would deal with them were they to shut their desks up behind barricades.

But I am bound to say that my letters were sent after me with that despatch and regularity which are the two first and greatest of post-official virtues. And the services in the Colony generally are very well performed, and performed well under great difficulties. The roads are bad, and the distances long, and the transit is necessarily rough. I was taken out to see such a cart as I should have to travel on for many a weary day before I had accomplished my task in South Africa. My spirit groaned within me as I saw it,—and for many a long and weary hour it has since expanded itself with external groanings though not quite on such a cart as I saw then. But the task has been done, and I can speak of the South African cart with gratitude. It is very rough,—very rough indeed for old bones. But it is sure.

I should weary my reader were I to tell him of all the civilized institutions,—one by one,—which are in daily use in Capetown. There is a Custom House, and a Sailors' Home, and there are hospitals, and an observatory,—very notable I believe as being well placed in reference to the Southern hemisphere,—and a Government Herbarium and a lunatic asylum at Robben Island. Of Mr. Stone, the Astronomer Royal and lord of the Observatory, I must say one word in special praise. "Do you care for the stars?" he asked me. In truth I do not care for the stars. I care, I think, only for men and women, and so I told him. "Then," said he, "I won't bother you to come to the Observatory. But if you wish to see stars I will show them to you." I took him at his word and did not then go to the Observatory. This I had said with some fear and trembling as I remembered well the disgust which Agazziz once expressed when I asked permission not to be shown his museum at Cambridge, Massachusetts. But Mr. Stone seemed to understand my deficiency, and if he pitied me he abstained from expressing his pity. Afterwards I did make a special visit to the Observatory,—which is maintained by the imperial Government and not by the Colony,—and was shown all the wonders of the Southern Heavens. They were very beautiful, but I did not understand much about them.

There is a comfortable and hospitable club at Capetown, to which, as at all colonial clubs, admission is given to strangers presumed to be of the same social standing as the members. The hour of lunch seems to be the hour of the day at which these institutions are most in request. This is provided in the form of a table d'hôte, as is also a dinner later on in the day. This is less numerously attended, but men of heroic mould are thus enabled to dine twice daily.

Capetown would be no city without a railway. The Colony at present has three starting-points for railways from the coast, one of which runs out of Capetown, with a branch to Wynberg which is hardly more than a suburb and is but eight miles distant, and a second branch to Worcester which is intended to be carried up the country to the distant town of Graaf Reynet and so on through the world of Africa. The line to Wynberg is of infinite importance to the city as giving to the inhabitants easy means of access to a charming locality. Capetown itself is not a lovely spot on which to reside, but the district at the back of the Table Mountain where are Mowbray, Rondebusch, Wynberg and Constantia,—which district is reached by the railway,—supplies beautiful sites for houses and gardens. There are bits of scenery which it would be hard to beat either in form or colour, so grand are the outlines of the mountain, and so rich and bountiful the verdure of the shrubs and timbers. It would be difficult to find a site for a house more charming than that occupied by the bishop, which is only six miles from town and hardly more than a mile distant from a railway station. Beyond Wynberg lies the grape district of Constantia so well known in England by the name of its wine;—better known, I think, forty years ago than it is now.

All these places, Rondebusch, Wynberg, Constantia and the rest lie on that promontory which when we look at the map we regard as the Cape of Good Hope. The Dutch had once an idea of piercing a canal across the isthmus from sea to sea, from Table Bay to False Bay,—in which lies Simon's Bay where is our naval station,—and maintaining only the island so formed for its own purposes, leaving the rest of South Africa to its savagery. And, since the time of the Dutch, it has been suggested that if England were thus to cut off the Table Mountain with its adjacent land, England would have all of South Africa that it wants. The idea is altogether antagonistic to the British notion of colonization, which looks to a happy home for colonists or the protection natives, rather than the benefit or glory of the Mother Country. But were such a cutting off to be effected, the morsel of land so severed would be very charming, and would demand I think a prettier town than Capetown.

Beyond and around Wynberg there is a little world of lovely scenery. Simonstown is about twelve miles from Wynberg, the road passing by the now growing bathing place of Kalk bay. It is to Kalk bay that the ladies of Capetown go with their children when in summer they are in search of fresh air, and sea breezes, and generally improved sanitary arrangements. A most delightful spot it would be if only there were sufficient accommodation. The accommodation of course will come as years roll on. Beyond Kalk bay are Simonstown and Simon's Bay, where lives the British Commodore who has the command of these waters. The road, the whole way down, lies between the mountain and the sea. Beyond Simonstown I rode out for six or seven miles with the Commodore along the side of the hill and through the rocks till we could see the lighthouse at the extremity of the Cape. It is impossible to imagine finer sea scenery or a bolder coast than is here to be seen. There is not a yard of it that would not be the delight of tourists if it were in some accessible part of Europe,—not a quarter of a mile that would not have its marine villa if it were in England.

Before I returned home I stayed for a week or two at an Inn, a mile or two beyond Wynberg, called Rathfelders. I suppose some original Dutchman of that name once kept the house. It is of itself an excellent place of resort, cool in summer being on the cool side of the Table Mountains, and well kept;—a comfortable refuge to sojourners who do not object to take their meals at a public table; but peculiarly pleasant as being in the midst of the mountain scenery. From here there is a ride through the mountains to Hout's Bay,—a little inlet on the other side of the Cape promontory,——which cannot be beaten for beauty of the kind. The distance to be ridden may be about ten miles each way, and good riding horses are kept at Rathfelders. But I did not find that very many had crossed the pass. I should say that in the neighbourhood of Wynberg there are various hotels and boarding houses so that accommodation may always be had. The best known of these is Cogill's Hotel close to the Wynberg Railway Station. I did not stay there myself, but I heard it well spoken of.

Altogether the scenery of the Promontory on which the Dutch landed, the southern point of which is the Cape of Good Hope, and on which stands Capetown, is hardly to be beaten for picturesque beauty by any landskip charms elsewhere within the same area.

I was taken down to Constantia where I visited one of the few grape growers among whom the vineyards of this district are divided. I found him with his family living in a fine old Dutch residence,—which had been built I was told by one of the old Dutch Governors when a Governor the Cape was a very aristocratic personage. Here he keeps a few ostriches, makes a great deal of wine, and has around him as lovely scenery as the eye of man can desire. But he complained bitterly as to the regulations,—or want of regulations,—prevailing in regard to labour. "If an idle people could only be made to work for reasonable wages the place would become a very Paradise!" This is the opinion as to labour which is left behind in all lands in which slavery has prevailed. The man of means, who has capital either in soil or money, does not actually wish for a return to slavery.

The feelings which abolished slavery have probably reached his bosom also. But he regrets the control over his fellow creatures which slavery formerly gave him, and he does not see that whether a man be good or bad, idle by nature and habits or industrious, the only compulsion to work should come from hunger and necessity,—and the desire of those good things which industry and industry alone will provide.

On the other side of Capetown,—the other side from the direction towards Wynberg,—there is another and the only other road out of Capetown which leads down to Sea Point, where there is a second pleasant suburb and a second clustering together of villa residences. Here the inhabitants look direct on to Table Bay and have the surges of the Atlantic close to their front doors. The houses at Sea Point are very nice, but they have nothing of the Elysian scenery of Wynberg. Continuing the road from Sea Point the equestrian, or energetic walker, may return by the Kloof,—anglice Cleft,—which brings him back to town by a very picturesque route between the Lion and Table Mountains. This is almost too steep for wheels, or it would claim to be called a third road out of the town.

I was taken to see two schools, the high school at Rondebusch, and a school in the town for coloured lads. At the high school the boys were away for their holidays and therefore I could see nothing but the outside material. I do not doubt but that lads are educated there quite as well as at similar institutions in England. It is under the guidance of a clergyman of the Church of England, and is thoroughly English in all its habits. I found a perfect menagery of interesting animals attached to it, which is an advantage which English schools seldom possess. The animals, which, though wild by nature, were at this place remarkably tame, had, fortunately for me, not gone home for their holidays,—so that, wanting the boys, I could amuse myself with them. I will not speak here of the coloured school, as I must, as I progress, devote a short chapter to the question of Kafir education.

In speaking of the Capital of the Colony I need only further remark that it possesses a completed and adequate dock for the reception of large ships, and a breakwater for the protection of the harbour. The traffic from England to the Cape of Good Hope is now mainly conducted by two Steam Ship Companies, the Union and Donald Currie & Co., which carry the mails with passengers and cargo each way weekly. Many of these vessels are of nearly 3,000 tons burden, some even of more, and at Capetown they are brought into the dock so that passengers walk in and out from the quay without the disagreeable aid of boats. The same comfort has not as yet been afforded at any other port along the coast.

CHAPTER VI

The Legislature and Executive

It has come to be understood that the appropriate mode of governing a Colony is to have a King, Lords and Commons as we do at home. And if a Colony be a Colony in the fashion described by me when endeavouring to define the nature of a Colony proper, there cannot be a doubt that this is the best mode. Where Englishmen,—or white men whether they be of English or other descent,—have gone to labour and have thus raised a community in a distant land under the British flag, the old constitutional mode of arranging things seems always to act well, though it may sometimes be rough at first, and sometimes at starting may be subject to difficulties. It has been set on foot by us, or by our Colonists, with a population perhaps not sufficient to give two members to an English borough,—and has then started with a full-fledged appanage of Governor, aide-de-camps, private secretaries, Legislative Council, Legislative Assembly, Prime Minister and Cabinet,—with a surrounding which one would have thought must have swamped so small a boat;—but the boat has become almost at once a ship and has ridden safely upon the waves. The little State has borrowed money like a proud Empire and has at once had its stocks quoted in the share lists. There have been causes for doubt, but I do not remember an instance of failure. This has been so universally the result that the British Government at home have become averse to Crown Colonies, and has of late invited her children to go out alone into the world, to enjoy their own earnings, and pay their own bills, and do as may seem good to them each in his own sight. I find that there are many in the Cape Colony who say that she undertook to govern herself in the proper parliamentary way not because she especially desired the independence to be thus obtained, but because the Colonial Office at home was anxious on the subject and put pressure on the Colony.

At any rate in 1872 the Cape began to rule itself. The process of ruling themselves rarely begins with Colonies all at once. The acme of independence is reached when a Colony levies and spends its own taxes and when the country is ruled by Ministers who are appointed because they have a parliamentary majority at their back and who go out of office when they are no longer so supported. There are various preliminary steps before this state of perfection be reached and in no Colony, I think, have these various steps been more elaborated than at the Cape. In 1825 the Governor ruled almost as a despot. He was of course subject to the Secretary of State at home,—by whom he might be dismissed or, if competent, would be promoted; but he was expected to be autocratic and imperious. I may say that he rarely fell short of the expectation. Lord Charles Somerset, who was the last of those Governors at the Cape, did and said things which are charming in the simplicity of their tyranny. In 1825 an Executive Council was appointed. These were, of course, nominees of the Government; but they divided the responsibility with the Governor, and were a check upon the exercise of his individual powers. The next step, in 1834, was to a Legislative Council. These were to be the lawmakers, but all of them were elected by the Governor. Six of the Council were the Governor's executive ministers, and the other six,—for the Council consisted of twelve,—were unofficial nominees.

But the existence of such a Council—a little Parliament elected by the Crown—created a desire for a popular Parliament and the people of the Colony petitioned for a representative House of Assembly. Then there was much hesitation, one Secretary of State after another and one Governor after another, struggling to produce a measure which should be both popular and satisfactory. For the element of colour,—the question as to white men and black men, which has been inoperative in Canada, in the Australia's, and even in New Zealand,—was as early as in those days felt to create a peculiar difficulty in South Africa. But at length the question was decided in favour of the black man and a low franchise. Sir Harry Smith the then Governor expressed an opinion that "by showing to all classes that no man's station was in this free country,"—meaning South Africa,—"determined by the accident of his colour, all ranks of men might be stimulated to improve and maintain their relative position." The principle enunciated is broad and seems, at the first hearing of it, to be excellent; but it would appear on examination to be almost as correct to declare to candidates for the household cavalry that the accident of height should have nothing to do with their chances. It may be open to argument whether the Queen would not be as well defended by men five feet high as by those who are six,—but the six-feet men are wanted. There may be those who think that a Kafir Parliament would be a blessing;—but the white men in the Colony are determined not to be ruled by black men.[1] It was intended, no doubt, simply to admit a few superior Kafirs to the franchise,—a select body whose appearance at the hustings would do good to the philanthropic heart; but it has led to the question whether there may not be more Kafirs than European voters. When it leads to the question whether there shall be Kafir members of Parliament, then there will be a revolution in the Colony. One or two the House might stand, as the House in New Zealand endures four or five Maoris who sit there to comfort the philanthropic heart; but should the number increase materially then there would be a revolution in the Cape Colony. In New Zealand the number is prescribed and, as the Maoris are coming to an end, will never be increased. In the Cape Colony every electoral district might return a Kafir; but I think those who know the Colony will agree with me when I say that the European would not consent to be so represented.

After much discussion, both at Cape and in England, two Houses of Parliament both elective were established and met together for the first time in July 1854. The franchise was then established on the basis which still prevails. To vote either for a member of the Legislative Council, or of the House of Assembly, a man must occupy land or a building alleged to be worth £25; or he must earn £50 per annum; or he must earn £25 per annum,—about 10s. a week,—and his diet. The English reader must understand that wages are very much higher in the Colony than in England, and that the labouring Kafir who works for wages frequently earns as much as the required sum. And the pastoral Kafir who pays rent for his land, does very often occupy a tract worth more than £25. There are already districts in which the Kafirs who might be registered as voters exceed in number the European voters. And the number of such Kafirs is increasing from day to day.

But even yet parliamentary government had not been attained in the Cape. Under the Constitution, as established in 1854, the power of voting supplies had been given, but the manner in which the supplies should be used was still within the Governor's bosom. His ministers were selected by him as he pleased, and could not be turned out by any parliamentary vote. That is the system which is now in existence in the United States,—where the President may maintain his ministers in opposition to the united will of the nation. At the Cape, after 1854, the Governor's ministers could sit and speak either in one House or in the other,—but were not members of Parliament and could not vote. Nor, which was more important, could they be turned out!

The next and last step was not taken till 1872, and was perhaps somewhat pressed on the Colony by the Home Government, who wished to assimilate the form of parliamentary constitution in all the Colonies which were capable of enjoying it. The measure however was carried at the Cape by majorities in both

Houses,—by a majority of 34 to 27 votes in the House of Assembly,—which on such a subject was a slender majority as showing the wish of the Colony, and by 11 votes against 10 in the Legislative Council. I think I am right in saying that two out of these eleven were given by gentlemen who thought it right to support the Government though in opposition to their own opinions. There were many who considered that in such a condition of things the measure should have been referred back to the people by a general dissolution. But so did not think the late Governor, Sir Henry Barkly, or the Secretary of State at home. The question was settled in favour of our old well-beloved form of constitutional government; and the Cape Colony became like to the Canadas and the Australias. The Governor has really little or nothing to say to the actual government of the country,—as the Sovereign has not with us. The Ministers are responsible, and must be placed in power or turned out of power as majorities may direct. And the majorities will of course be created by the will of the people, or, as it would be more fair to say, by the will of the voters.

But there are two points in which, with all these Colonies, the resemblance to England ceases. I have said that there were in the Cape Colony, Kings, Lords and Commons. With us, at home, the Lords are hereditary. A hereditary Upper House in a Colony would be impossible, and if possible would be absurd. There are two modes of selecting such a body,—one that of election by the people as is the case in Victoria, and the other that of nomination by the Crown, as is the practice in New South Wales. At the Cape the more democratic method has been adopted. It may be a question whether in regard to the special population of the Country, the other plan would not have been preferable. The second difference is common to all our Colonies, and has reference to the power which is always named first and which, for simplicity, I have described as the King. With us the Crown has a veto on all parliamentary enactments, but is never called upon to exercise it. The Crown with us acts by its Ministers who either throw out a measure they disapprove by the use of the majority at their back, or go out themselves. But in the Colonies the veto of the third party to legislation is not infrequently exercised by the Secretary of State at home, and here there is a safeguard against intemperate legislation.

Such is the form of government at the Cape of Good Hope. Of all forms known to us it is perhaps the most liberal, as the franchise is low enough to enable the ordinary labourer to vote for members of both Houses. For in truth every working man in the Colony may without difficulty earn l0s. a week and his diet; and no small holder of land will occupy a plot worth less than £25. Had the matter in question been the best form for the maintenance of liberty and assurance of liberty among white people, I, at least, should have nothing to say against it; but, seeing that the real people of the country is and will remain a coloured population, I cannot but think that there is room for doubt. I will not,—as I said before, venture to enquire into the far distant future of the black races of South Africa. There are many who think that the black man should not only be free but should be, and by his nature is, the equal of the white man. As I am glad to see all political inequalities gradually lessened among men of European descent, so should I be glad to think that the same process should take place among all men. But not only has not that time come yet, but I cannot think that it has so nearly come as to justify us in legislating upon the supposition that it is approaching. I find that the very men who are the friends of the negro hold the theory but never entertain the practice of equality with the negro. The stanchest disciple of Wilberforce and Buxton does not take the negro into partnership, or even make him a private secretary. The conviction that the white man must remain in the ascendant is as clear in his mind as in that of his opponent; and though he will give the black man a vote in hope of this happy future, he is aware that when black men find their way into any Parliament or Congress that Parliament or Congress is to a degree injured in public estimation. A power of voting in the hands of negroes has brought the time-honoured constitution of Jamaica to an end. The same power in the Southern States of the American Union is creating a political confusion of which none of us can foretell the end, but as to which we are all convinced that in one way or another a minority of white men will get the better of a majority of coloured men. In British South Africa the majority of coloured men is so great that the country has to be compared to India or Ceylon rather than to the Southern American States. When once the Kafir shall have learned what voting means there will be no withstanding him, should the system of voting which now prevails in the Cape Colony be extended over a South African Confederation. The Kafir is not a bad fellow. Of the black African races the South Eastern people whom we call Kafirs and Zulus are probably the best. They are not constitutionally cruel, they learn to work readily, and they save property. But they are as yet altogether deficient in that intelligence which is needed for the recognition of any political good. There can be no doubt that the condition of the race has been infinitely improved by the coming of the white man; but, were it to be put to the vote tomorrow among the Kafirs whether the white man should be driven into the sea, or retained in the country, the entire race would certainly vote for the white man's extermination. This may be natural; but it is not a decision which the white man desires or by which he intends to abide.

I will quote here a few words from an official but printed report, sent by Mr. Bowker, the late Commandant of the Frontier Mounted Police, to the Chairman of the Frontier Defence Committee in 1876, merely adding, that perhaps no one in the Cape Colony better understands the feeling between the Kafirs and their white neighbours than the gentleman whose words I use. "It must not be forgotten that while collectively the Border farmers look upon the natives as their bitterest foes, individually they have greater confidence in their Kafir servants than in any European immigrant whose services can be obtained in the Colony. It is much the same with the native servants. As a nation they hate the white man, and look forward to the day when he will be expelled from the country; while individually they are as much or more attached to their masters than would be the case with European servants." This represents exactly the condition of feeling in South Africa;—and, if so, it certainly is not to such feeling that we can safely entrust an equality of franchise with ourselves, seeing that they outnumber us almost by five to one. It is said that they cannot combine. If they could the question would be settled against us,—without any voting. But nothing will teach men to combine so readily as a privilege of voting. The franchise is intended to teach men to combine for a certain object, and when freely given has always succeeded in its intention.

As far as it has yet gone Parliamentary Government has worked well in the Cape Colony. There had been so long a period of training that a sufficient number of gentlemen were able to undertake the matter at once. I attended one hot debate and heard the leaders of the Opposition attack the Prime Minister and his colleague in the proper parliamentary manner. The question was one of defence against the border Kafirs;—and the Premier who had brought in a measure which the Opposition, as it appeared, was desirous of slaughtering peacemeal, was suspected of an intention to let the measure drop. And yet he was asking for an increased vote for defence, which,—so said the opposition,—ought not to be granted till he had declared his entire purpose in that respect. The object of the opposition of course was to say all the severe words which parliamentary manners allowed, and it succeeded as well as do our practised swordsmen at home. It was made to appear that the Prime Minister was a very wicked man indeed, whose only object it was to rob the Colony of its money. Of Mr. Paterson, who was the keenest of the swordsmen, I must say that he was very eloquent. Of Mr. Southey and Mr. Sprigg that they were very efficacious. It was of course the object of the Ministers to get the vote passed with as little trouble as possible, knowing that they had a majority at their back. Mr. Molteno the Premier declared that he really did not know what gentlemen on the other side wanted. If they could throw out the vote let them do it,—but what was the use of their reiterating words if they had no such power. That seemed to be the gist of the Premier's arguments,—and it is the natural argument for a Prime Minister who has never yet been turned out. Of course he got his vote,—as to which I presume that no one had the least doubt.

Mr. Molteno, who has been in parliamentary life for many years, having held a seat since the creation of the first House of Assembly in 1854, has been a very useful public servant and thoroughly understands the nature of the work required of him; but I fancy that in a parliamentary constitutional government things cannot go quite straight till there has been at least one change,—till a Minister has been made to feel that any deviation from responsibility may bring upon him at a moment's notice a hostile majority. We at home talk about a strong Government; but a very strong Government is likely to be a fainéant Government, and is rarely a faithful Government. A Minister should have before him a lively dread. Mr. Molteno seemed to be too confident,—and to be almost fretful because gentlemen made him sit there in the House when he would have preferred being in his office or at home. I am far from saying that the Cape can have a better Minister;—but if he could go out for a short while and then come back it would probably be for his comfort.

I cannot finish these remarks without saying that the most sensible speech I heard in the House was from Mr. Saul Solomon. Mr. Solomon has never been in the Government and rarely in opposition, but he has been perhaps of as much use to the Colony as any living man. He is one who certainly should be mentioned as a very remarkable personage, having risen to high honours in an occupation perhaps of all the most esteemed among men, but for which he must have seemed by nature to be peculiarly ill adapted. He is a man of very small stature,—so small that on first seeing him the stranger is certainly impressed with the idea that no man so small has ever been seen by him before. His forehead however is fine, and his face full of intelligence. With all this against him Mr. Solomon has gone into public life, and as a member of Parliament in the Cape Colony has gained a respect above that of Ministers in office. It is not too much to say that he is regarded on both sides as a safe adviser; and I believe that it would be hardly possible to pass any measure of importance through the Cape Legislature to which he offered a strenuous opposition. He reminded me of two other men whom it has been my privilege to know and who have been determined to seize and wear parliamentary honours in the teeth of misfortunes which would have closed at any rate that profession against men endowed with less than Herculean determination. I mean Mr. Fawcett who in our own House at home has completely vanquished the terrible misfortune of blindness, and my old friend John Robertson of Sydney,—Sir John I believe he is now,—who for many years presided over the Ministry in New South Wales, leading the debates in a parliamentary chamber, without a palate to his mouth. I regard these three men as great examples of what may be done by perseverance to overcome the evils which nature or misfortune have afflicted.

The people of Capetown think of the two chambers in which the two Houses sit with something of shame, declaring that they are not at all what they ought to be,—that they are used as makeshifts, and that there has never yet been time, or perhaps money at hand, for constructing proper Houses of Parliament. Had I not heard this I should have thought that each of them was sufficiently commodious and useful, if not quite sufficiently handsome or magnificent.

1.I do not intend to suggest that any man should be excluded by his colour from the hustings. I am of opinion that no allusion should be made to colour in defining the franchise for voters in any British possession. But in colonies such as those of South Africa,—in which the bulk of the population is coloured,—the privilege should be conferred on black and white alike, with such a qualification as will admit only those who are fit.

CHAPTER VII

KNYSNA, GEORGE, AND THE CANGO CAVES

WHEN I HAD SPENT A few weeks in Capetown and the immediate neighbourhood I went into the Eastern Province of the Cape Colony, and thence on to Natal, the Transvaal, the Diamond Fields, and the Orange Free State Republic,—as I hope to tell my readers in this and the next volume; but as I afterwards came back to the Western Province,—of which I had as yet seen but little,—and used what remainder of time was at my command in visiting what was easiest reached, I will now go forwards so as to complete my narrative as to the West before I speak of the East. In this way my story may be more intelligible than if I were to follow strictly the course of my own journeyings. I have already alluded to the political division of the Cape Colony, and to the great desire which has pervaded the men of the East to separate themselves from the men of the West;—and when, a few chapters further on, I shall have brought myself eastwards I shall have to refer to it again. This desire is so strong that it compels a writer to deal separately with the two Provinces, and to divide them almost as completely as though they had been separated. South Africa is made up of different parts. And as there are the four divisions which I have named above, so are there the two Provinces of the Cape Colony, which are joined under the same Parliament and the same Governor but which can hardly be said to have identical interests. The West no doubt is contented with the union, having the supremacy; but the East has been always clamorous for Separation.

After a very long coach journey from Bloemfontein down to Fort Elizabeth, of which I shall have to say a few words further on, I went by steamer to Mossel Bay on my way back to Capetown. Mossel Bay is the easternmost harbour the Western Province, collecting a Custom Revenue of £20,000. It is fourth in importance of the ports of the Colony, those ranking higher being Capetown itself, Fort Elizabeth, and East London,—the two latter belonging to the Eastern Province. It contains about 1,400 inhabitants; and has three hotels, a bank, a Custom House, and a Resident Magistrate. I doubt, however, whether all these attractions would have taken me to Mossel Bay had I not been told of the scenery of the Outeniqua mountains and of the Knysna river. It had been averred to me that I should do injustice to South Africa generally if I did not visit the prettiest scenery known in South Africa. Having done so I feel that I should have done injustice at any rate to myself if I had not taken the advice given me.

Of all the beneficent Institutions of Mossel Bay which I have named I became personally acquainted with but one,—the Resident Magistrate, who was so beneficent that at a moment's notice he offered to make the trip to the Knysna with me. By this I gained a guide, philosopher, and friend,—and a very pleasant companion for my excursion. In such tourings solitude will often rob them of all delight, and ignorance of all instruction. It is impossible to see the things immediately under the eye, unless there be some one to tell you where to look for them. A lone wanderer may get up statistics, and will find persons to discuss politics with him in hotel parlours and on the seats of public conveyances. He may hear, too, the names of mountains and of rivers. But of the inner nooks of social life or of green hills he will know nothing unless he can fall into some intimacy, even though it be short-lived, with the people among whom he is moving.

We had to be in a hurry because a Cape Colony Resident Magistrate cannot be absent long from his seat of justice. If he be not on the spot there is no one to whom misfortune can appeal or whom iniquity need dread. In an English town a Mayor has his aldermen, and the Chairman of the Bench his brother magistrates;—but at Mossel Bay the Resident is as necessary at ten o'clock on a Monday morning as is the Speaker to the House of Commons at four o'clock in the afternoon. So we started at once with a light cart and a pair of horses,—which was intended to take us as far as George, a distance of 30 miles.

We went through a country teeming with ostriches. Ostrich-farming on a great scale I will describe further on. Here the work was carried on in a smaller way, but, as I was told, with great success. The expenses were small, and the profits very great,—unless there should come misfortunes, as when a valuable bird will break his leg and so destroy himself, or when a hen supposed to be worth £50 or £60 won't lay an egg. I think that in ostrich-farming, as in all commercial pursuits, the many little men who lose a little money,—perhaps their little all,—and then go quietly to the wall, attract less attention than the prosperous few. I am bound however to say that in this district I saw many ostriches and heard of much success.

As evening was coming on, when we had got half way to George, we found that our horses were knocked up. We stopped therefore at a woolwashing establishment, and sent round the country to beg for others. Here there was also a large shop, and a temperance hotel, and an ostrich farm, all kept by the same person or by his son. Word came to us that all the horses in the place had done, each of them, an extra hard day's work that day; but, so great a thing is it to be a Resident Magistrate, that in spite of this difficulty two horses were promised us! But they had to be caught! So we walked up to see the woolwashers finish their day's work, the sun having already set.

Their mode of woolwashing was quite new to me. The wool, which seemed to have been shorn in a very rough manner,—cut off in locks after a fashion which would have broken the heart of an Australian Squatter, wool chopped as you would chop a salad,—was first put into a square caldron of boiling, or nearly boiling water. Then it was drawn out in buckets, and brought to troughs made in a running stream, in which the dirt was trodden out of it by coloured men. These were Hottentots, and Negroes,—the children of the old slaves,—and one or two Kafirs from the East. The wool is squeezed and laid out on drying grounds to dry. The most interesting part of the affair was the fact that these coloured men were earning 4s. 6d. a day wages each. Some distance further on the next day we came on two white men,—navvies,—who were making a dam and were earning only 1s. 7d. a day, and their diet. That might together be worth 2s. 6d. They explained to us that they had found it very hard to get any job, and had taken this almost in despair. But they wouldn't have trod the wool along with the black men, even for 4s. 6d.

Just as the night was set in we started at a gallop with our tired horses. I know so well the way in which a poor weary brute may be spirited up for five minutes; not, alas, without the lash. A spur to a tired horse is like brandy to a worn-out man. It will add no strength, but it will enable the sufferer to collect together and to use quickly what little remains. We had fifteen miles to do, and wearily, with sad efforts, we did twelve of them. Then we reached a little town, Blanco, and were alive with hopes of a relay. But everybody in Blanco was in bed, and there was nothing for us but to walk, the driver promising that if we would allow the poor animals twenty minutes to look about them, they would be able to crawl on with the cart and our portmanteaus. And so we walked on to George, and found our dinner of mutton chops ready for us at eleven o'clock. A telegram had been sent on so that a vehicle might be prepared for us before daybreak on the morrow.

As I entered George,—the geographers I believe call the place Georgetown, but the familiar name is George,—by starlight, just able to discern the tops of the mountains above it, I felt that it was a pretty place. On the following morning, as I walked up and down its so-called principal street, waiting between 5 and 6, for, the wicked mules which were an hour late, I swore that it was the prettiest village on the face of the earth,—the prettiest village at any rate that I had ever seen. Since that I have moderated my enthusiasm so far that I will admit some half dozen others to the same rank. George will probably resent the description, caring more for its importance than its prettiness. George considers itself to be a town. It is exactly what in England we would describe to be a well-to-do village. Its so-called street consists of a well made broad road, with a green sward treble the width of the road on each side. And here there are rows of oak trees,—real English oak trees, planted by some most beneficent because patient inhabitant of the earlier days. A man who will plant a poplar, a willow, or even a blue-gum in a treeless country,—how good is he! But the man who will plant an oak will surely feel the greenness of its foliage and the pleasantness of its shade when he is lying down, down beneath the sod!

In an English village there are gentlemen's houses, and cottages, and shops. Shops are generally ugly, particularly shops in a row, and the prettiness of a village will depend mostly on the number of what may be called gentlemen's houses, and on the grouping of them. Cottages may be lovely to look at;—sometimes are; but it is not often. 15s. a week and roses form a combination which I have seen, but of which I have read in poetry much more than I have seen. Perhaps the ugliest collection of ruined huts I ever visited was "Sweet Auburn, loveliest village of the plain." But the pretty English villages will have a parson, a doctor, an officer's widow, a retired linen-draper, and perhaps the Dowager Squiress, living in houses of different patterns, each standing in its own garden, but not so far from the road as to stand in its own ground. And there will be an inn, and the church of course, and probably a large brick house inhabited by some testy old gentleman who has heaps of money and never speaks to any body. There will be one shop, or at the most two, the buying and selling of the place being done in the market-town two miles off. In George the houses are all of this description. No two are alike. They are all away from the road. They have trees around them. And they are quaint in their designs, many of them having been built by Dutch proprietors and after Dutch patterns. And they have an air of old fashioned middle class comfort,—as though the inhabitants all ate hot roast mutton at one o'clock as a rule of their lives. As far as I could learn they all did.

There are two churches,—a big one for the Dutch, and a little one for the English. Taking the village and the country round, the Dutch are no doubt in a great majority; but in George itself I heard nothing but English spoken. Late on a Sunday evening, when I had returned from the Knysna, I stood under an oak tree close to the corner of the English church and listened to a hymn by star light. The air was so soft and balmy that it was a pleasure to stand and breathe it. It was the longest hymn I ever heard; but I thought it was very sweet; and as it was all that I heard that Sunday of sacred service, I did not begrudge its length. But the South Africans of both colours are a tuneful people in their worship.

The comfort of the houses, and the beauty of the trees, and the numbers of the gardens, and the plentiful bounty of the green swards have done much for George;—but its real glory is in the magnificent grouping of the Outiniqua mountains under which it is clustered. These are altogether unlike the generality of South African hills, which are mostly flat-topped, and do not therefore seem to spring miscellaneously one from another,—but stand out separately and distinctly, each with its own flat top. The Outiniquas form a long line, running parallel with the coast from which they are distant perhaps 20 miles, and so group themselves,—as mountains should do,—that it is impossible to say where one ends and another begins. They more resemble some of the lower Pyrenees than any other range that I know, and are dark green in colour, as are the Pyrenees.

The Knysna, as the village and little port at the mouth of the Knysna river are called, is nearly 60 miles from George. The rocks at the entrance from the sea are about that distance, the village being four or five miles higher up. We started with four mules at 6.30,—but for the natural wickedness of the animals it would have been at 5.30,—and went up and down ravines and through long valleys for 50 miles to a place called Belvidere on the near side of the Knysna river. It would be hard to find 50 miles of more continuously picturesque scenery, for we were ever crossing dark black streams running down through the close ravines from the sides of the Outiniqua mountains. And here the ravines are very thickly wooded, in which respect they differ much from South African hill sides generally. But neither would it be easy to find 50 miles more difficult to travel. As we got nearer to the Knysna and further up from the little streams we had crossed, the ground became sandy,—till at last for a few miles it was impossible to do more than walk. But the mules, which had been very wicked in the morning, now put forth their virtues, and showed how superior they could be under stress of work to their nobler half-brother the horse.

At Belvidere we found an Inn and a ferry, and put them both to their appropriate use, drinking at the one and crossing the other. Here we left our mules and proceeded on foot each with his own bag and baggage. On the further side there was to be a walk of three miles, and it was very hot, and we had already trudged through some weary miles of sand. And though we had compelled the ferryman to carry our bags, we were laden with our great coats. But, lo, Providence sent the mounted post-boy along our path, when the resource of giving him the great coats to carry, and taking his pony for my own use was too evident to require a moment's thought. He saw it in the same light and descended as though it were a matter of course. And so I rode into the village, with the post boy and the post boy's dog, the ferryman and the Resident Magistrate following at my heels.

Here was another English village, but quite of a different class;—and yet picturesque beyond expression. "The" Knysna as the place is called is a large straggling collection of houses which would never be called other than a village in England, but would strike an investigating visitor as a village rising townwards. It is, in a very moderate way, a seaport, and possesses two inns. The post boy with unflinching impartiality refused to say which was the better, and we went to the wrong one,—that which mariners frequented. But such is South African honesty that the landlord at once put us right. He could put us up no doubt;—but Mr. Morgan at the other house could do it better. To Mr. Morgan, therefore, we went, and were told at once that we could have a leg of mutton, potatoes, and cabbages for dinner. "And very glad you ought to be to get them," said Mrs. Morgan. We assented of course, and every thing was pleasant.

In fifteen minutes we were intimate with everybody in the place, including the magistrate, the parson, and the schoolmaster; and in half an hour we were on horse back,—the schoolmaster accompanying us on the parson's nag,—in order that we might rush out to the Heads before dark. Away we scampered, galloping through salt water plashes, because the sun was already disappearing. We had just time to do it,—to gallop through the salt water and up the hills and round to the headland, so that we might look down into the lovely bright green tide which was rushing in from the Indian ocean immediately beneath our feet. From where I stood I could have dropped a penny into the sea without touching a rock.

The spot is one of extreme beauty. The sea passes in and out between two rocks 160 yards apart, and is so deep that even at low tide there are 18 feet of water. Where we stood the rocks were precipitous, but on the other side it was so far broken that we were told that bucks when pressed by hounds would descend it, so as to take the water at its foot. This would have seemed to be impossible were it not that stags will learn to do marvellous things in the way of jumping. On our right hand, between us and the shore of the outer Ocean, there was a sloping narrow green sward, hardly broader than a ravine, but still with a sward at its foot, running down to the very marge of the high tide, seeming to touch the water as we looked at it. And beyond, further on the left, there were bright green shrubs the roots of which the sea seemed to wash. A little further out was the inevitable "bar,"—injurious to commerce though adding to the beauty of the spot, for it was marked to us only by the breakers which foamed across it.

The schoolmaster told us much of the eligibility of the harbour. Two men of war,—not probably first-class ironclads, modest little gun boats probably—had been within the water of the Knysna. And there were always 18 feet of water on the bar because of the great scour occasioned by the narrow outlet, whereas other bars are at certain times left almost waterless. A great trade was done,—in exporting wood. But in truth the entrance to the Knysna is perhaps more picturesque and beautiful than commercially useful. For the former quality I can certainly speak; and as I stood there balancing between the charms of the spot and the coming darkness, aggravated by thoughts which would fly off to the much needed leg of mutton, I felt it to be almost hard that my friend the magistrate should have punctilious scruples as to his duties on Monday morning.

The description given to me as to trade at the Knysna was not altogether encouraging. The people were accustomed to cut wood and send it away to Capetown or Fort Elizabeth, and would do nothing else. And they are a class of Dutch labourers, these hewers of wood, who live a foul unholy life, very little if at all above the Hottentots in civilization. The ravines between the spurs of the mountains which run down to the sea are full of thick timber, and thus has grown up this peculiarity of industry by which the people of the Knysna support themselves. But wood is sometimes a drug,—as I was assured it was at the time of my visit,—and then the people are very badly off indeed. They will do nothing else. The land around will produce anything if some little care be taken as to irrigation. Any amount of vegetables might be grown and sent by boat to Capetown or Algoa Bay. But no! The people have learned to cut wood, and have learned nothing else. And consequently the Knysna is a poor place,—becoming poorer day by day. Such was the description given to us; but to the outward eye everybody seemed to be very happy,—and if the cabbage had been a little more boiled everything would have been perfect. The rough unwashed Dutch woodcutters were no doubt away in their own wretched homes among the spurs of the mountains. We, at any rate, did not see them.

Cutting timber is a good wholesome employment; and if the market be bad to-day it will probably be good to-morrow. And even Dutch woodcutters will become civilized when the schoolmaster gradually makes his way among them. But I did express myself as disappointed when I was told that nothing was ever done to restore the forests as the hill-sides are laid bare by the axe. There will be an end to the wood even on the spurs of the Outiniqua range, if no care be taken to assist the reproduction of nature. The Government of the Cape Colony should look to this, as do the Swiss Cantons and the German Duchies.

The Knysna is singularly English, being, as it is, a component part of a Dutch community, and supported by Dutch labour. I did not hear a Dutch word spoken while I was there,—though our landlady told us that her children played in Dutch or in English, as the case might be. Our school master was English, and the parson, and the magistrate, and the innkeeper, and the tradesmen of the place who called in during the evening to see the strangers and to talk with the magistrate from distant parts about Kreli and the Kafirs who were then supposed to be nearly subdued. It is a singularly picturesque place, and I left it on the following morning at 5 A.M. with a regret that I should never see the Knysna again.

There was to have been a cart to take us; but the horse had not chosen to be caught, and we walked to the ferry. Then, at the other side, at Belvidere, the wicked eggs would not get themselves boiled for an hour, though breakfast at an appointed time, 6 A.M., had been solemnly promised to us. Everything about the George and the Knysna gratified me much. But here, as elsewhere in South Africa, punctuality is not among the virtues of the people. Six o'clock means seven, or perhaps twenty minutes after seven. If a man promises to be with you at nine, he thinks that he has done pretty well if he comes between ten and eleven. I have frequently been told that a public conveyance would start at four in the morning,—or at five, as it might be,—and then have had to walk about for half an hour before a horse has made its appearance. And it is impossible for a stranger to discount this irregularity, so as to take advantage of it. It requires the experience of a life to ascertain what five o'clock will mean in one place, and what in another. When the traveller is assured that he certainly will be left behind if he be not up an hour before dawn, he will get up, though he knows that it will be in vain. The long minutes that I have passed, during my late travels, out in the grey dawn, regretting the bed from which I have been uselessly torn, have been generally devoted to loud inward assertions that South Africa can never do any good in the world till she learns to be more punctual. But we got our breakfast at Belvidere at last, and returned triumphantly with our four mules to George.

In the neighbourhood of George there is a mission station called Pacaltsdorp, for Hottentots, than which I can imagine nothing to be less efficient for any useful purpose. About 500 of these people live in a village,—or straggling community,—in which they have huts and about an acre of land for each family. There is a church attached to the place with a Minister, but when I visited the place there was no school. The stipend of the minister is paid by some missionary society at home, and it would seem that it is supported chiefly because for many years past it has been supported.

The question has frequently been raised whether the Hottentots are or are not extinct as a people. Before the question can be answered some one must decide what is a Hottentot. There is a race easily recognized throughout South Africa,—found in the greatest numbers in the Western Province of the Cape Colony,—who are at once known by their colour and physiognomy, and whom the new-comer will soon learn to call Hottentots whether they be so or not. They are of a dusty dusky hue, very unlike the shining black of the Kafir or Zulu, and as unlike the well shaded black and white of the so-called "Cape Boy" who has the mixed blood of Portuguese and Negroes in his veins. This man is lantern-jawed, sad-visaged, and mild-eyed,—quite as unlike a Kafir as he is to a European. There can be no doubt but that he is not extinct. But he is probably a bastard Hottentot,—a name which has become common as applied to his race,—and comes of a mingled race half Dutch and half South African.

These people generally perform the work of menial servants. They are also farm labourers,—and sometimes farmers in a small way. They are not industrious; but are not more lazy than men of such a race may be expected to be. They are not stupid, nor, as I think, habitually dishonest. Their morals in other respects do not rank high. Such as they are they should be encouraged in all ways to work for hire. Nothing can be so antagonistic to working as such a collection of them as that at Pacaltsdorp, where each has land assigned to him just sufficient to enable him to live,—with the assistance of a little stealing. As for church services there are quite enough for their wants in the neighbourhood, of various denominations. The only excuse for such an establishment would be the existence of a good school. But here there was none. Pacaltsdorp is I believe more than half a century old. When it was commenced the people probably had no civilizing influences round them. Now the Institution hardly seems to be needed.

From George I went over the Montague Pass to Oudtshoorn. My travels hitherto had chiefly been made with the view of seeing people and studying the state of the country,—and at this time, as I have explained above, my task was nearly completed. But now I was in search of the picturesque. It is not probable that many tourists will go from England to South Africa simply in quest of scenery. The country is not generally attractive, and the distances are too long. But to those who are there, either living in the Colony, or having been carried thither in search of health or money, the district of which I am now speaking offers allurements which will well repay the trouble of the journey. I am bound however to say that the beauties of this region cannot be seen at a cheap rate. Travelling in South Africa is costly. The week which I spent in the neighbourhood of George cost me £30, and would have cost me much more had I been alone. And yet I was not overcharged. The travellers in South Africa are few in number, and it is much travelling which makes cheap travelling.

Montague Pass is a road through the Outiniqua mountains,—which was made by Mr. White and called by the name of Mr. Montague who was the Colonial Secretary when the line was opened. It is very fine, quite equal to some of the mountain roads through the Pyrenees. There are spots on which the traveller will quite forget South African ugliness and dream that he is looking at some favoured European landskip. Throughout the whole of those mountains the scenery must be very grand, as they group themselves with fantastic intermingling peaks, and are green to the top. The ascent from the side nearest to George, which the tourist will probably walk, is about four miles, and the views are varied at almost every step,—as is the case in all really fine mountain scenery.

From the foot of the hill on the side away from George the road to Oudtshoorn passes for about thirty miles through the Karoo. The Karoo is a great Institution in the Cape Colony and consists of enormous tracts of land which are generally devoted to the pasture of sheep. The karoo properly is a kind of shrub, which sheep will eat, such as is the salt bush in Australia. Various diminutive shrubs are called "karoo," of which most are aromatic with a rich flavour as of some herb, whereas others are salt. But the word has come to signify a vast flowery plain, which in seasons of drought is terribly arid, over which the weary traveller has often to be dragged day after day without seeing a tree, or a green blade of grass; but which in spring becomes covered with wild flowers. A large portion of the Western Province is called Karoo, and is very tedious to all but sheep. That over which I passed now was "Karoo" only in its produce, being closely surrounded by mountains. The sheep, however, had in most places given way to ostriches,—feathers at present ruling higher in the world than wool. I could not but hope as I saw the huge birds stalking about with pompous air,—which as you approached them they would now and again change for a flirting gait, looking back over their shoulders as they skipped along with ruffled tails;—I have seen a woman do very much the same;—that they might soon be made to give place again to the modest sheep.

Oudtshoorn,—a place with a most uncomfortably Dutch name,—is an uninteresting village about two miles long; which would, at least, be uninteresting were it not blessed with a superlatively good hotel kept by one Mr. Holloway. Mr. Holloway redeems Oudtshoorn, which would otherwise have little to say for its own peculiar self. But it is the centre of a rich farming district, and the land in the valleys around it is very fertile. It must be remembered that fertility in South Africa does not imply a broad area of cultivated land, or even a capacity for it. Agriculture is everywhere an affair of patches, and frequently depends altogether on irrigation. Near Oudtshoorn I saw very fine crops,—and others which were equally poor,—the difference having been caused altogether by the quantity of water used. The productiveness of South Africa is governed by the amount of skill and capital which is applied to the saving of rain when rain does fall, and to the application of it to the land when no rain is falling. How far the water sent by God may, with the assistance of science, be made sufficient for the cultivation of the broad plains, I, at least, am unable to say. They who can measure the rainfalls, and the nature of the slopes by which the storms and showers may be led to their appointed places, will after a while tell us this. But it is patent to all that extensive cultivation in South Africa must depend on irrigation.

I had come to Oudtshoorn chiefly to see the Cango Caves. I wish some of my readers would write the name of the village in order that they may learn the amount of irritation which may be produced by an unfortunately awkward combination of letters. The Cango Caves are 24 miles distant from the place, and are so called after the old name of the district. Here too they make brandy from grapes,—called euphoniously "Old Cango." The vituperative have christened the beverage Cape Smoke. "Now I'll give you a glass of real fine Old Cango," has been said to me more than once. I would strongly advise weak-headed Europeans, not to the manner born, to abstain from the liquor under whatever name it may make its appearance. But the caves may be seen without meddling with the native brandy. We brought ours with us, and at any rate believed that it had come from France.

The road from the village to the caves is the worst, I think, over which wheels were ever asked to pass. A gentleman in Oudtshoorn kindly offered to take us. No keeper of post horses would let animals or a carriage for so destructive a journey. At every terrific jolt and at every struggle over the rocks my heart bled for our friend's property,—of which he was justly proud. He abstained even from a look of dismay as we came smashing down from stone to stone. Every now and then we heard that a bolt had given way, but were assured in the same breath that there were enough to hold us together. We were held together; but the carriage I fear never can be used again. The horses perhaps with time may get over their ill usage. We were always going into a river or going out of it, and the river had succeeded in carrying away all the road that had ever been made. Unless the engineers go seriously to work I shall be the last stranger that will ever visit the Cango Caves in a carriage.

I have made my way into various underground halls, the mansions of bats and stalactites. Those near Deloraine in Tasmania are by far the most spacious in ascertained length that I have seen. Those at Wonderfontein in the Transvaal, of which I will speak in the next volume, may be, and probably are, larger still, but they have never been explored. In both of these the stalactites are much poorer in form than in the caves of the Cheddar cliffs,—which however are comparatively small. The Mammoth Caves in Kentucky I have not visited; but I do not understand that the subterranean formations are peculiarly grand. In the Cango Grottoes the chambers are very much bigger than in the Tasmanian Caves.

They also have not been fully explored. But the wonderful forms and vagaries of the stalactites are infinitely finer than anything I have seen elsewhere. We brought with us many blue lights,—a sort of luminary which spreads a powerful glare to a considerable distance for three or four minutes,—without which it would be impossible to see the shapes around. The candles which we carried with us for our own guidance had little or no effect.

In some places the droppings had assumed the shape of falling curtains. Across the whole side of a hall, perhaps sixty feet long, these would hang in regular pendent drapery, fold upon fold, seeming to be as equal and regular as might be the heavy folds protecting some inner sacred chapel. And in the middle of the folds there would be the entrance, through which priests and choristers and people might walk as soon as the machinery had been put to work and the curtain had been withdrawn. In other places there would hang from the roof the collected gathered pleats, all regular, as though the machinery had been at work. Here there was a huge organ with its pipes, and some grotesque figure at the top of it as though the constructor of all these things had feared no raillery. In other places there were harps against the walls, from which, as the blue lights burned, one expected to hear sounds of perhaps not celestial minstrelsy. And pillars were erected up to the ceiling,—not a low grovelling ceiling against which the timid visitor might fear to strike his head, but a noble roof, perfected, groined, high up, as should be that of a noble hall. That the columns had in fact come drop by drop from the rock above us did not alter their appearance. There was one very thick, of various shapes, grotesque and daring, looking as though the base were some wondrous animal of hideous form that had been made to bear the superstructure from age to age. Then as the eye would struggle to examine it upwards, and to divide the details each from the others, the blue light would go out and the mystery would remain. Another blue light would be made to burn; but bats would come flitting through, disturbing all investigation;—and the mystery would still remain.

There were various of these halls or chambers, all opening one to another by passages here and there, so that the visitor who is never compelled to travel far, might suppose them all to be parts of one huge dark mansion underground. But in each hall there were receding closets, guarded by jutting walls of stalactite breast high, round which however on closer search, a way would be found,—as though these might be the private rooms in which the ghouls would hide themselves when thus disturbed by footsteps and voices, by candles and blue lights from above. I was always thinking that I should come upon a ghoul; but there were inner chambers still into which they crept, and whither I could not follow them.

Careful walking is necessary, as the ground is uneven; and there are places in which the ghouls keep their supply of water,—stone troughs wonderfully and beautifully made. But except in one place there is no real difficulty in moving about, when once the visitor to the Caves has descended into them. At this place the ascent is perplexing, because the ground is both steep and slippery. I can imagine that a lady or an old man might find it difficult to be dragged up. Such lady or old man should either remain below or allow us companions to drag him up. There is very little stoop necessary anywhere. But it has to be borne in mind that after entering the mouth of the cave and reaching the first chamber, the realms I have described have to be reached by an iron ladder which holds 38 steps. To get onto this ladder requires some little care and perhaps a dash of courage. The precautions taken, however, suffice, and I think I may say that there is no real danger.

We called at a Dutch Boer's house about a mile from the Caves, and were accompanied by three members of the Boer's family. This is usual, and, I believe, absolutely necessary. I paid one of the men a sovereign for his trouble,—which sum he named as his regular price for the assistance provided. He found the candles, but some of our party took the blue lights with them. Nothing could have been seen without them.

From Oudtshoorn I travelled back through the Outiniqua mountains by Robinson's pass to Mossel Bay, and thence returned by steamer to Capetown.

CHAPTER VIII

The Paarl, Ceres, and Worcester

My last little subsidiary tours in South Africa were made from Capetown to the country immediately across the Hottentot mountains after my return from Oudtshoorn and the Cango Caves. It had then become nearly midsummer and I made up my mind that it would be very hot. I prepared myself to keep watch and ward against musquitoes and comforted myself by thinking how cool it would be on my return journey, in the Bay of Biscay for instance on the first of January. I had heard, or perhaps had fancied, that the South African musquito would be very venomous and also ubiquitous. I may as well say here as elsewhere that I found him to be but a poor creature as compared with other musquitoes,—the musquito of the United States for instance. The South African December, which had now come, tallies with June on the other side of the line;—and in June the musquito of Washington is as a roaring lion.

On this expedition I stopped first at The Paarl, which is not across the Hottentot mountains but in the district south of the mountains to which the Dutch were at first inclined to confine themselves when they regarded the apparently impervious hills at their back as the natural and sufficient barrier of their South African dominions.

There is now a railway out of Capetown which winds its way through these mountains, or rather circumvents them by a devious course. It branches from the Wynberg line a mile or two out of Capetown, and then pursues its way towards the interior of Africa with one or two assistant branches on the southern side of the hills. The Wynberg line is altogether surburban and pleasant. The first assistant branch goes to Malmesbury and is agricultural. Malmesbury is a corn producing country in the flats north of Capetown, and will, I hope, before long justify the railway which has been made. At present I am told that the branch hardly pays for the fuel it consumes. It no doubt will justify the railway as wheat can be grown in the district without irrigation, and it will therefore become peopled with prosperous farmers. Then there is a loop line to Stellenbosch, an old and thriving little Dutch town which I did not visit. It is very old, having been founded in 1684. In 1685 the French Refugees came of whom a large proportion were settled at Stellenbosch. The main line which is intended to cross the entire Colony then makes its way on to The Paarl and Wellington,—from whence it takes its passage among the mountains. This is of course in the Western Province,—which I must persist in so designating though I know I shall encounter the wrath of many South African friends of the West. In the Eastern Province there are two lines which have been commenced from the coast with the same mission of making their way up into the whole continent of Africa, one of them starting from Fort Elizabeth, intending to go on by Cradock, with a branch already nearly finished to Grahamstown, and the other from East London travelling north by King Williamstown and Queenstown. The rivalry between the three is great. It is so great even between the two latter as to have much impaired the homogeneity of the Eastern Province. At present the chief object of them all is to secure the trade to Kimberley and the Diamond Fields. That by which I was now travelling is already open to Worcester, across the mountain, for all traffic, and for goods traffic forty miles beyond Worcester, up the valley of the Hex River.

I stopped at The Paarl to see the vineyards and orange groves, and also the ostriches. These are the industries of The Paarl, which is in its way a remarkable and certainly a very interesting place. It was only during the last month of my sojourn in South Africa that I came to see how very much lovely scenery there is within reach of the residents of Capetown. As in all countries of large area, such as South Africa, the United States, the interior of Australia, and Russia generally,—of which I speak only from hearsay,—the great body of the landskip is uninteresting. The Transvaal, the Orange Free State, Griqua Land West, and the Karoos of the Cape Colony are not beautiful. This the traveller hears, and gradually sees for himself. But if he will take the trouble he may also see for himself spots that are as entrancing as any among the more compressed charms of European scenery. The prettinesses of The Paarl, however, come from the works of man almost as much as from those of Nature.

It is a very long town,—if town it is to be called,—the main street running a length of eight miles. Through all this distance one spot is hardly more central than another,—though there is a market-place which the people of The Paarl probably regard as the heart of the town. It is nowhere contiguous, the houses standing, almost all, separately. It is under the paarl, or pearl rock,[1]—which strangers are invited to ascend, but are warned at the same time that the ascent in summer may be very hot. I thanked my friend for the caution and did not ascend the mountain. I was of course told that without ascending I could not see The Paarl aright. I did not therefore see it aright, and satisfy my conscience by instructing others how they may do so. The town from one end to the other is full of oak trees, planted as I was told by the Dutch. They did not look to be over seventy years of age, but I was assured that the growth though certain had been slow. It is perhaps the enormous number of oak trees at The Paarl which more than anything else makes the place so graceful. But many of the houses too are graceful, being roomy old Dutch buildings of the better class, built with gables here and there, with stables and outhouses around them, and with many oaks at every corner, all in full foliage at the time of my visit. At The Paarl there are no bad houses. The coloured people who pick the grapes and tread the wine vats and hoe the vines live in pretty cottages up the hill side. There is nothing squalid or even untidy at The Paarl. For eight miles you are driven through a boskey broad well-shaded street with houses on each side at easy intervals, at every one of which you are tempted to think that you would like to live.

What do the people do? That is of course the first question. It was evident from the great number of places of worship that they all went to church very often;—and from the number of schools that they were highly educated. Taking the population generally, they are all Dutch, and are mostly farmers. But their farming is very unlike our farming,—and still more unlike that of the Dutch Boers up the country,—the main work of each individual farmer being confined to a very small space, though the tract of adjacent land belonging to him may extend to one or two or three thousand acres. The land on which they really live and whereby they make their money is used chiefly for the growth of grapes,—and after that for oranges and ostriches. The district is essentially wine making,—though at the time of my visit the low, price of wine had forced men to look to other productions to supplement their vines.

I was taken to the house of one gentleman,—a Dutchman of course,—whose homestead in the middle of the town was bosomed amidst oaks. His vineyard was a miracle of neatness, and covered perhaps a dozen acres;—but his ostriches were his pride. Wine was then no more than £3 the "ligger,"—the ligger, or leaguer, being a pipe containing 126 gallons. This certainly is very cheap for wine,—so cheap that I was driven to think that if I lived at The Paarl I would prefer ostriches. It seemed to be thought, however, that a better time would come, and that the old price of £5 or £6 the ligger might again be reached. I am afraid there is some idea that this may be done by the maternal affection of the Mother

Country,—which is to be shewn in a reduction of the duties, so that Cape wine may be consumed more freely in England. I endeavoured to explain that England cannot take wine from the Colonies at a lower rate of duty than from foreign countries. I did not say anything as to the existing prejudice against South African sherries. I was taken into this gentleman's house and had fruit and wine of his own producing. The courtesy and picturesque old-fashioned neatness of it all was very pleasing. He himself was a quiet well-mannered man, shewing no excitement about anything, till it was suggested to him that a mode of incubating ostriches eggs different to his own might be preferable. Then he shewed us that on a subject which he had studied he could have a strong opinion of his own. This was in the town. The owner, no doubt, had a considerable tract of land lying far back from the street; but all his operations seemed to be carried on within a quarter of a mile of his house.

I was afterwards driven out to two country farms, but at both of them the same thing prevailed. Here there were large vineyards, and oranges in lieu of ostriches. At one beautiful spot, just under the mountains, there was a grove of 500 orange trees from which, the proprietor told me, he had during the last year made a net profit of £200 after paying all expenses. £200 will go a long way towards the expenditure of a Dutch farmer's house. Of course there was no rent to be paid as the whole place belonged to him,—and had probably belonged to his ancestors for many generations. He was lord also of a large vineyard which he told me had cost a great deal of labour to bring to its present perfection of cleanliness and fertility.

Here too we were taken into the house and had wine given to us,—wine that was some years old. It certainly was very good, resembling a fine port that was just beginning to feel its age in the diminution of its body. We enquired whether wine such as that was for sale, but were told that no such wine was to be bought from any grower of grapes. The farmers would keep a little for their own use, and that they would never sell. Neither do the merchants keep it,—not finding it worth their while to be long out of their money,—nor the consumers, there being no commodity of cellarage in the usual houses of the Colony. It has not been the practice to keep wine,—and consequently the drinker seldom has given to him the power of judging whether the Cape wines may or may not become good. At dinner tables at the Cape hosts will apologise for putting on their tables the wines of the Colony, telling their guests that that other bottle contains real sherry or the like. I am inclined to think that the Cape wines have hardly yet had a fair chance, and have been partly led to this opinion by the excellence of that which I drank at Great Draghenstern, which was the name either of the farm or of the district in question.

As we had wandered through the grove we saw oranges still hanging on the trees, high up out of reach. The season was over but still there were a few. It is a point of honour to keep them as long as possible,—so that towards December they become valuable treasures. I had one given to me when we started, as being the oldest of the party. It was scrupulously divided, and enjoyed no doubt very much more than had we been sent away with our cart full.

Here too the house was exceedingly picturesque, being surrounded by oak trees. There was no entrance hall, such as has been common with us for many years; but the rooms were lofty, spacious, and well built, and the neighbouring wilderness of a garden was wonderfully sweet with flowers. The owner was among the vines when we arrived, and as he walked up to us in the broad place in front of his house, he informed us that he was "jolly old ——" This he said in Dutch. His only word of English was spoken as we parted. "Good bye, old gentleman," he holloaed out to me as I shook hands with him. Here as elsewhere there was no breadth of cultivation. The farm was large, but away from the house, and on it there were only a few cattle. There can be no cultivation without irrigation, and no extended irrigation without much labour. Like other farmers in South Africa jolly old —— complained that his industry was sadly crippled by want of labour. Nevertheless jolly old —— seemed to me to be as well off as a man need be in this world. Perhaps it was that I envied him his oaks, and his mountains, and his old wine,—and the remaining oranges.

We visited also a wool-washing establishment which had just been set up with new fashioned machinery, and then we had seen all that The Paarl had to shew us in the way of its productions. I should perhaps say that I visited the stores of a great wine company, at which, in spite of the low price of the article in which they deal, good dividends are being paid. At the wine stores I was chiefly interested in learning that a coloured cooper whom I saw at work on a cask,—a black man,—was earning £300 a year. I enquired whether he was putting by a fortune and was told that he and his family lived from hand to mouth and that he frequently overdrew his wages. "But what does he do with the money?" I asked. "Hires a carriage on Sundays or holy days and drives his wife about," was the reply. The statement was made as though it were a sad thing that a coloured man should drive his wife about in a carriage while labour was so scarce and dear, but I was inclined to think that the cooper was doing well with his money. At any rate it pleased me to learn that a black man should like to drive his wife about;—and that he should have the means.

I was very much gratified with The Paarl, thinking it well for a Colony to have a town and a district so pretty and so prosperous. The population of the district is about 16,000, and of the town about 8000. It is, however, much more like a large village than a small town,—the feeling being produced by the fact that the houses all have gardens attached to them and are built each after its own fashion and not in rows.

From this place I and the friend who was travelling with me went on by cart to Ceres. It would have been practicable to go by railway at any rate to the Ceres Road Station, but we were anxious to travel over two of the finest mountain roads in South Africa, Bain's Kloof, and Mitchell's Pass, both of which lay on the road from The Paarl to Ceres. To do so we passed through Wellington and Wagon-maker's valley, which lay immediately under the Hottentot mountains. I have described grapes and oranges as being the great agricultural industries of The Paarl district;—but I must not leave the locality without recording the fact that the making of Cape carts and wagons is a specialty of The Paarl and of the adjacent country. It is no more possible to ignore the fact in passing through its streets than it is to ignore the building of carriages in Long Acre. The country up above The Paarl has been called Wagon-maker's valley very far back among the Dutch of the Cape, and the trade remains through the whole district. And at Wellington there is I believe the largest orange grove in the country. Time did not allow me to see it, but I could look down upon it from some of the turns in the wonderful road by which Mr. Bain made his way through the mountains.

Rising up from Wellington is the Bain's Kloof road which traverses the first instalment of the barrier mountains. It is the peculiarity of these hills that they seem to lie in three folds,—so that when you make your way over the first you descend into the valley of the Breede River,—and from thence ascend again on high, to come down into the valley of Ceres, with the third and last range of the Hottentots still before you. Bain's Kloof contains some very grand scenery, especially quite at the top;—but is not equal either to Montague Pass,—or to Mitchell's Pass which we were just about to visit. Descending from this we crossed at the fords two branches of the Breede River,—at one of which the bridge was impassable, there never having been a bridge at the other,—and immediately ascended Mitchell's Pass. The whole of the country north and east of Capetown as far as the mountains extend is made remarkable by these passes which have been carried through the hills with great engineering skill and at an enormous cost to the Colony. It has chiefly been done by convict labour,—the labour of its own convicts—for the Colony, as my reader will I hope remember, has never received a convict from the Mother Country. But convict labour is probably dearer than any other. The men certainly are better fed than they would be if they were free. Houses have to be built for them which are afterwards deserted. And when the man has been housed and fed he will not work as a freeman must do if he means to keep his place. But the roads have been made, and Mitchell's Pass into the valley of Ceres is a triumph of engineering skill.

To see it aright the visitor should travel by it from Ceres towards the Railway. We passed it in both directions and I was never more struck by the different aspect which the same scenery may bear if your face be turned one way or the other. The beauty here consists of the colour of the rocks rather than of the shape of the hills. There is a world of grey stone around you as you ascend from the valley which becomes almost awful as you look at it high above your head and then low beneath your feet. As you begin the ascent from Ceres, near the road but just out of sight of it, there is a small cataract where the Breede runs deep through a narrow channel,—so narrow that a girl can jump from rock to rock. Some years since a girl was about to jump it when her lover, giving her a hand to help her, pulled her in. She never lived to become his bride but was drowned there in the deep black waters of the narrow Breede.

Ceres is one of those village-towns by which this part of the Colony is populated, and lies in a Rasselas happy valley,—a basin so surrounded by hills as to shew no easy way out. The real Rasselas valley, however, was, we suppose, very narrow, whereas this valley is ten miles long by six broad, and has a mail cart road running through it. It lies on the direct route from Capetown to Fraserburg, and thence, if you choose to go that way, to the Diamond Fields and the Orange Free State. Nevertheless the place looks as though it were, or at least should be, delightfully excluded from all the world beyond. Here again the houses stand separate among trees, and the river flowing through it makes everything green. I was told that Ceres had been lately smitten with too great a love of speculation, had traded beyond her means, and lost much of her capital. It was probably the reaction from this condition of things which produced the peculiarly sleepy appearance which I observed around me. A billiard room had been lately built which seemed just then to monopolize the energy of the place. The hotel was clean and pleasant,—and would have been perfect but for a crowd of joyous travellers who were going down to see somebody married two or three hundred miles off. On our arrival we were somewhat angry with the very civil and considerate landlady who refused to give us all the accommodation we wanted because she expected twelve other travellers. I did not believe in the twelve travellers, and muttered something as to trying the other house even though she devoted to the use of me and my friend a bedroom which she declared was as a rule kept for ladies. We of course demanded two rooms,—but as to that she was stern. When a party of eleven did in truth come I not only forgave her, but felt remorse at having occupied the best chamber. She was a delightful old lady, a German, troubled much in her mind at the time by the fact that a countryman of hers had come to her house with six or seven dozen canaries and had set up a shop for them in her front sitting room. She did not know how to get rid of them; and, as all the canaries sang continuously the whole day through, their presence did impair the comfort of the establishment. Nevertheless I can safely recommend the hotel at Ceres as the canaries will no doubt have been all sold before any reader can act on this recommendation.

The name of Ceres has been given to the valley in a spirit of prophecy which has yet to be fulfilled. The soil no doubt is fertile, but the cereal produce is not as yet large. Here, as in so large a proportion of South Africa, irrigation is needed before wheat can be sown with any certainty of repaying the sower. But the valley is a smiling spot, green and sweet among the mountains, and gives assurance by its aspect of future success and comfort. It has a reputation for salubrity, and should be visited by those who wish to see the pleasant places of the Cape Colony.

From Ceres we went back over Mitchell's Pass to the railway, and so to Worcester. Worcester is a town containing 4,000 inhabitants, and is the capital of a "Division." The whole Colony is portioned out into Divisions, in each of which there is located a Resident Magistrate or Commissioner, who lives at the chief town. The Division and the Capital have, I believe always, the same name. Worcester is conspicuous among other things for its huge Drotsdy, or Chief Magistrate's mansion. In the old Dutch days the Drotsdy was inhabited by the Landroost, whose place is now filled by the English Commissioner. I grieve to say that with the spirit of economy which pervades self-governing Colonies in these modern days, the spacious Drotsdy houses have usually been sold, and the Commissioners have been made to find houses for themselves,—just as a police magistrate does in London. When I was at George I could not but pity the Commissioner who was forced day after day to look at the beautiful Drotsdy house, embowered by oak trees, which had been purchased by some rich Dutch farmer. But at Worcester the Drotsdy, which was certainly larger than any other Drotsdy and apparently more modern, was still left as a residence for the Commissioner. When I asked the reason I was told that no one would buy it.

It is an enormous mansion, with an enormous garden. And it is approached in front through a portico of most pretentious and unbecoming columns. Nothing could be imagined less like Dutch grandeur or Dutch comfort. The house, which might almost contain a regiment, certainly contained a mystery which warranted enquiry. Then I was told the story. One of the former great Governors, Lord Charles Somerset,—the greatest Governor the Colony ever had as far as a bold idea of autocratic authority can make a Governor great,—had wanted a shooting lodge under the mountains, and had consequently caused the Drotsdy house at Worcester to be built,—of course at the expense of the Crown. I can never reflect that such glorious days have gone for ever without a soft regret. There was something magnificent in those old, brave, unhidden official peculations by the side of which the strict and straight-laced honesty of our present Governors looks ugly and almost mean.

Worcester is a broad town with well arranged streets, not fully filled up but still clean,—without that look of unkempt inchoation which is so customary in Australian towns and in many of the young municipalities of the United States. The churches among its buildings are conspicuous,—those attracting the most notice being the Dutch Reformed Church, that of the Church of England,—and a Church for the use of the natives in which the services are also in accordance with the Dutch Reformed religion. The latter is by far the most remarkable, and belongs to an Institution which, beyond even the large Drotsdy house, makes Worcester peculiarly worth visiting.

Of the Institution the Revd. Mr. Esselin is the Head, but was not the founder. There were I think two gentlemen in charge of a native mission before he came to Worcester;—but the church and schools have obtained their great success under his care. He is a German clergyman who came to the place in 1848, and has had charge of the Institution since that date. That he has done more than any one else as a teacher and preacher among the coloured races, at any rate in the Western Province, I think will hardly be denied. But for Lovedale in the East of which I shall speak further on, I should have claimed this pre-eminence for him as to all South Africa. This I believe is owing to the fact that under his guidance the coloured people have been treated as might any poor community in England or elsewhere in Europe which required instruction either secular or religious. There has been a distinct absence of the general missionary idea that coloured people want special protection, that they should be kept separate, and that they should have provided for them locations,—with houses and grounds. The ordinary missionary treatment has I think tended to create a severance between the natives and the white people who are certainly destined to be their masters and employers,—at any rate for many years to come; whereas M. Esselin has from the first striven to send them out into the world to earn their bread, giving them such education as they have been able to receive up to the age of fifteen. Beyond that they have not, except on rare occasions, been kept in his schools.

The material part of the Institution consists of a church, and four large school-rooms, and of the pastor's residence. There are also other school-rooms attached of older date. The church has been built altogether by contributions from the coloured attendants, and is a spacious handsome building capable of containing 900 persons. M. Esselin told me that his ordinary congregation amounted to 500. I went to the morning service on Sunday, and found the building apparently full.

I think there was no white person there besides the clergyman, my companion, and myself. As the service was performed in Dutch I did not stay long, contenting myself with the commencing hymn—which was well sung, and very long, more Africano. I had at this time been in various Kafir places of worship and had become used to the Kafir physiognomies. I had also learned to know the faces of the Hottentots, of old Cape negroes, of the coloured people from St. Helena, and of the Malays. The latter are not often Christians; but the races have become so mixed that there is no rule which can be accepted in that respect. Here there were no Kafirs, the Kafirs not having as yet made their way in quest of wages as far west as Worcester.[2] The people were generally Hottentot, half negro,—with a considerable dash of white blood through them. But in the church I could see no Europeans. It is a coloured congregation, and supported altogether by contributions from the coloured people.

The school interested me, however, more than the church. I do not know that I ever saw school-rooms better built, better kept, or more cleanly. As I looked at them one after another I remembered what had been the big room at Harrow in my time, and the single school-room which I had known at Winchester,—for there was only one; and the school-room, which I had visited at Eton and Westminster; and I was obliged to own that the coloured children of Worcester are very much better housed now during their lessons than were the aristocracy of England forty or fifty years ago. There has been an improvement since, but still something might be learned by a visit to Worcester. At Worcester the students pay a penny a week. At the other schools I have named the charges are something higher.

There are 500 children at these schools among whom I saw perhaps half a dozen of white blood. M. Esselin said that he took any who came who would comply with the general rules of the school. The education of coloured children is, however, the intention of the place. In addition to the pence, which do not amount to £100 a year, the Government grant,—given to this school, as to any other single school kept in accordance with Government requirements,—amounts to £70 per annum. The remaining cost, which must be very heavy, is made up out of the funds raised by the congregation of the church. Under M. Esselin there is but one European master. The other teachers are all females and all coloured. There were I think seven of them. The children, as I have said before, are kept only till they are fifteen and are then sent out to the work of the world without any pretence of classical scholarship or ecstatic Christianity.

Having heard of a marvellous hot spring or Geyser in the neighbourhood of Worcester I had myself driven out to visit it. It is about 8 miles from the town at, or rather beyond, a marshy little lake called Brand Vley, the name of which the hot spring bears. It is adjacent to a Dutch farmhouse to which it belongs, and is to some small extent used for sanitary purposes. If, as I was told, the waters are peculiarly serviceable to rheumatic affections, it is a pity that such sanitary purposes should not be extended, and be made more acceptable to the rheumatic world at large.

There is but one spring of boiling water. In New Zealand they are very numerous, bubbling up frequently in close proximity to each other, sometimes so small and unpronounced as to make it dangerous to walk among them lest the walker's feet should penetrate through the grass into the boiling water. Here the one fountain is very like to some of the larger New Zealand springs. The water as it wells up is much hotter than boiling, and fills a round pool which may perhaps have a circumference of thirty feet. It is of a perfectly bright green colour, except where the growth of a foul-looking weed defaces the surface. From this well the still boiling water makes its way under ground, a distance of a few yards into a much larger pool where it still boils and bubbles, and still maintains that bright green colour which seems to be the property of water which springs hot from the bowels of the earth.

At a little distance a house has been built intended to contain baths, and conduits have been made to bring a portion of the water under cover for the accommodation of bathers,—while a portion is carried off for irrigation. We made our way into the house where we found a large Dutch party, whether of visitors or residents at the house we did not know; and one of them, a pretty Dutch girl prettily dressed, who could speak English was kind enough to show us the place. We accompanied her, though the stench was so foul that it was almost impossible to remain beneath the roof.[3] It was difficult to conceive how these people could endure it and live. The girl opened the bath rooms, in which the so-called baths, constructed on the floor, were dilapidated and ruined. "They are all just now near broke to pieces," she said. I asked her what the patients paid. "Just sixpence a day," she replied, "because one cannot in these hard days charge the people too much." I presume that the patients were expected to bring their diet with them,—and probably their beds.

And yet an invaluable establishment might be built at this spot, and be built in the midst of most alluring scenery! The whole district of which I am now speaking is among the mountains, and the Worcester railway station is not more than eight or ten miles distant. The Auckland Geysers in New Zealand cannot be reached except by long journeys on horseback, and accommodation for invalids could be procured only at great cost. But here an establishment of hot baths might be made very easily. It seemed at any rate to be a pity that such a provision of hot water should be wasted,—especially if it contain medicinal properties of value. We were forced to return to Worcester without trying it, as there were not means of bathing at our command. No possible medicinal properties would have atoned for the horrors of undressing within that building.

1. So called from a block of granite lying on the mountain over the town, to which has been given the name of The Pearl.
2. Mr. Esselin told us that since he had been at Worcester he had had a few but only a very few Kafir children in his schools.
3. This did not come at all from any property of the water but simply from the foulness of the place.

CHAPTER IX

ROBERTSON, SWELLENDAM AND SOUTHEY'S PASS

FROM WORCESTER WE WENT ON to a little town called Robertson, which is also the capital of an electoral division. The country here is altogether a country of mountains, varying from three to seven thousand feet high. The valleys between them are broad, so as to give ample space for agriculture,—if only agriculture can be made to pay. Having heard much of the continual plains of South Africa I had imagined that everything beyond the hills immediately surrounding Capetown would be flat; but in lieu of that I found myself travelling through a country in which one series of mountains succeeds another for hundreds of miles. The Cape Colony is very large,—especially the Western Province, which extends almost from the 28th to much below the 34th degree of latitude S., and from the 7th to the 23rd of longitude E. Of this immense area I was able to see comparatively only a small part;—but in what I did see I was never out of the neighbourhood of mountains. The highest mountain in South Africa is Cathkin Peak, in Natal, and that is over 10,000 feet. In the districts belonging to the Cape Colony the highest is in Basuto, and is the Mont aux Sources. The highest in the Western Province is called The Seven Weeks Poort, which is in the neighbourhood of Swellendam and belongs to the district of which I am now speaking. It is 7,600 feet high. As the first and most important consequence of this the making of roads within a couple of hundred miles of Capetown has been a matter of great difficulty. In every direction passes through the mountains have had to be found, which when found have required great skill and a very heavy expenditure before they could be used for roads. But a second consequence has been that a large extent of magnificent scenery has been thrown open, which, as the different parts of the world are made nearer to each other by new discoveries and advancing science, will become a delight and a playground to travellers,—as are the Alps and the Pyrenees and the Apennines in Europe. At present I think that but few people in England are aware that among the mountains of the Cape Colony there is scenery as grand as in Switzerland or the south-west of France. And the fact that such scenery is close to them attracts the notice of but a small portion of the inhabitants of the Colony itself. The Dutch I fancy regarded the mountains simply as barriers or disagreeable obstacles, and the English community which has come since has hardly as yet achieved idleness sufficient for the true enjoyment of tourist travelling.

Robertson itself is not an interesting town, though it lies close under the mountains. Why it should have missed the beauty of The Paarl, of Ceres, and of Swellendam which we were about to visit, I can hardly say. Probably its youth is against it. It has none of the quaintness of Dutch architecture; and the oaks,—for it has oaks,—are not yet large enough to be thoroughly delightful. We found, however, in its neighbourhood a modern little wood large enough to enable us to lose ourselves, and were gratified by the excitement.

I have said that in these districts, mountainous as they are, the valleys are broad enough for agriculture, if only agriculture can be made to pay. The fertility of the soil is apparent everywhere. Robertson itself is devoted to the making of brandy, and its vineyards are flourishing. Patches of corn were to be seen and trees had grown luxuriantly here and there. It seemed that almost anything would grow. But little or nothing useful will grow without the aid of other water than that bestowed in the regular course of nature. "I plant as many trees," said the magistrate of the district, speaking to me of the streets of the town, "as I can get convicts to water." "Wheat;—oh yes, I can grow any amount of wheat," a farmer said to me in another place, "where I can lead water." In Messrs. Silver and Co.'s Guide book, page 99, I find the following passage in reference to the Cape Colony. "The whole question of the storing of water by means of scientifically constructed dams is one that cannot be too strongly urged on the Cape Government." Of the truth of this there can be no doubt, nor is the district one in which the fall of rain is deficient, if the rain could be utilized. It amounts to something over 24 inches annually, which would suffice for all the purposes required if the supply given could be made to flow upon the lands. But it falls in sudden storms, is attracted by the mountains, and then runs off into the rivers and down to the sea without effecting those beneficent objects which I think we may say it was intended to produce. The consequence is that agriculture is everywhere patchy, and that the patches are generally small. The farmer according to his means or according to his energy will subject 10, 20, 30, or 40 acres to artificial irrigation. When he does so he can produce anything. When he does not do so he can produce nothing.[1]

There are the mountains and the rains fall upon them, running off uselessly to the ocean with their purpose unaccomplished. When we want to store the rain water from our roof for domestic uses we construct pipes and tanks and keep the blessing by us so as to have it when we want it. The side of a mountain is much like the roof of a house,—only larger. And the pipes are for the most part made to our hand by nature in the shape of gullies, kloofs, and rivulets. It is but the tanks that we want, and some adjustment as to the right of using them. This, if ever done, must be done by the appliance of science, and I of all men am the last to suggest how such appliance should be made. But that it is practicable appears to be probable, and that if done it would greatly increase the produce of the lands affected and the general well being of the Colony no one can doubt. But the work is I fear beyond the compass of private enterprise in a small community, and seems to be one which requires the fostering hand of Government. If a Governor of the Cape Colony,—or a Prime Minister,—could stop the waters as they rush down from the mountains and spread them over the fields before they reach the sea he would do more for the Colony than has been effected by any conqueror of Kafirs.

From Robertson we went a little off our road to Montague for the sake of seeing Cogman's Pass. That also is interesting though not as fine as some others. Whence it has taken its name I could not discover. It was suggested to me that it was so called because of its lizards;—and the lizards certainly were there in great numbers. I could not find that Cogman meant lizard either in Hottentot language or in Dutch. Nor did it appear that any man of note of the name of Cogman had connected himself with the road. But there is the Pass with its ugly name leading gallantly and cleverly through the rocks into the little town of Montague.

Montague like Oudtshoorn and Robertson makes brandy, the Montague brandy being, I was assured, equal to the Cango brandy which comes from Oodtshoorn, and much superior to that made at Robertson. I tasted them all round and declare them to be equally villainous. I was assured that it was an acquired taste. I hope that I may not be called on to go through the practice necessary for acquiring it. I shall perhaps be told that I formed my judgment on the new spirit, and that the brandy ought to be kept before it is used. I tried it new and old. The new spirit is certainly the more venemous, but they are equally nasty. It is generally called Cape Smoke. Let me warn my readers against Cape Smoke should they ever visit South Africa.

At Montague, as we were waiting outside the inn for our cart, two sturdy English beggars made their appearance before us, demanding charity. They could get no work to do,—so they said,—in this accursed land, and wanted money to buy bread. No work to do! And yet every farmer, every merchant, every politician

I had met and spoke with since I had put my foot on South African soil, had sworn to me that the country was a wretched country simply because labour could not be had! The two men had Cape Smoke plainly developed in every feature of their repulsive faces. As we were seated and could not rid ourselves of our country men without running away, we entered into conversation with them. Not get work! It was certainly false! They were on their way, they said, from the Eastern Province. Had they tried the railway? We knew that at the present moment labour was peculiarly wanted on the railway because of the disturbance created by Kreli and his Galekas. For the disturbance of which I shall speak in one of the concluding chapters of my work was then on hand. "Yes," said the spokesman who, as on all such occasions, was by far the more disreputable of the two. "They had tried the railway, and had been offered 2s. 6d. a day. They were not going to work along side of niggers for 2s. 6d., which would only supply them with grub! Did we want real Englishmen to do that?" We told them that certainly we did want real Englishmen to earn their grub honestly and not to beg it and then, having endeavoured to shame them by calling them mean fellows, we were of course obliged to give them money.

Such rascals might turn up anywhere,—in any town in England much more probably than in South Africa. But their condition as we saw them, and the excuse which they made for their condition, were typical of the state of labour in South Africa generally. The men, if worth anything, could earn more than 2s. 6d. a day,—as no doubt those other men could have done of whom I spoke some chapters back;—but an Englishman in South Africa will not work along side of a coloured man on equal terms with the coloured man. The English labourer who comes to South Africa either rises to more than the labouring condition, or sinks to something below it. And he will not be content simply to supply his daily wants. He at once becomes filled with the idea that as a Colonist he should make his fortune. If he be a good man, industrious, able to abstain from drink and with something above ordinary intelligence,—he does make some fortune, more or less adequate. At any rate he rises in the world. But if he have not those gifts,—then he falls as had done those two ugly reprobates.

On our way from Montague to Swellendam, where was to be our next short sojourn, our Cape cart broke down. The axle gave way, and we were left upon the road;—or should have been left, some fifteen miles from Montague in one direction and the same distance from Swellendam in the other, had not the accident happened within sight of a farm house. As farm houses occur about once in every six or seven miles, this was a blessing; and was felt so very strongly when a young Dutch farmer came at once to our rescue with another cart. "I might as well take it," he said with a smile when we offered him half a sovereign, "but, you'd have had the cart all the same without it." This was certainly true as we were already taking our seats when the money was produced. I am bound to say that I was never refused anything which I asked of a Dutchman in South Africa. I must remark also that often as I broke down on, my travels,—and I did break down very often and some times in circumstances that were by no means promising,—there always came a Deus ex machina for my immediate relief. A generous Dutchman would lend me a horse or a cart;—or a needy Englishman would appear with an animal to sell when the getting of a horse under any circumstances had begun to appear impossible. On one occasion a jibbing brute fell as he was endeavouring to kick everything to pieces, and nearly cut his leg in two;—but a kindhearted colonist appeared immediately on the scene, with a very pretty girl in his cart, and took me on to my destination. And yet one often travels hour after hour, throughout the whole day, without meeting a fellow traveller.

Swellendam is such another village as The Paarl, equally enticing, equally full of oaks, though not equally long. From end to end it is but three miles, while The Paarl measures eight. But the mountains at Swellendam are finer than the mountains at The Paarl, and with the exception of those immediately over George, are the loveliest which I saw in the Colony. Swellendam is close under the Langeberg range,—so near that the kloofs or wild ravines in the mountains can be reached by an easy walk. They are very wild and picturesque, being thickly wooded, but so deep that from a little distance the wood can hardly be seen. Here at the foot of the hills were exquisite sites for country houses,—to be built, perhaps, by the future coloured millionaires of South Africa,—with grand opportunities for semi-tropical gardens, if only the water from the mountains could be used. Oranges, grapes, and bananas grow with the greatest profusion wherever water has been "led on." And yet it seems that the district is the very country for oaks. I had found more oaks during this last little tour through a portion of the Western Province of the Cape Colony than I have ever seen during the same time in England.

My kind host at Swellendam told me that it was imperative to go to the Tradouw,—or Southey's Pass through the mountains. The Tradouw is the old Dutch name for the ravine which was used for a pass before the present road was made. An energetic traveller will do as he is bid, especially when he is in the hands of an energetic host. The traveller wishes to see whatever is to be seen but has to be told what he should see. To such commands I have generally been obedient. He is too often told also what he should believe. Against this I have always rebelled;—mutely if possible, but sometimes, under coercion, with outspoken vehemence. "If it be true," I have had to say, "that I mean to write a book, I shall write my book and not yours." But as to the seeing of sights absolute obedience is the best.

Therefore I allowed my host to take me to the Tradouw, though my bones were all bruised and nearly dislocated with tape cart travelling and the sweet idea of a day of rest under the Swellendam oaks had taken strong hold of my imagination. I was amply repaid for my compliance.

On our way to the Tradouw we passed through a long straggling village inhabited exclusively by coloured people, and called the Caledon Missionary Institution. It had also some native name which I heard but failed to note. It was under the charge of a Dutch pastor upon whom we called and from whom I learned something of the present condition of the location. I will say, however, before I describe the Institution, that it is already doomed and its days numbered. That this should be its fate was not at all marvellous to me. That it should have been allowed to live so long was more surprising.

The place is inhabited by and belongs to persons of colour to whom it was originally granted as a "location" in which they might live. The idea of course has been that as the Colonists made the lands of the Colony their own, driving back the Hottentots without scruple, exercising the masterdom of white men for the spoliation of the natives, something should be secured to the inferior race, the giving of which might be a balm to the conscience of the invader and at the same time the means of introducing Christianity among the invaded. Nothing can be better than the idea,—which has been that on which the South African missionaries have always worked. Nor will I in this place assail the wisdom of the undertaking at the time at which it was set on foot. Whether anything better could then have been done may, perhaps, be doubted. I venture only to express an opinion that in the present condition of our South African Colonies all such Institutions are a mistake. As the Caledon Institution is about to be brought to an end, I may say this with the less chance of giving offence.

The last census taken of the population of the village gave its numbers as 3,000. I was told that at present there might be perhaps 2,000 coloured persons living there. I should have thought that to be a very exaggerated number, judging from the size of the place and the number of ruined and deserted huts, were it not that the statement was made to me in a tone of depreciation rather than of boasting. "They call it three thousand," said the pastor, "but there are not more than two." Looking at the people as I passed through the village I should be inclined to describe them as Hottentots, were it not for the common assertion that the Hottentot race is extinct in these parts. The Institution was originally intended for Hottentots, and the descendants of Hottentots are now its most numerous inhabitants. That other blood has been mixed with the Hottentot blood,—that of the negroes who were brought to the Cape as slaves and of the white men who were the owners of the slaves,—is true here as elsewhere. There is a church for the use of these people,—and a school. Without these a missionary institution would be altogether vain;—though, as I have stated some pages back, the school belonging to the Institution at Pacaltsdorp had gone into abeyance when I visited that place. Here the school was still maintained; but I learned that the maximum number of pupils never exceeded a hundred. Considering the amount of the population and the fact that the children are not often required to be absent on the score of work, I think I am justified in saying that the school is a failure. M. Esselin in his schools at Worcester, which is a town of 4,000 inhabitants of whom a large proportion are white, has an average attendance of 500 coloured children. The attendance at the missionary church is no better, the number of customary worshippers being the same as that of the scholars,—namely a hundred. With these people there is nothing to compel them to send their children to school, and nothing but the eloquence of the pastor to induce them to go to church. The same may be said as to all other churches and all other congregations. But we are able to judge of the utility of a church by the force of example which it creates. Among these people the very fashion of going to church is dying out.

But I was more intent, perhaps, on the daily employment than the spiritual condition of these people, and asked whether it sent out girls as maid-servants to the country around. The pastor assured me that he was often unable to get a girl to assist his wife in the care of their own children. The young women from the Missionary Institution do not care for going into service.

"But how do they live?" Then it was explained to me that each resident in the Institution had a plot of ground of his own, and that he lived on its produce, as far as it went, like any other estated gentleman. Then the men would go out for a little sheep-shearing, or the picking of Buchus in the Buchu season. The Buchu is a medicinal fruit which is gathered in these parts and sent to Europe. Such an arrangement cannot be for the welfare either of the Colony or of the people concerned. Nothing but work will bring them into such communion with civilization as to enable them to approach the condition of the white man. The arcadian idea of a coloured man with his wife and piccaninnies living happily under the shade of his own fig tree and picking his own grapes and oranges is very pretty in a book, and may be made interesting in a sermon. But it is ugly enough in that reality in which the fig tree is represented by a ruined mud-hut and the grapes and oranges by stolen mutton. The sole effect of the missionary's work has too often been that of saving the Native from working for the white man. It was well that he should be saved from slavery;—but to save him from other work is simply to perpetuate his inferiority.

The land at the Caledon Institution is the property of the resident Natives. Each landowner can at present sell his plot with the sanction of the Governor. In ten years' time he will be enabled to sell it without such sanction. The sooner he sells it and becomes a simple labourer the better for all parties. I was told that the Governor's sanction is rarely if ever now refused.

Then we went on to the Tradouw, and just at the entrance of the ravine we came upon a party of coloured labourers, with a white man over them, making bricks in the close vicinity of an extensive building. A party of convicts was about to come to the spot for the purpose of mending the road, and the bricks were being made so that a kitchen might be built for the cooking of their food. The big building, I was told, had been erected for the use of the convicts who a few years since had made the road. But it had fallen out of repair, and the new kitchen was considered necessary, though the number of men needed for the repair would not be very large, and they would be wanted only for a few months. I naturally asked what would become of the kitchen afterwards,—which seemed to be a spacious building containing a second apartment, to be used probably as scullery. The kitchen would again be deserted and would become the property of the owner of the land. I afterwards heard by chance of a contract for supplying mutton to the convicts at 6½d. a pound,—a pound a day for each man;—and I also heard that convict labour was supposed to be costly. The convicts are chiefly coloured people. With such usage as they receive the supply, I should imagine, would be ample. The ordinary Hottentot with his daily pound of mutton, properly cooked in a first-class kitchen and nothing but convict labour to do, would probably find himself very comfortable.

Southey's Pass,—so called from Mr. Southey who was Colonial Secretary before the days of parliamentary government, and is now one of the stoutest leaders of the opposition against the Ministers of the day,—is seven miles from end to end and is very beautiful throughout. But it is the mile at the end,—furthest from Swellendam,—in which it beats in sublimity all the other South African passes which I saw, including even the Montague Pass which crosses the Outiniqua mountains near George. South Africa is so far off that I cannot hope to be able to excite English readers to visit the Cape Colony for the sake of the scenery,—though for those whose doctors prescribe a change of air and habits and the temporary use of a southern climate I cannot imagine that any trip should be more pleasant and serviceable;—but I do think that the inhabitants of Capetown and the neighbourhood should know more than they do of the beauties of their own country. I have never seen rocks of a finer colour or twisted about into grander forms than those which make the walls of that part of Southey's Pass which is furthest from Swellendam.

When we were in the ravine two small bucks called Klip—springers,—springers that is among the stones,—were disturbed by us and passing down from the road among the rocks made their way to the bottom of the ravine. Two dogs had followed the Hottentot who was driving us, a terrier and a large mongrel hound, and at once got upon the scent of the bucks. I shall never forget the energy of the Hottentot as he rushed down from the road to a huge prominent rock which stood over the gorge, so as to see the hunt as near as possible, or my own excitement as I followed him somewhat more slowly. The ravine was so narrow that the clamour of the two dogs sounded like the music of a pack of hounds. The Hottentot as he leant forward over his perch was almost beside himself with anxiety. Immediately beneath us, perhaps twenty feet down, were two jutting stones separated from each other by about the same distance, between which was a wall of rock with a slant almost perpendicular and perfectly smooth, so that there could be no support to the foot of any animal. Up to the first of these stones one of the klip-springers was hunted with the big hound close at his heels. From it the easiest escape was by a leap to the other rock which the buck made without a moment's hesitation. But the dog could not follow. He knew the distance to be too great for his spring, and stood on his rock gazing at his prey. Nor could the buck go further. The stone it occupied just beneath ourselves was altogether isolated, and it stood there looking up at us with its soft imploring eyes, while the Hottentot in his excitement cheered on the dog to make the leap which the poor hound knew to be too much for him. I cannot say which interested me most, the man beside me, the little buck just below my feet, or the anxious eager palpitating hound with his short sharp barks. There was no gun with us, but the Hottentot got fragments of stone to throw at the quarry. Then the buck knew that he must shift his ground if he meant to save himself, and, marking his moment, he jumped back at the dog, and was then up among the almost perpendicular rocks over our heads before the brute could seize it. I have always been anxious for a kill when hunting, but I was thoroughly rejoiced when that animal saved himself. The Hottentot who was fond of venison did not at all share my feelings.

This occurred about 22 miles from Swellendam, and delayed us a little. My host, who had accompanied me, had asked a house full of friends to dine with him at seven, and it was five when the buck escaped. South African travelling is generally slow; but under the pressure of the dinner party our horses were made to do the distance in an hour and fifty minutes.

From Swellendam we went on to Caledon another exquisitely clean little Dutch town. The distance from Swellendam to Caledon is nearly eighty miles, through the whole of which the road runs under the Zondereinde mountains through a picturesque country which produces some of the best wool of the Colony. Caledon is another village of oak trees and pleasant detached Dutch-looking houses, each standing in its own garden and never mounting to a story above the ground. In winter no doubt the feeling inspired by these village-towns would be different; but when they are seen as I saw them, with, the full foliage and the acorns on the oaks, and the little gardens over-filled with their luxuriance of flowers, with the streets as clean and shaded as the pet road through a gentleman's park, the visitor is tempted to repine because Fate did not make him a wine-growing, orange-planting, ostrich-feeding Dutch farmer. From Caledon we returned through East Somerset, a smaller village and less attractive but still of the same nature, to Capetown, getting on to the railway about twenty miles from the town at the Eerste River Station. In making this last journey we had gone through or over two other Passes, called How Hoek and Sir Lowry's Pass. They are, both of them, interesting enough for a visit from Capetown, but not sufficiently so to be spoken of at much length after the other roads through the mountains which I had seen. The route down from Sir Lowry's Pass leads to the coast of False Bay,—of which Simon's Bay is an inlet. Between False Bay to the South and Table Bay to the North is the flat isthmus which forms the peninsula, on which stands Cape town and the Table Mountains, the Southern point of which is the Cape of Good Hope.

In this journey among the Dutch towns which lie around the capital I missed Stellenbosch, which is, I am told, the most Dutch of them all. As good Americans when dead go to Paris, so do good Dutchmen while still alive go to Stellenbosch,—and more especially good Dutchwomen, for it is a place much affected by widows. The whole of this country is so completely Dutch that an Englishman finds himself to be altogether a foreigner. The coloured people of all shades talk Dutch as their native language. It is hard at first to get over the feeling that a man or woman must be very ignorant who in an English Colony cannot speak English, but the truth is that many of the people are much less ignorant than they are at home with us, as they speak in some fashion both English and Dutch. In the Eastern Province of the Colony, as in the other Colonies and divisions of South Africa, the native speaks some native language,—the Kafir, Zulu, or Bechuana language as the case may be but in the part of the Western Province of which I am speaking,—part which the Dutch have long inhabited,—there is no native language left among the coloured people. Dutch has become their language. The South African language from the mouths of Kafirs and Zulus does not strike a stranger as being odd;—but Dutch volubility from Hottentot lips does do so.

I must not finish this short record of my journeys in the Western Province of the Cape Colony without repeating the expression of my opinion as to the beauty of the scenery and the special charms of the small towns which I had visited.

1. At the present time about a hundredth part of the area of the Cape Colony is under cultivation. The total area comprises 20,454,602 morgen, whereas only 217,692 morgen are cultivated. The morgen is a little more than two acres. Of the proportion cultivated, nearly a half is under wheat.

CHAPTER X

Fort Elizabeth and Grahamstown

From Capetown I went on by sea to Fort Elizabeth or Algoa Bay, thus travelling from the Western to the Eastern Province,—leaving the former when I had as yet seen but little of its resources because it was needful that I should make my tour through Natal and the Transvaal before the rainy season had commenced.[1] The run is one which generally occupies from thirty to forty hours, and was effected by us under the excellent auspices of Captain Travers in something but little in excess of the shorter period. It rained during the whole of our little journey, so that one could not get out upon the deck without a ducking;—which was chiefly remarkable in that on shore every one was complaining of drought and that for many weeks after my first arrival in South Africa this useless rain at sea was the only rain that I saw. Persons well instructed in their geography will know that Algoa Bay and Fort Elizabeth signify the same seaport,—as one might say that a ship hailed from the Clyde or from Glasgow. The Union Steam Ship Company sends a first-class steamer once a month from Southampton to Algoa Bay, without touching at Capetown.

Fort Elizabeth, as I walked away from the quay up to the club where I took up my residence, seemed to be as clean, as straight, and as regular as a first class American little town in the State of Maine. All the world was out on a holyday. It was the birthday of the Duke of Edinburgh, and the Fort-Elizabethians observed it with a loyalty of which we know nothing in England. Flags were flying about the ships in the harbour and every shop was closed in the town. I went up all alone with my baggage to the club, and felt very desolate. But everybody I met was civil, and I found a bedroom ready for me such as would be an Elysium, in vain to be sought for in a first class London hotel. My comfort, I own, was a little impaired by knowing that I had turned a hospitable South African out of his own tenement. On that first day I was very solitary, as all the world was away doing honour somewhere to the Duke of Edinburgh.

In the evening I went out, still alone, for a walk and without a guide, found my way to the public park and the public gardens. I cannot say that they are perfect in horticultural beauty and in surroundings, but they are spacious, with ample room for improvement, well arranged as far as they are arranged, and with a promise of being very superior to anything of the kind at Capetown. The air was as sweet, I think, as any that I ever breathed. Through them I went on, leaving the town between me and the sea, on to a grassy illimitable heath on which, I told myself, that with perseverance I might walk on till I came to Grand Cairo. I had my stick in my hand and was prepared for any lion that I might meet. But on this occasion I met no lion. After a while I found myself descending into a valley,—a pretty little green valley altogether out of sight of the town, and which as I was wending along seemed at first to be an interruption in my way to the centre of the continent. But as I approached the verge from which I could look down into its bosom, I heard the sound of voices, and when I had reached a rock which hung over it, I saw beneath me a ring, as it might be of fairy folk, in full glee,—of folk, fairy or human, running hither and thither with extreme merriment and joy. After standing awhile and gazing I perceived that the young people of Fort Elizabeth were playing kiss in-the-ring. Oh,—how long ago it was since I played kiss-in-the-ring, and how nice I used to think it! It was many, many years since I had even seen the game. And these young people played it with an energy and an ecstasy which I had never seen equalled. I walked down, almost amongst them, but no one noticed me. I felt among them like Rip Van Winkle. I was as a ghost, for they seemed not even to see me. How the girls ran, and could always have escaped from the lads had they listed, but always were caught round some corner out of the circle! And how awkward the lads were in kissing, and how clever the girls in taking care that it should always come off at last, without undue violence! But it seemed to me that had I been a lad I should have felt that when all the girls had been once kissed, or ay twice,—and when every girl had been kissed twice round by every lad, the thing would have become tame, and the lips unhallowed. But this was merely the cynicism of an old man, and no such feeling interrupted the sport. There I left them when the sun was setting, still hard at work, and returned sadly to my dinner at the club.

The land round the town, though well arranged for such purpose as just described, is not otherwise of a valuable nature. There seems to be an unlimited commonage of grass, but of so poor and sour a kind that it will not fatten and will hardly feed cattle. For sheep it is of no use whatever. This surrounds the town, and when the weather is cool and the air sweet, as it was when I visited the place, even the land round Fort Elizabeth is not without its charms. But I can understand that it would be very hot in summer and that then, the unshaded expanse would not be attractive. There is not a tree to be seen.

The town is built on a steep hill rising up from the sea, and is very neat. The town hall is a large handsome building, putting its rival and elder sister Capetown quite to shame. I was taken over a huge store in which, it seemed to me, that every thing known and wanted in the world was sold, from American agricultural implements down to Aberdeen red herrings. The library and reading room, and public ballroom or concert hall, were perfect. The place contains only 15,000 inhabitants, but has every thing needed for instruction, civilization and the general improvement of the human race. It is built on the lines of one of those marvellous American little towns in which philanthropy and humanity seem to have worked together to prevent any rational want.

Ostrich feathers and wool are the staples of the place. I witnessed a sale of feathers and was lost in wonder at the ingenuity of the auctioneer and of the purchasers. They seemed to understand each other as the different lots were sold, with an average of 30 seconds allowed to each lot. To me it was simply marvellous, but I gathered that the feathers were sold at prices varying from £5 to £25 a pound. They are sold by the pound, but in lots which may weigh perhaps not more than a few ounces each. I need only say further of Fort Elizabeth that there are churches, banks; and institutions fit for a town of ten times its size,—and that its club is a pattern club, for all Colonial towns.

Twenty miles north west of Fort Elizabeth is the pleasant little town of Uitenhage,—which was one of the spots peopled by the English emigrants who came into the Eastern Province in 1820. It had previously been settled and inhabited by Dutch inhabitants in 1804, but seems to have owed its success to the coming of the English,—and is now part of an English, as distinct from a Dutch Colony. It is joined to Fort Elizabeth by a railway which is being carried on to the more important town of Graff Reynet. It is impossible to imagine a more smiling little town than Uitenhage, or one in which the real comforts of life are more accessible. There is an ample supply of water. The streets are well laid out, and the houses well built. And it is surrounded by a group of mountains, at thirty miles distance, varying from 3,000 to 6,000 feet in height, which give a charm to the scenery around. It has not within itself much appearance of business, but everything and everybody seems to be comfortable. I was told that it is much affected by well-to-do widows who go thither to spend the evenings of their lives and enjoy that pleasant tea-and-toast society which is dear to the widowed heart. Timber is generally scarce in South Africa;—but through the streets of Uitenhage there are lovely trees, which were green and flowering when I was there in the month of August, warning me that the spring and then the heats of summer were coming on me all too soon.

During the last few years a special industry has developed itself at Uitenhage,—that of washing wool by machinery. As this is all carried on, not in stores or manufactories within the place, but at suburban mills placed along the banks of the river Swartzcop outside the town, they do not affect the semi-rural and widow-befitting aspect of the place. I remarked to the gentleman who was kindly driving me about the place that the people I saw around me seemed to be for the most part coloured. This he good-humouredly resented, begging that I would not go away and declare that Uitenhage was not inhabited by a white population. I have no doubt that my friend has a large circle of white friends, and that Uitenhage has a pure-blooded aristocracy. Were I to return there, as I half promised, for the sake of meeting the charming ladies whom he graciously undertook to have gathered together for my gratification, I am sure that I should have found this to be the case. But still I maintain that the people are a coloured people. I saw no white man who looked as though he earned his bread simply with his hands. I was driven through a street of pleasant cottages, and in asking who lived in the best looking of the lot I was told that he was an old Hottentot. The men working at the washing machines were all Kafirs,—earning on an average 3s. 6d. a day. It is from such evidence as this that we have to form an opinion whether the so called savage races of South Africa may or may not ultimately be brought into habits of civilization. After visiting one of the washing mills and being driven about the town we returned to Fort Elizabeth to dine.

Starting from Fort Elizabeth I had to commence the perils of South African travel. These I was well aware would not come from lions, buffaloes, or hippopotamuses,—nor even, to such a traveller as myself, from Kafirs or Zulus,—but simply from the length, the roughness and the dustiness of roads. I had been told before I left England that a man of my age ought not to make the attempt because the roads were so long, so rough,—and so dusty. In travelling round the coast there is nothing to be dreaded. The discomforts are simply of a marine nature, and may easily be borne by an old traveller. The terrible question of luggage does not disturb his mind. He may carry what he pleases and revel in clean shirts. But when he leaves the sea in South Africa every ounce has to be calculated. When I was told at Capetown that on going up from Natal to the Transvaal I should be charged 4s. extra for every pound I carried above fifteen I at once made up my mind to leave my bullock trunk at Government House. At Fort Elizabeth a gentleman was very kind in planning my journey for me thence up to Grahamstown, King William'stown &c.,—but, on coming into my bed room, he strongly recommended me to leave my portmanteau and dispatch box behind me, to be taken on, somewhither, by water, and to trust myself to two bags. So I tied on addresses to the tabooed receptacles of my remaining comforts, and started on my way with a very limited supply of wearing apparel. In the selection which one is driven to make with an agonized mind,—when the bag has been stamped full to repletion with shirts, boots, and the blue books which are sure to be accumulated for the sake of statistics, the first thing to be rejected is one's dress suit. A man can live without a black coat, waistcoat, and trousers. But so great is colonial hospitality wherever the traveller goes, and so similar are colonial habits to those at home, that there will always come a time,—there will come many times,—in which the traveller will feel that he has left behind him the very articles which he most needed, and that the blue books should have been made to give way to decent raiment. These are difficulties which at periods become almost heart breaking. Nevertheless I made the decision and rejected the dress suit. And I trusted myself to two pair of boots. And I allowed my treasures to be taken from me, with a hope that I might see them again some day in the Colony of Natal.

From Fort Elizabeth there is a railway open on the road to Grahamstown as far as a wretched place called Sand Flat. From thence we started in a mail cart,—or Cobb's omnibus as it is called. The whole distance to Grahamstown is about 70 miles, and the journey was accomplished in eleven hours. The country through which we passed is not favourable for agriculture or even for pasture. Much of it was covered with bush, and on that which is open the grass is too sour for sheep. It is indeed called the Zuurveld, or sour-field country. But as we approached Grahamstown it improved, and farming operations with farm steads,—at long distances apart,—came in view. For some miles round Fort Elizabeth there is nothing but sour grass and bush and the traveller inspecting the country is disposed to ask where is the fertility and where the rural charms which produced the great effort at emigration in 1820, when 5,000 persons were sent out from England into this district. The Kafirs had driven out the early Dutch settlers, and the British troops had driven out the Kafirs. But the country remained vacant, and £50,000 was voted by Parliament to send out what was then a Colony in itself, that the land might be occupied. But it is necessary to travel forty or fifty miles from Fort Elizabeth, or Algoa Bay, before the fertility is discovered.

Grahamstown when it is reached is a smiling little town lying in a gentle valley on an elevated plateau 1,700 feet above the sea. It contains between eight and nine thousand inhabitants of whom a third are coloured. The two thirds are almost exclusively British, the Dutch element having had little or no holding in this small thriving capital of the Eastern Province. For Grahamstown is the capital of the East, and there are many there who think that it should become a Capital of a Colony, whether by separation of the East from the West, or by a general federation of South African States—in which case the town would, they think, be more eligible than any other for all the general honours of government and legislation. I do not know but that on the whole I am inclined to agree with them. I think that if there were an united South Africa, and that a site for a capital had to be chosen afresh, as it was chosen in Canada, Grahamstown would receive from an outside commission appointed to report on the matter, more votes than any other town. But I am far from thinking that Grahamstown will become the capital of a South African Confederation.

The people of Grahamstown are very full of their own excellencies. No man there would call his town a "beastly place." The stranger on the other hand is invited freely to admire its delights, the charm of its position up above the heat and the musquitoes, the excellence of its water supply, the multiplicity of its gardens, the breadth and prettiness of its streets, its salubrity,—for he is almost assured that people at Grahamstown never die,—and the perfection of its Institutions. And the clock tower appended to the cathedral! The clock tower which is the work of the energetic Dean was when I was there,—not finished indeed for there was the spire to come,—but still so far erected as to be a conspicuous and handsome object to all the country round. The clock tower was exercising the minds of men very much, and through a clever manœuvre,—originating I hope with the Dean,—is supposed to be a town-clock tower and not an appanage of the cathedral. In this way all denominations have been got to subscribe, and yet, if you were not told to the contrary, you would think that the tower belongs to the cathedral as surely as its dome belongs to St. Paul's.

In truth Grahamstown is a very pretty town, and seen, as it is on all sides, from a gentle eminence, smiles kindly on those who enter it. The British troops who guarded the frontier from our Kafir enemies were formerly stationed here. As the Kafirs have been driven back eastwards, so have the troops been moved in the same direction and they are now kept at King Williamstown about 50 miles to the North East of Grahamstown, and nearer to the Kei river which is the present boundary of the Colony;—or was till the breaking out of the Kafir disturbance in 1877. The barracks at Grahamstown still belong to the Imperial Government, as does the castle at Capetown, and are let out for various purposes. Opening from the barrack grounds are the public gardens which are pretty and well kept. Grahamstown altogether gives the traveller an idea of a healthy, well-conditioned prosperous little town, in which it would be no misfortune to be called upon to live. And yet I was told that I saw it under unfavourable circumstances, as there had been a drought for some weeks, and the grasses were not green.

I was taken from Grahamstown to see an ostrich farm about fifteen miles distant. The establishment belongs to Mr. Douglas, who is I believe among the ostrich farmers of the Colony about the most successful and who was if not the first, the first who did the work on a large scale. He is, moreover, the patentee for an egg-hatching machine, or incubator, which is now in use among many of the feather-growers of the district. Mr. Douglas occupies about 1,200 acres of rough ground, formerly devoted to sheep-farming. The country around was all used not long since as sheep walks, but seems to have so much deteriorated by changes in the grasses as to be no longer profitable for that purpose. But it will feed ostriches.

At this establishment I found about 300 of those birds, which, taking them all round, young and old, were worth about £30 a piece. Each bird fit for plucking gives two crops of feathers a year, and produces, on an average, feathers to the value of £15 per annum. The creatures feed themselves unless when sick or young, and live upon the various bushes and grasses of the land. The farm is divided out into paddocks, and, with those which are breeding, one cock with two hens occupies each paddock. The young birds,—for they do not breed till they are three years old,—or those which are not paired, run in flocks of thirty or forty each. They are subject to diseases which of course require attention, and are apt to damage themselves, sometimes breaking their own bones, and getting themselves caught in the wire fences. Otherwise they are hardy brutes, who can stand much heat and cold, can do for long periods without water, who require no delicate feeding, and give at existing prices ample returns for the care bestowed upon them.

But, nevertheless, ostrich farming is a precarious venture. The birds are of such value, a full grown bird in perfect health being worth as much as £75, that there are of course risks of great loss. And I doubt whether the industry has, as yet, existed long enough for those who employ it to know all its conditions. The two great things to do are to hatch the eggs, and then to pluck or cut the feathers, sort them, and send them to the market. I think I may say that ostrich farming without the use of an incubator can never produce great results. The birds injure their feathers by sitting and at every hatching lose two months. There is, too, great uncertainty as to the number of young birds which will be produced, and much danger as to the fate of the young bird when hatched. An incubator seems to be a necessity for ostrich farming. Surely no less appropriate word was ever introduced into the language, for it is a machine expressly invented to render unnecessary the pro cess of incubation. The farmer who devotes himself to artificial hatching provides himself with an assortment of dummy eggs,—consisting of eggshells blown and filled with sand,—and with these successfully allures the hens to lay. The animals are so large and the ground is so open that there is but little difficulty in watching them and in obtaining the eggs. As each egg is worth nearly £5 I should think that they would be open to much theft when the operation becomes more general, but as yet there has not come up a market for the receipt of stolen goods. When found they are brought to the head quarters and kept till the vacancy occurs for them in the machine.

The incubator is a low ugly piece of deal furniture standing on four legs, perhaps eight or nine feet long. At each end there are two drawers in which the eggs are laid with a certain apparatus of flannel, and these drawers by means of screws beneath them are raised or lowered to the extent of two or three inches. The drawer is lowered when it is pulled out, and is capable of receiving a fixed number of eggs. I saw, I think, fifteen in one. Over the drawers and along the top of the whole machine there is a tank filled with hot water, and the drawer when closed is screwed up so as to bring the side of the egg in contact with the bottom of the tank. Hence comes the necessary warmth. Below the machine and in the centre of it a lamp, or lamps, are placed which maintain the heat that is required. The eggs lie in the drawer for six weeks, and then the bird is brought out.

All this is simple enough, and yet the work of hatching is most complicated and requires not only care but a capability of tracing results which is not given to all men. The ostrich turns her egg frequently, so that each side of it may receive due attention. The ostrich farmer must therefore turn his eggs. This he does about three times a day. A certain amount of moisture is required, as in nature moisture exudes from the sitting bird. The heat must be moderated according to circumstances or the yolk becomes glue and the young bird is choked. Nature has to be followed most minutely, and must be observed and understood before it can be followed. And when the time for birth comes on the ostrich farmer in must turn midwife and delicately assist the young one to open its shell, having certain instruments for the purpose. And when he has performed his obstetrical operations he must become a nursing mother to the young progeny who can by no means walk about and get his living in his earliest days. The little chickens in our farm yards seem to take the world very easily; but they have their mother's wings, and we as yet hardly know all the assistance which is thus given to them. But the ostrich farmer must know enough to keep his young ones alive, or he will soon be ruined,—for each bird when hatched is supposed to be worth £10. The ostrich farmer must take upon himself all the functions of the ostrich mother, and must know all that instinct has taught her, or he will hardly be successful.

The birds are plucked before they are a year old, and I think that no one as yet knows the limit of age to which they will live and be plucked. I saw birds which had been plucked for sixteen years and were still in high feather. When the plucking time has come the necessary number of birds are enticed by a liberal display of mealies,—as maze or Indian corn is called in South Africa,—into a pen one side of which is moveable. The birds will go willingly after mealies, and will run about their paddocks after any one they see, in the expectation of these delicacies. When the pen is full the moveable side is run in, so that the birds are compressed together beyond the power of violent struggling. They cannot spread their wings or make the dart forward which is customary to them when about to kick. Then men go in among them, and taking up their wings pluck or cut their feathers. Both processes are common but the former I think is most so, as being the more profitable. There is a heavier weight to sell when the feather is plucked; and the quil begins to grow again at once, whereas the process is delayed when nature is called upon to eject the stump. I did not see the thing done, but I was assured that the little notice taken by the animal of the operation may be accepted as proof that the pain, if any, is slight. I leave this question to the decision of naturalists and anti-vivisectors.

The feathers are then sorted into various lots, the white primary outside rim from under the bird's wing being by far the most valuable,—being sold, as I have said before, at a price as high as £25 a pound. The sorting does not seem to be a difficult operation and is done by coloured men. The produce is then packed in boxes and sent down to be sold at Fort Elizabeth by auction.

As far as I saw all labour about the place was done by black men except that which fell to the lot of the owner and two or three young men who lived with him and were learning the work under his care. These black men were Kafirs, Fingos, or Hottentots—so called, who lived each in his own hut with his wife and family. They received 26s. a month and their diet,—which consisted of two pound of meat and two pound of mealies a day each. The man himself could not eat this amount of food, but would no doubt find it little enough with his wife and children. With this he has permission to build his hut about the place, and to burn his master's fuel. He buys coffee if he wants it from his master's store, and in his present condition generally does want it. When in his hut he rolls himself in his blanket, but when he comes out to his work attires himself in some more or less European apparel according to regulation. He is a good humoured fellow, whether by nature a hostile Kafir, or a submissive Fingo, or friendly Basuto, and seems to have a pleasure in being enquired into and examined as to his Kafir habits. But, if occasion should arise, he would probably be a rebel. On this very spot where I was talking to him, the master of the farm had felt himself compelled during the last year,—1876—to add a couple of towers to his house so that in the event of an attack he might be able to withdraw his family from the reach of shot, and have a guarded platform from whence to fire at his enemies. Whether or not the danger was near as he thought it last year I am unable to say; but there was the fact that he had found it necessary so to protect himself only a few months since within twenty miles of Grahamstown! Such absence of the feeling of security must of course be injurious if not destructive to all industrial operations.

I may add with regard to ostrich farming that I have heard that 50 per cent. per annum on the capital invested has been not uncommonly made. But I have heard also that all the capital invested has not been unfrequently lost. It must be regarded as a precarious business and one which requires special adaptation in the person who conducts it. And to this must be added the fact that it depends entirely on a freak of fashion. Wheat and wool, cotton and coffee, leather and planks men will certainly continue to want, and of these things the value will undoubtedly be maintained by competition for their possession. But ostrich feathers may become a drug. When the nurse-maid affects them the Duchess will cease to do so.

Grahamstown is served by two ports. There is the port of Fort Elizabeth in Algoa Bay which I have already described as a thriving town and one from which a railway is being made across the country, with a branch to Grahamstown. All the mail steamers from England to Capetown come on to Algoa Bay, and there is also a direct steamer from Plymouth once a month. The bulk of the commerce for the whole adjacent district comes no doubt to Fort Elizabeth. But the people of Grahamstown affect Port Alfred, which is at the mouth of the Kowie river and only 35 miles distant from the Eastern Capital. I was therefore taken down to see Port Alfred.

I went down on one side of the river by a four-horsed cart as far as the confluence of the Mansfield, and thence I was shewn the beauties of the Kowie river by boat. Our party dined and slept at Port Alfred, and on the following day we came back to Grahamstown by cart on the other side of the river. I was perhaps more taken with the country which I saw than with the harbour, and was no longer at a loss to know where was the land on which the English settlers of 1820 were intended to locate themselves. We passed through a ruined village called Bathurst,—a village ruined while it was yet young, than which nothing can be more painful to behold. Houses had been built again, but almost every house had at one time,—that is in the Kafir war of 1850,—been either burnt or left to desolation. And yet nothing can be more attractive than the land about Bathurst, either in regard to picturesque situation or fertility. The same may be said of the other bank of this river. It is impossible to imagine a fairer district to a farmer's eye. It will grow wheat, but it will also grow on the slopes of the hills, cotton and coffee. It is all possessed, and generally all cultivated;—but it can hardly be said to be inhabited by white men, so few are they and so far between. A very large proportion of the land is let out to Kafirs who pay a certain sum for certain rights and privileges. He is to build his hut and have enough land to cultivate for his own purposes, and grass enough for his cattle;—and for these he contracts to pay perhaps £10 per annum, or more, or less, according to circumstances. I was assured that the rent is punctually paid. But this mode of disposing of the land, excellent for all purposes as it is, has not arisen of choice but of necessity. The white farmer knows that as yet he can have no security if he himself farms on a large scale. Next year there may be another scare, and then a general attack from the Kafirs; or the very scare if there be no attack, frightens away his profits;—or, as has happened before, the attack may come without the scare. The country is a European country,—belongs that is to white men,—but it is full of Kafirs;—and then, but a hundred miles away to the East, is Kafraria Proper where the British law does not rule even yet.

No one wants to banish the Kafirs. Situated as the country is and will be, it cannot exist without Kafirs, the Kafirs are the only possible labourers. To utilize the Kafir and not to expel him must be the object of the white man. Speaking broadly it may be said of the Colony, or at any rate of the Eastern district, that it has no white labourers for agricultural purposes. The Kafir is as necessary to the Grahamstown farmer as is his brother negro to the Jamaica sugar grower. But, for the sake both of the Kafir and of the white man, some further assurance of security is needed. I am inclined to think that more evil is done both to one and the other by ill defined fear than by actual danger.

Along the coast of the Colony there are various sea ports, none of which are very excellent as to their natural advantages, but each of which seems to have a claim to consider itself the best. There is Capetown of course with its completed docks, and Simon's Bay on the other side of the Cape promontory which is kept exclusively for our men of war. Then the first port, eastwards, at which the steamers call is Mossel Bay. These are the chief harbours of the Western Province. On the coast of the Eastern Province there are three ports between which a considerable jealousy is maintained, Fort Elizabeth, Port Alfred, and East London. And as there is rivalry between the West and East Provinces, so is there between these three harbours. Fort Elizabeth I had seen before I came up to Grahamstown. From Grahamstown I travelled to Port Alfred, taken thither by two patriotic hospitable and well-instructed gentlemen who thoroughly believed that the commerce of the world was to flow into Grahamstown viâ Port Alfred, and that the overflowing produce of South Africa will, at some not far distant happy time, be dispensed to the various nations from the same favoured harbour. "Statio bene fida carinis," was what I heard all the way down,—or rather promises of coming security and marine fruitfulness which are to be results of the works now going on. It was all explained to me,—how ships which now could not get over the bar would ride up the quiet little river in perfect safety, and take in and discharge their cargoes on comfortable wharves at a very minimum of expense. And then, when this should have been completed, the railway from the Kowie's mouth up to Grahamstown would be a certainty, even though existing governments had been so shortsighted as to make a railway from Fort Elizabeth to Grahamstown—carrying goods and passengers ever so far out of their proper course.

It is a matter on which I am altogether unable to speak with any confidence. Neither at Fort Elizabeth, or at the mouth of the Kowie where stands Port Alfred, or further eastwards at East London of which I must speak in a coming chapter, has Nature done much for mariners, and the energy shown to overcome obstacles at all these places has certainly been very great. The devotion of individuals to their own districts and to the chances of prosperity not for themselves so much as for their neighbours, is almost sad though it is both patriotic and generous. The rivalry between places which should act together as one whole is distressing;—but the industry of which I speak will surely have the results which industry always obtains. I decline to prophesy whether there will be within the next dozen years a railway from Port Alfred to Grahamstown,—or whether the goods to be consumed at the Diamond Fields and in the Orange Free State will ever find their way to their destinations by the mouth of the Kowie;—but I think I can foresee that the enterprise of the people concerned will lead to success.

1.It should be understood that the places described in the last three chapters were not visited till after my return from Natal, the Transvaal, the Diamond Fields, and the Orange Free State.

CHAPTER X

British Kafraria

It is not improbable that many Englishmen who have not been altogether inattentive to the course of public affairs as affecting Great Britain may be unaware that we once possessed in South Africa a separate colony called British Kafraria, with a governor of its own, and a form of government altogether distinct from that of its big brother the Cape Colony. Such however is the fact, though the territory did not, perhaps, attract much notice at the time of its annexation. Some years after the last Kafir war which may have the year 1850 given to it as its date, and after that wonderful Kafir famine which took place in 1857,—the famine which the natives created for themselves by destroying their own cattle and their own food, Kafraria was made a separate colony and was placed under the rule of Colonel Maclean. The sanction from England for the arrangement had been long given, but it was not carried out till 1860. It was not intended that the country should be taken away from the Kafirs;—but only the rule over the country, and the privilege of living in accordance with their own customs. Nor was this privilege abrogated all at once, or abruptly. Gradually and piecemeal they were to be introduced to what we call civilization. Gradually and piecemeal the work is still going on,—and so progressing that there can hardly be a doubt that as far as their material condition is concerned we have done well with the Kafirs. The Kafir Chiefs may feel,—certainly do feel,—that they have been aggrieved. They have been as it were knocked about, deprived of their power, humiliated and degraded, and, as far as British Kafraria is concerned, made almost ridiculous in the eyes of their own people. But the people themselves have been relieved from the force of a grinding tyranny. They increase and multiply because they are no longer driven to fight and be slaughtered in the wars which the Chiefs were continually waging for supremacy among each other. What property they acquire they can hold without fear of losing it by arbitrary force. They are no longer subject to the terrible superstitions which their Chiefs have used for keeping them in subjection. Their huts are better, and their food more constantly sufficient. Many of them work for wages. They are partially clothed,—sometimes with such grotesque partiality as quite to justify the comical stories which we have heard at home as to Kafir full dress. But the habit of wearing clothes is increasing among them. In the towns they are about as well clad as the ordinary Irish beggar,—and as the traveller recedes from the towns he perceives that this raiment gradually gives way to blankets and red clay. But to have got so far as the Irish beggar condition in twenty years is very much, and the custom is certainly spreading itself. The Kafir who has assiduously worn breeches for a year does feel, not a moral but a social shame, at going without them. As I have no doubt whatever that the condition of these people has been improved by our coming, and that British rule has been on the whole beneficent to them, I cannot but approve of the annexation of British Kafraria. But I doubt whether when it was done the justification was as complete as in those former days, twenty years before, when Lord Glenelg reprimanded Sir Benjamin D'Urbin for the extension he made in the same territory, and drew back the borders of British sovereignty, and restored their lands and their prestige and their customs to the natives, and declared himself willing to be responsible for all results that might follow,—results which at last cost so much British blood and so much British money!

The difficult question meets one at every corner in South Africa. What is the duty of the white man in reference to the original inhabitant? The Kafir Chief will say that it is the white man's duty to stay away and not to touch what does not belong to him. The Dutch Colonist will say that it is the white man's duty to make the best he can of the good things God has provided for his use,—and that as the Kafir in his natural state is a bad thing he should either be got rid of, or made a slave. In either assertion there is an intelligible purpose capable of a logical argument. But the Briton has to go between the two, wavering much between the extremes of philanthropy and expansive energy. He knows that he has to get possession of the land and use it, and is determined that he will do so;—but he knows also that it is wrong to take what does not belong to him and wrong also to treat another human being with harshness. And therefore with one hand he waves his humanitarian principles over Exeter Hall while with the other he annexes Province after Province. As I am myself a Briton I am not a fair critic of the proceeding;—but it does seem to me that he is upon the whole beneficent, though occasionally very unjust.

After the wars, when this Kafraria had become British, a body of German emigrants were induced to come here who have thriven wonderfully upon the land,—as Germans generally do. The German colonist is a humble hard working parsimonious man, who is content as long as he can eat and drink in security and put by a modicum of money. He cares but little for the form of government to which he is subjected, but is very anxious as to a market for his produce. He is unwilling to pay any wages, but is always ready to work himself and to make his children work. He lives at first in some small hovel which he constructs for himself, and will content himself with maze instead of meat till he has put by money enough for the building of a neat cottage. And so he progresses till he becomes known in the neighbourhood as a man who has money at the bank. Nothing probably has done more to make Kafraria prosperous than this emigration of Germans.

But British Kafraria did not exist long as a separate possession of the Crown, having been annexed to the Cape Colony in 1864. From that time it has formed part of the Eastern Province. It has three thriving English towns, King the capital, East London the port, and Queenstown, further up the country than King-Williamstown;—towns which are peculiarly English though the country around is either cultivated by German farmers or held by Kafir tenants. The district is still called British Kafraria. I myself have some very dim remembrance of British Kafraria as a Colony, but like other places in the British empire it has been absorbed by degrees without much notice at home.

Starting from Grahamstown on a hired Cape cart I entered British Kafraria somewhere between that town and Fort Beaufort. A "Cape cart" is essentially a South African vehicle, and is admirably adapted for the somewhat rough roads of the country. Its great merit is that it travels on only two wheels;—but then so does our English gig. But the English gig carries only two passengers while the Cape cart has room for four,—or even six. The Irish car no doubt has both these merits,—carries four and runs on two wheels; but the wheels are necessarily so low that they are ill adapted for passing serious obstructions. And the Cape cart can be used with two horses, or four as the need may be. A one-horse vehicle is a thing hardly spoken of in South Africa, and would meet with more scorn than it does even in the States. But the chief peculiarity of the Cape cart is the yoke of the horses, which is somewhat similar in its nature to that of the curricle which used to be very dangerous and very fashionable in the days of George IV. With us a pair of horses is now always connected with four wheels, and with the idea of security which four wheels give. Though the horse may tumble down the vehicle stands. It was not so with the curricle. When a horse fell, he would generally bring down his comrade, horse with him, and then the vehicle would go,—to the almost certain destruction of the pole and the imminent danger of the passengers. But with the Cape cart the bar, instead of passing over the horse's back—the bar on which the vehicle must rest when for a moment it loses its balance on the two wheels with a propulsion forwards—passes under the horses' necks with straps appended to the collars. I have never seen a horse fall with one of them;—but I can understand that when such an accident happens the falling horse should not bring the other animal down with him. The advantage of having two high wheels,—and only two,—need not be explained to any traveller.

On the way to Fort Beaufort I passed by Fort Brown,—a desolate barrack which was heretofore employed for the protection of the frontier when Grahamstown was the frontier city. I arrived there by a fine pass, excellently well engineered, through the mountains, called the Queen's Road,—very picturesque from the shape of the hills, though desolate from the absence of trees. But at Fort Brown the beauty was gone and nothing but the desolation remained. The Fort stands just off the road, on a plain, and would hold perhaps 40 or 50 men. I walked up to it and found one lonely woman who told me that she was the wife of a policeman stationed at some distant place. It had become the fate of her life to live here in solitude, and a more lonely creature I never saw. She was clean and pleasant and talked well;—but she declared that unless she was soon liberated from Fort Brown she must go mad. She was eloquent in favour of hard work, declaring that there was nothing else which could give a real charm to life;—but perhaps she had been roused to that feeling by knowing that there was not a job to be done upon the earth to which in her present circumstances she could turn her hand. Optat arare caballus. She told me of a son who was employed in one of the distant provinces, and bade me find him if I could and tell him of his mother. "Tell him to think of me here all alone," she said. I tried to execute my commission but failed to find the man.

I had intended sleeping at Fort Beaufort and on going from thence up the Catsberg Mountain. But I was prevented by the coming of a gentleman, a Wesleyan minister, who was very anxious that I should see the Kafir school at Healdtown over which he presided. From first to last through my tour I was subject to the privileges and inconveniences of being known as a man who was going to write a book. I never said as much to any one in South Africa,—or even admitted it when interrogated. I could not deny that I possibly might do so, but I always protested that my examiner had no right to assume the fact. All this, however, was quite vain as coming from one who had written so much about other Colonies, and was known to be so inveterate a scribbler as myself. Then the argument, though never expressed in plain words, would take, in suggested ideas, the following form. "Here you are in South Africa, and you are going to write about us. If so I,—or we, or my or our Institution, have an absolute claim to a certain portion of your attention. You have no right to pass our town by, and then to talk of the next town merely because such an arrangement will suit your individual comfort!" Then I would allege the shortness of my time. "Time indeed! Then take more time. Here am I,—or here are we, doing our very best; and we don't intend to be passed by because you don't allow yourself enough of time for your work." When all this was said on behalf of some very big store, or perhaps in favour of a pretty view, or—as has been the case,—in pride at the possession of a little cabbage garden, I have been apt to wax wroth and to swear that I was my own master;—but a Kafir missionary school, to which some earnest Christian man, with probably an earnest Christian wife, devotes a life in the hope of making fresh water flow through the dry wilderness, has claims, however painful they may be at the moment. This gentleman had come into Fort Beaufort on purpose to catch me. And as he was very eloquent, and as I did feel a certain duty, I allowed myself to be led away by him. I fear that I went ungraciously, and I know that I went unwillingly. It was just four o'clock and, having had no luncheon, I wanted my dinner. I had already established myself in a very neat little sitting-room in the Inn, and had taken off my boots. I was tired and dusty, and was about to wash myself. I had been on the road all day, and the bed-room offered to me looked sweet and clean;—and there was a pretty young lady at the Inn who had given me a cup of tea to support me till dinner should be ready. I was anxious also about the Catsberg Mountain, which under the minister's guidance I should lose, at any rate for the present. I spoke to the minister of my dinner;—but he assured me that an hour would take me out to his place at Healdtown. He clearly thought,—and clearly said,—that it was my duty to go, and I acceded. He promised to convey me to the establishment in an hour,—but it was two hours and a half before we were there. He allured me by speaking of the beauty of the road,—but it was pitch dark all the way. It was eight o'clock before my wants were supplied, and by that time I hated Kafir children thoroughly.

Of Healdtown and Lovedale,—a much larger Kafir school,—I will speak in the next chapter, which shall be exclusively educational. Near to Lovedale is the little town of Alice in which I stayed two days with the hospitable doctor. He took me out for a day's hunting as it is called, which in that benighted country means shooting. I must own here to have made a little blunder. When I was asked some days previously whether I would like to have a day's hunting got up for me in the neighbourhood of Alice, I answered with alacrity in the affirmative. Hunting, which is the easiest of all sports, has ever been an allurement to me. To hunt, as we hunt at home, it is only necessary that a man should stick on to the back of a horse,—or, failing that, that he should fall off. When hunting was offered to me I thought that I could at any rate go out and see. But on my arrival at Alice I found that hunting meant—shooting, an exercise of skill in which I had never even tried to prevail. "I haven't fired off a gun," I said, "for forty years." But I had agreed to go out hunting, and word had passed about the country, and a hundred naked Kafirs were to be congregated to drive the game. I tried hard to escape. "Might I not be allowed to go and see the naked Kafirs without a gun,—especially as it was so probable that I might shoot one of them if I were armed?" But this would not do. I was told that the Kafirs would despise me. So I took the gun and carried it ever so many miles, on horseback, to my very great annoyance.

At a certain spot on a hill side,—where the hill downwards was covered with bush and shrubs, we met the naked Kafirs. There were a hundred of them, I was told, more or less, and they were as naked as my heart could desire,—but each carrying some fragment of a blanket wound round on his arm, and many of them were decorated with bracelets and earrings. There were some preliminary ceremonies, such as the lying down of a young Kafir and the pretence of all the men around him,—and of all the dogs, of which there was a large muster,—the prostrate figure was a dead buck over whom it was necessary to lick their lips and shake their weapons;—and after this the Kafirs went down, into the bush. Then I was led away by my white friend, carrying my gun and leading my horse, and after a while was told that the very spot had been found. If I would remain there with my gun cocked and ready, a buck would surely come by almost at once so that I might shoot him. I did as I was bid, and sat alert for thirty minutes holding my gun as though something to be shot would surely come every second. But nothing came and I gradually went to sleep.

Then of a sudden I heard the Kafirs approaching. They had beaten the woods for a mile along the valley; and then a gun was fired and then another, and gradually my white friends reappeared among the Kafirs. One had shot a bird, and another a hare; and the most triumphant of the number had slaughtered a very fat monkey of a peculiarly blue colour about his hinder quarters. This was the great battue of the day. There were two or three other resting places at which I was instructed to stand and wait; and then we would be separated again, and again after a while would come the noise of the Kafirs. But no one shot anything further, and during the whole day nothing appeared before my eyes at which I was even able to aim my gun. But the native Kafirs with their red paint and their blankets wound round their arms, passing here and there through the bush hind beating for game, were real enough and very interesting. I was told that to them it was a day of absolute delight, and that they were quite satisfied with having been allowed to be there.

I have spoken before of the Kafir scare of 1876 during which it was certainly the general opinion at Grahamstown that there was about to be a general rising among the natives, and that it would behove all Europeans in the Eastern Province to look well to their wives and children and homesteads. I have described the manner in which my friend at the ostrich farm fortified his place with turrets, and I had heard of some settlers further east who had left their homes in the conviction that they were no longer safe. Gentlemen at Grahamstown had assured me that the danger had been as though men were going about a powder magazine with lighted candles. Here, where was our hunting party, we were in the centre of the Kafirs. A farmer who was with us owned the land down to the Chumie river which was at our feet, and on the other side there was a wide district which had been left by Government to the Kafirs when we annexed the land,—a district in which the Kafirs live after their old fashion. This man had his wife and children within a mile or two of hordes of untamed savages. When I asked him about the scare of last year, he laughed at it. Some among his neighbours had fled;—and had sold their cattle for what they would fetch. But he, when he saw that Kafirs were buying the cattle thus sold, was very sure that they would not buy that which they could take without price if war should come. But the Kafirs around him, he said, had no idea of war; and, when they heard of all that the Europeans were doing, they had thought that some attack was to be made on them.[1] The Kafirs as a body no doubt hate their invaders; but they would be well content to be allowed to hold what they still possess without further struggles with the white man, if they were sure of being undisturbed in their holdings. But they will be disturbed. Gradually, for this and the other reason, from causes which the white man of the day will be sure to be able to justify at any rate to himself more and more will be annexed, till there will not be a hill side which the Kafir can call his own dominion. As a tenant he will be admitted, and as a farmer, if he will farm the land, he will be welcomed. But the Kafir hill sides with the Kafir Kraals,—or homesteads,—and the Kafir flocks will all gradually be annexed and made subject to British taxation.

From Alice I went on to King Williamstown,—at first through a cold but grandly mountainous country, but coming, when half way, to a spot smiling with agriculture, called Debe Nek, where too there were forest trees and green slopes. At Debe Nek I met a young farmer who was full of the hardships to which he was subjected by the unjust courses taken by the Government. I could not understand his grievance, but he seemed to me to have a very pleasant spot of ground on which to sow his seed and reap his corn. His mother kept an hotel, and was racy with a fine Irish brogue which many years in the Colony had failed in the least to tarnish. She had come from Armagh and was delighted to talk of the beauty and bounty and great glory of the old primate, Beresford. She sighed for her native land and shook her head incredulously when I reminded her of the insufficiency of potatoes for the needs of man or woman. I never met an Irishman out of his own country, who, from some perversity of memory, did not think that he had always been accustomed to eat meat three times a day, and wear broad cloth when he was at home.

King Williamstown was the capital of British Kafraria, and is now the seat of a British Regiment. I am afraid that at this moment it is the Head Quarters of much more than one. This perhaps will be the best place in which to say a few words on the question of keeping British troops in the Cape Colony. It is held to be good colonial doctrine that a Colony which governs itself, which levies and uses its own taxes, and which does in pretty nearly all things as seems good to itself in its own sight, should pay its own bills;—and among other bills any bill that may be necessary for its own defence. Australia has no British soldiers,—not an English redcoat; nor has Canada, though Canada be for so many miles flanked by a country desirous of annexing it. My readers will remember too that even while the Maoris were still in arms the last regiment was withdrawn from New Zealand, so greatly to the disgust of New Zealand politicians that the New Zealand Minister of the day flew out almost in mutiny against our Secretary of State at the time. But the principle was maintained, and the measure was carried, and. the last regiment was withdrawn. But at that time ministerial responsibility and parliamentary government had not as yet been established in the Cape Colony, and there were excuses for British soldiers at the Cape which no longer existed in New Zealand.

Now parliamentary government and ministerial responsibility are as strong at Capetown as at Wellington, but the British troops still remain in the Cape Colony. There will be, I think, when this book is published more than three regiments in the Colony or employed in its defence. The parliamentary system began only in 1872, and it may be alleged that the withdrawal of troops should be gradual. It may be alleged also that the present moment is peculiar, and that the troops are all this time specially needed. It should, however, be remembered that when the troops were finally withdrawn from New Zealand, disturbance among the Maoris was still rampant there. I suppose there can hardly be a doubt that it is a subject on which a so called Conservative Secretary of State may differ slightly from a so called Liberal Minister. Had Lord Kimberley remained in office there might possibly be fewer soldiers in the Cape Colony. But the principle remains, and has I think so established itself that probably no Colonial Secretary of whatever party would now deny its intrinsic justice.

Then comes the question whether the Cape Colony should be made an exception, and if so why. I am inclined to think that no visitor travelling in the country with his eyes open, and with capacity for seeing the things around him, would venture to say that the soldiers should be withdrawn now, at this time. Looking back at the nature of the Kafir wars, looking round at the state of the Kafir people, knowing as he would know that they are armed not only with assegais but with guns, and remembering the possibilities of Kafir warfare, he would hesitate to leave a quarter of a million of white people to defend themselves against a million and a half of warlike hostile Natives. The very withdrawal of the troops might itself too probably cause a prolonged cessation of that peace to which the Kafir Chiefs have till lately felt themselves constrained by the presence of the red coats, and for the speedy re-establishment of which the continued presence of the red coats is thought to be necessary. The capable and clearsighted stranger of whom I am speaking would probably decline to take such responsibility upon himself even though he were as strong in the theory of colonial self-defence as was Lord Granville when he took the soldiers away from New Zealand.

But it does not follow that on that account he should think that the Cape Colony should be an exception to a rule which as to other Colonies has been found to be sound. It may be wise to keep the soldiers in the Colony, but have been unwise to saddle the Colony with full parliamentary institutions before it was able to bear their weight. "If the soldiers be necessary, then the place was not ripe for parliamentary institutions." That may be a very possible opinion as to the affairs of South Africa generally.

I am again driven to assert the difference between South Africa, and Canada, or Australia, or New Zealand. South Africa is a land peopled with coloured inhabitants. Those other places are lands peopled with white men. I will not again vex my reader with numbers,—not now at least. He will perhaps remember the numbers, and bethink himself of what has to be done before all those negroes can be assimilated and digested and made into efficient parliamentary voters, who shall have civilization, and the good of their country, and "God save the Queen" generally, at their hearts' core. A mistake has perhaps been made;—but I do not think that because of that mistake the troops should be withdrawn from the Colony.

I cannot, however, understand why they should be kept at Capetown, to the safety of which they are no more necessary than they would be to that of Sydney or Melbourne. It is alleged that they can be moved more easily from Capetown, than they might be from any inland depot. But we know that if wanted at all they will be wanted on the frontier,—say within 50 miles of the Kei river which is the present boundary of the Colony. If the Kafirs east of the Kei can be kept quiet, there will be no rising of those to the west of the river. It was the knowledge that there were troops at King Williamstown, not that there were troops at Capetown, which operated so long on the minds of Kreli and other Transkeian Kafirs. And now that disturbance has come all the troops are sent to the frontier. If this be so, it would seem that British Kafraria is the place in which they should be located. But Capetown has been Head Quarters since the Colony was a Colony, and Head Quarters are never moved very easily. It is right that I should add that the Colony pays £10,000 a year to the mother country in aid of the cost of the troops. I need hardly say that that sum does not go far towards covering the total expense of two or more regiments on foreign service.

Another difficulty is apt to arise,—which I fear will now be found to be a difficulty in South Africa. If imperial troops be used in a Colony which enjoys parliamentary government, who is to be responsible for their employment? The Parliamentary Minister will expect that they shall be used as he may direct;—but so will not the authorities at home! In this way there can hardly fail to be difference of opinion between the Governor of the Colony and his responsible advisers.

King Williamstown is a thoroughly commercial little city with a pleasant club, with a railway to East London, and with smiling German cultivation all around it. But it has no trees. There is indeed a public garden in which the military band plays with great éclat, and in which horses can be ridden, and carriages with ladies be driven about,—so as to look almost like Hyde Park in June. I stayed three or four days at the place and was made very comfortable; but what struck me most was the excellence of the Kafir servant who waited upon me. A gentleman had kindly let me have the use of his house, and with his house the services of this treasure. The man was so gentle, so punctual, and so mindful of all things that I could not but think what an acquisition he would be to any fretful old gentleman in London.

When I was at King Williamstown I was invited to hold a conference with two or three Kafir Chiefs, especially with Sandilli, whose son I had seen at school, and who was the heir to Gaika, one of the great kings of the Kafirs, being the son of Gaika's "great wife," and brother to Makomo the Kafir who in the last war had done more than Kafir had ever done before to break the British power in South Africa. It was Makomo who had been Sir Harry Smith's too powerful enemy,—and Sandilli, who is still living in the neighbourhood of King Williamstown, was Makomo's younger but more royal brother. I expressed, of course, great satisfaction at the promised interview, but was warned that Sandilli might not improbably be too drunk to come.

On the morning appointed about twenty Kafirs came to me, clustering round the door of the house in which I was lodging,—but they declined to enter. I therefore held my levee out in the street. Sandilli was not there. The reason for his absence remained undivulged, but I was told that he had sent a troop of cousins in his place. The spokesman on the occasion was a chief named Siwani, who wore an old black coat, a flannel shirt, a pair of tweed trousers and a billycock hat,—comfortably and warmly dressed,—with a watch-key of ordinary appearance ingeniously inserted into his ear as an ornament. An interpreter was provided; and, out in the street, I carried on my colloquy with the dusky princes. Not one of them spoke but Siwani, and he expressed utter dissatisfaction with everything around him. The Kafirs, he said, would be much better off if the English would go away and leave them to their own customs. As for himself, though he had sent a great many of his clansmen to work on the railway,—where they got as he admitted good wages,—he had never himself received the allowance per head promised him. "Why not appeal to the magistrate?" I asked. He had done so frequently, he said, but the Magistrate always put him off and then, personally, he was treated with very insufficient respect. This complaint was repeated again and again. I, of course, insisted on the comforts which the Europeans had brought to the Kafirs,—trousers for instance,—and I remarked that all the royal princes around me were excellently well clad. The raiment was no doubt of the Irish beggar kind but still admitted of being described as excellent when compared in the mind with red clay and a blanket. "Yes,—by compulsion," he said. "We were told that we must come in and see you, and therefore we put on our trousers. Very uncomfortable they are, and we wish that you and the trousers and the magistrates, but above all the prisons, would go away out of the country together." He was very angry about the prisons, alleging that if the Kafirs did wrong the Kafir Chiefs would know how to punish them. None of his own children had ever gone to school,—nor did he approve of schools. In fact he was an unmitigated old savage, on whom my words of wisdom had no effect whatever, and who seemed to enjoy the opportunity of unburdening his resentment before a British traveller. It is probable that some one had given him to understand that I might possibly write a book when I returned home.

When, after some half hour of conversation, he declared that he did not want to answer any more questions, I was not sorry to shake hands with the prominent half dozen, so as to bring the meeting to a close. But suddenly there came a grin across Siwani's face,—the first look of good humour which I had seen,—and the interpreter informed me that the Chief wanted a little tobacco. I went back into my friend's house and emptied his tobacco pot, but this, though accepted, did not seem to give satisfaction. I whispered to the interpreter a question, and on being told that Siwani would not be too proud to buy his own tobacco, I gave the old beggar half a crown. Then he blessed me, as an Irish beggar might have done, grinned again and went off with his followers. The Kafir boy or girl at school and the Kafir man at work are pleasing objects; but the old Kafir chief in quest of tobacco,—or brandy,—is not delightful.

King Williamstown is the head quarters of the Cape mounted frontier police, of which Mr. Bowker, whose opinion respecting Kafirdom I have already quoted, was at the period of my visit the Commandant. This is a force, consisting now of about 1,200 men, maintained by the Colony itself for its own defence, and was no doubt established by the Colony with a view of putting its own foot forward in its own behalf and doing something towards the achievement of that colonial independence of which I have spoken. It has probably been thought that the frontier police might at last stand in lieu of British soldiers. The effort has been well made, and the service is of great use. The brunt of 'the fighting in the late disturbance has been borne by the mounted police. The men are stationed about the country in small parties,—never I think more than thirty or forty together, and often in smaller numbers. They are very much more efficacious than soldiers, as every man is mounted,—and the men themselves come from a much higher class than that from which our soldiers are enlisted. But the troop is expensive, each private costing on an average about 7s. a day. The men are paid 5s. 6d. a day as soon as they are mounted,—out of which they have to buy and keep their horses and furnish everything for them selves. When they join the force their horses and equipments are supplied to them, but the price is stopped out of their pay. They are recruited generally, though by no means universally, in England, under the care of an emigration agent who is maintained at home. I came out myself with six or seven of them,—three of whom I knew chief in quest of tobacco,—or brandy,—is not delightful.

King Williamstown is the head quarters of the Cape mounted frontier police, of which Mr. Bowker, whose opinion respecting Kafirdom I have already quoted, was at the period of my visit the Commandant. This is a force, consisting now of about 1,200 men, maintained by the Colony itself for its own defence, and was no doubt established by the Colony with a view of putting its own foot forward in its own behalf and doing something towards the achievement of that colonial independence of which I have spoken. It has probably been thought that the frontier police might at last stand in lieu of British soldiers. The effort has been well made, and the service is of great use. The brunt of the fighting in the late disturbance has been borne by the mounted police. The men are stationed about the country in small parties,—never I think more than thirty or forty together, and often in smaller numbers. They are very much more efficacious than soldiers, as every man is mounted,—and the men themselves come from a much higher class than that from which our soldiers are enlisted. But the troop is expensive, each private costing on an average about 7s. a day. The men are paid 5s. 6d. a day as soon as they are mounted,—out of which they have to buy and keep their horses and furnish everything for themselves. When they join the force their horses and equipment are supplied to them, but the price is stopped out of their pay. They are recruited generally, though by no means universally, in England, under the care of an emigration agent who is maintained at home. I came out myself with six or seven of them,—three of whom I knew to be sons of gentlemen, and all of whom may have been so. So terrible is the struggle at home to find employment for young men that the idea of £100 a year at once has charms, even though the receiver of it will have to keep not only himself, but a horse also, out of the money. But the prospect, if fairly seen, is not alluring. The young men when in the Colony are policemen and nothing more than police men. Many of them after a short compulsory service find a better employment elsewhere, and their places are filled up by new comers.

From King Williamstown I went to East London by railway and there waited till the ship came which was to take me on to Natal. East London is another of those ports which stubborn Nature seems to have made unfit for shipping, but which energy and enterprise are determined to convert to good purposes. As Grahamstown believes in Port Alfred, so does King Williamstown believe in East London, feeling sure that the day will come when no other harbour along the coast will venture to name itself in comparison with her. And East London has as firm a belief in herself with a trustworthy reliance on a future day when the commerce of nations will ride in safety within her at present ill-omened bar. I had heard much of East London and had been warned that I might find it impossible to get on board the steamer even when she was lying in the roads. At Fort Elizabeth it had been suggested to me that I might very probably have to come back there because no boat at East London would venture to take me out. The same thing was repeated to me along my route, and even at King Williamstown. But not the less on that account, when I found myself in British Kafraria of which East London is the port, was I assured of all that East London would hereafter perform. No doubt there was a perilous bar. The existence of the bar was freely admitted. No doubt the sweep of the sea in upon the mouth of the Buffalo river was of such a nature as to make all intercourse between ships and the shore both difficult and disagreeable. No doubt the coast was so subject to shipwreck as to have caused the insurance on ships to East London to be abnormally high. All these evils were acknowledged, but all these evils would assuredly be conquered by energy, skill, and money. It was thus that East London was spoken of by the friends who took me there in order that I might see the works which were being carried on with the view of overcoming Nature.

At the present moment East London is certainly a bad spot for shipping. A vessel had broken from her anchor just before my arrival and was lying on the shore a helpless wreck. There were the fragments to be seen of other wrecks;

and I heard of many which had made the place noted within the last year or two. Such was the character of the place. I was told by more than one voice that vessels were sent there on purpose to be wrecked. Stories which I heard made me believe in Mr. Plimsoll more than I had ever believed before. "She was intended to come on shore," was said by all voices that day in East London as to the vessel that was still lying among the breakers, while men were at work upon her to get out the cargo. "They know that ship will drag their anchor here; so, when they want to get rid of an old tub, they send her to East London." It was a terrible tale to hear, and especially so from men who themselves believe in the place with all the implicit confidence of expended capital. On the second day after my arrival the vessel that was to carry me on to Natal steamed into the roads. It had been a lovely morning and was yet early,—about eleven o'clock. I hurried down with a couple of friends to the man in authority who decides whether communication shall or shall not be had between the shore and the ship, and he, cocking a telescope to his eye, declared that even though the Governor wanted to go on board he would not let a boat stir that day. In my ill-humour I asked him why he would be more willing to risk the Governor's life than that of any less precious individual. I own I thought he was a tyrant,—and perhaps a Sabbatarian, as it was on a Sunday. But in half an hour the wind had justified him, even to my uneducated intelligence. During the whole of that day there was no intercourse possible between the ships and the shore. A boat from a French vessel tried it, and three men out of four were drowned! Early on the following day I was put on board the steamer in a life-boat. Again it was a lovely morning,—and the wind had altogether fallen,—but the boat shipped so much water that our luggage was wet through.

But it is yet on the cards that the East Londoners may prevail. Under the auspices of Sir John Coode a breakwater is being constructed with the purpose of protecting the river's mouth from the prevailing winds, and the river is being banked and altered so that the increased force of the water through a narrowed channel may scour away the sand. If these two things can be done then ships will enter the Buffalo river and ride there in delicious ease, and the fortune of the place will be made. I went to see the works and was surprised to find operations of such magnitude going on at a place which apparently was so insignificant. A breakwater was being constructed out from the shore,—not an isolated sea wall as is the breakwater at Plymouth and at Fort Elizabeth,—but a pier projecting itself in a curve from one of the points of the river's mouth so as to the other when completed. On this £120,000 had already been spent, and a further sum of £80,000 is to be spent. It is to be hoped that it will be well expended,—for which the name of Sir John Coode is a strong guarantee.

At present East London is not a nice place. It is without a pavement,—I may almost say without a street, dotted about over the right river bank here and there, dirty to look at and dishevelled, putting one in mind of the American Eden as painted by Charles Dickens,—only that his Eden was a river Eden while this is a marine Paradise. But all that no doubt will be mended when the breakwater has been completed. I have already spoken of the rivalry between South African ports, as between Port Alfred and Fort Elizabeth, and between South African towns, as between Capetown and Grahamstown. The feeling is carried every where, throughout everything. Opposite to the town of East London, on the left side of the Buffalo river, and connected with it by ferries, is the township of Panmure. The terminus of the railway is at Panmure and not at East London. And at Panmure there has gathered itself together an unpromising assemblage of stores and houses which declares of itself that it means to snuff East London altogether out. East London and Panmure together are strong against all the coast of South Africa to the right and, left; but between the two places themselves there is as keen a rivalry as between any two towns on the continent. At East London I was assured that Panmure was merely "upstart;"—but a Panmurite had his revenge by whispering to me that East London was a nest of musquitoes. As to the musquitoes I can speak from personal experience.

And yet I ought to say a good word of East London for I was there but three days and was invited to three picnics. I went to two of them, and enjoyed myself thoroughly, seeing some beautiful scenery up the river, and some charming spots along the coast. I was, however, very glad to get on board the steamer, having always had before my eyes the terrible prospect of a return journey to Fort Elizabeth before I could embark for Natal.

1. This conversation occurred and the above words were written before the disturbance of 1877. But the Kafirs here spoken of are the very Gaikas who have been expected to join the Galekas in their rebellion, but who have not as yet done so. Nor, as I think, will they do so.

CHAPTER XII

KAFIR SCHOOLS

THE QUESTION OF KAFIR EDUCATION is perhaps the most important that has to be solved in South Africa,—and certainly it is the one as to which there exists the most violent difference of opinion among those who have lived in South Africa. A traveller in the land by associating exclusively with one set of persons would be taught to think that here was to be found a certain and quick panacea for all the ills and dangers to which the country is subjected. Here lies the way by which within an age or two the population of the country may be made to drop its savagery and Kafirdom and blanket loving vagabondism and become a people as fit to say their prayers and vote for members of parliament as at any rate the ordinary English Christian constituent. "Let the Kafir be caught young and subjected to religious education, and he will soon become so good a man and so docile a citizen that it will be almost a matter of regret that more of us were not born Kafirs." That is view of the question which prevails with those who have devoted themselves to Kafir education,—and of them it must be acknowledged that their efforts are continuous and energetic. I found it impossible not to be moved to enthusiasm by what I saw at Kafir schools.

Another traveller falling into another and a different set will be told by his South African associates that the Kafir is a very good fellow, and may be a very good servant, till he has been taught to sing psalms and to take pride in his rapidly acquired book learning;—but that then he becomes sly, a liar and a thief whom it is impossible to trust and dangerous to have about the place. "He is a Kafir still," a gentleman said to me, "but a Kafir with the addition of European cunning without a touch of European conscience." As far as I could observe, the merchants and shopkeepers who employ Kafirs about their stores, and persons who have Kafirs about their houses, do eschew the school Kafir. The individual Kafir when taken young and raw out of his blanket, put into breeches and subjected to the general dominion of a white master, is wonderfully honest, and, as far as he can speak at all, he speaks the truth. There can I think be no question about his virtues. You may leave your money about with perfect safety, though he knows well what money will do for him; you may leave food,—and even drink in his way and they will be safe. "Is there any housebreaking or shoplifting?" I asked a tradesman in King Williamstown. He declared that there was nothing of the kind known,—unless it might be occasionally in reference to a horse and saddle. A Kafir would sometimes be unable to resist the temptation of riding back into Kafirdom, the happy possessor of a steed. But let a lad have passed three or four years at a Kafir school, and then he would have become a being very much altered for the worse and not at all fit to be trusted among loose property. The saints in Kafirland will say that I have heard all this exclusively among the sinners. If so I can only say that the men of business are all sinners.

For myself I found it very hard to form an opinion between the two. I do believe most firmly in education. I should cease to believe in any thing if I did not believe that education if continued will at least civilize. I can conceive no way of ultimately overcoming and dispelling what I must call the savagery of the Kafirs, but by education. And when I see the smiling, oily, good humoured, docile, naturally intelligent but still wholly uneducated black man trying to make himself useful and agreeable to his white employers, I still recognise the Savage. With all his good humour and spasmodic efforts at industry he is no better than a Savage. And the white man in many cases does not want him to be better. He is no more anxious that his Kafir should reason than he is that his horse should talk. It requires an effort of genuine philanthropy even to desire that those beneath us should become more nearly equal to us. The man who makes his money by employing Kafir labour is apt to regard the commercial rather than the philanthropic side of the question. I refuse therefore to adopt his view of the matter. A certain instinct of independence, which in the eyes of the employer of labour always takes the form of rebellion, is one of the first and finest effects of education. The Kafir who can argue a question of wages with his master has already become an objectionable animal.

But again the education of the educated Kafir is very apt to "fall off." So much I have not only heard asserted generally by those who are antikafir-educational in their sympathies, but admitted also by many of those who have been themselves long exercised in Kafir education. And, in regard to religious teaching, we all know that the singing of psalms is easier than the keeping of the ten commandments. When we find much psalm-singing and at the same time a very conspicuous breach of what has to us been a very sacred commandment, we are apt to regard the delinquent as a hypocrite. And the Kafir at school no doubt learns something of that doctrine,—which in his savage state was wholly unknown to him, but with which the white man is generally more or less conversant,—that speech has been given to men to enable them to conceal their thoughts. In learning to talk most of us learn to lie before we learn to speak the truth. While dropping some thing of his ignorance the Savage drops something also of his simplicity. I can understand therefore why the employer of labour should prefer the unsophisticated Kafir, and am by no means sure that if I were looking out for black labour in order that I might make money out of it I should not eschew the Kafir from the schools.

The difficulty arises probably from our impatience. Nothing will satisfy us unless we find a bath in which we may at once wash the blackamoor white, or a mill and oven in which a Kafir may be ground and baked instantly into a Christian. That much should be lost,—should "fall off" as they say,—of the education imparted to them is natural. Among those of ourselves who have spent, perhaps, nine or ten years of our lives over Latin and Greek how much is lost! Perhaps I might say how little is kept! But something remains to us,—and something to them. There is need of very much patience. Those who expect that a Kafir boy, because he has been at school, should come forth the same as a white lad, all whose training since, and from long previous to his birth, has been a European training, will of course be disappointed. But we may, I think, be sure that no Kafir pupil can remain for years or even for months among European lessons and European habits, without carrying away with him to his own people, when he goes, something of a civilizing influence.

My friend, the Wesleyan Minister, who by his eloquence prevailed over me at Fort Beaufort in spite of my weariness and hunger, took me to Healdtown, the Institution over which he himself presides. I had already seen Kafir children and Kafir lads under tuition at Capetown. I had visited Miss Arthur's orphanage and school, where I had found a most interesting and cosmopolitan collection of all races, and had been taken by the Bishop of Capetown to the Church of England Kafir school at Zonnebloom, and had there been satisfied of the great capability which the young Kafir has for learning his lessons. I had been assured that up to a certain point and a certain age the Kafir quite holds his own with the European. At Zonnebloom a master carpenter was one of the instructors of the place, and, as I thought, by no means the least useful. The Kafir lad may perhaps forget the names of the "five great English poets with their dates and kings," by recapitulating which he has gained a prize at Lovedale,—or may be unable some years after he has left the school to give an "Outline of Thomson's Seasons," but when he has once learned how to make a table stand square upon four legs he has gained a power of helping his brother Kafirs which will never altogether desert him.

At Healdtown I found something less than 50 resident Kafir boys and young men, six of whom were in training as students for the Wesleyan Ministry. Thirteen Kafir girls were being trained as teachers, and two hundred day scholars attended from the native huts in the neighbourhood,—one of whom took her place on the school benches, with her own little baby on her back. She did not seem to be in the least inconvenienced by the appendage. I was not lucky in my hours at Healdtown as I arrived late in the evening, and the tuition did not begin till half-past nine in the morning, at which time I was obliged to leave the place. But I had three opportunities of hearing the whole Kafir establishment sing their hymns. The singing of hymns is a thoroughly Kafir accomplishment and the Kafir words are soft and melodious. Hymns are very good, and the singing of hymns, if it be well done, is gratifying. But I remember feeling in the West Indies that they who devoted their lives to the instruction of young negroes thought too much of this pleasant and easy religious exercise, and were hardly enough alive to the expediency of connecting conduct with religion. The black singers of Healdtown were, I was assured, a very moral and orderly set of people; and if so the hymns will not do them any harm.

For the erudition of such of my readers as have not hitherto made themselves acquainted with the religious literature of Kafirland I here give the words of a hymn which I think to be peculiarly mellifluous in its sounds. I will not annex a translation, as I cannot myself venture upon versifying it, and a prose version would sound bald and almost irreverent. I will merely say that it is in praise of the Redeemer, which name is signified by the oft-repeated word Umkululi.

ICULO 38.
Elamashumi matatu anesibozo.

Ungu-Tixo Umkululi,
Wenza into zonke;
Ungu-Tixo Umkululi,
Ungopezu konke.

Waba ngumntu Umkululi,
Ngezizono zetu;
Waba ngumntu Umkululi,
Wafa ngenxa yetu.

Unosizi Umkululi
Ngabasetyaleni;
Unosizi Umkululi
Ngabasekufeni.

Unxamile Umkululi
Ukusiguqula;
Unxamile Umkululi
Ukusikulula.

Unamandla Umkululi
Ukusisindisa;
Unamandla Umkululi
Ukusonwabisa.

Unotando Umkululi,
Uuofefe kuti;
Unotando Umkululi,
Masimfune futi.

If the lover of sweet sounds will read the lines aloud, merely adding a half pronounced U at the beginning of those words which are commenced with an otherwise unpronounceable ng, so as to make a semi-elided syllable, I think he will understand the nature of the sweetness of sound which Kafirs produce in their singing. When he finds that nearly all the lines and more than half the words begin with the same letter he will of course be aware that their singing is monotonous.

I was glad to find that the Kafir-scholars at Healdtown among them paid £200 per annum towards the expense of the Institution. The Government grants £700, and the other moiety of the total cost—which amounts to £1,800,—is defrayed by the Wesleyan missionary establishment at home. As the Kafir contribution is altogether voluntary, such payment shews an anxiety on the part of the parents that their children should be educated. As far as I 1 remember nothing was done at Healdtown to teach the children any trade. It is altogether a Wesleyan missionary establishment, combining a general school in which religious education is perhaps uppermost, with a training college for native teachers and ministers. I cannot doubt but that its effect is salutary. It has been built on a sweet healthy spot up among the hills, and nothing is more certain than the sincerity and true philanthropy of those who are engaged upon its work.

My friend who had carried me off from Fort Beaufort kept his word like a true man the next morning, in allowing me to start at the time named, and himself drove me over a high mountain to Lovedale. How we ever got up and down those hill sides with a pair of horses and a vehicle, I cannot even yet imagine;—but it was done. There was a way round, but the minister seemed to think that a straight line, to any place or any object must be the best way, and over the mountain we went. Some other Wesleyan minister before his days, he said, had done it constantly and had never thought anything about it. The horses did go up and did go down; which was only additional evidence to me that things of this kind are done in the Colonies which would not be attempted in England.

On my going down the hill towards Lovedale, when we had got well out of the Healdtown district, an argument arose between me and my companion as to the general effect of education on Kafir life. He was of opinion that the Kafirs in that locality were really educated, whereas I was quite willing to elicit from him the sparks of his enthusiasm by suggesting that all their learning faded as soon as they left school. "Drive up to that hut," I said, picking out the best looking in the village, "and let us see whether there be pens, ink and paper in it. It was hardly a fair test, because such accommodation would not be found in the cottage of many educated Englishmen. But again, on the other side, in my desire to be fair I had selected something better than a normal hut. We got out of our vehicle, undid the latch of the door,—which was something half way between a Christian doorway and the ordinary low hole through which the ordinary Kafir creeps in and out,—and found the habitation without its owners. But an old woman in the kraal had seen us, and had hurried across to exercise hospitality on behalf of her absent neighbours. Our desire was explained to her and she at once found pens and ink. With the pens and ink there was probably paper, on which she was unable to lay her hand. I took up, however, an old ragged quarto edition of St. Paul's epistles,—with very long notes. The test as far as it was carried certainly supported my friend's view.

Lovedale is a place which has had and is having very great success. It has been established under Presbyterian auspices but is in truth altogether undenominational in the tuition which it gives. I do not say that religion is neglected, but religious teaching does not strike the visitors as the one great object of the Institution. The schools are conducted very much like English schools,—with this exception, that no classes are held after the one o'clock dinner. The Kafir mind has by that time received as much as it can digest. There are various masters for the different classes, some classical, some mathematical, and some devoted to English literature. When I was there, there were eight teachers, independent of Mr. Buchanan who was the acting Head or President of the whole Institution. Dr. Stewart, who is the permanent Head, was absent in central Africa. At Lovedale, both with the boys and girls black and white are mixed when in school without any respect of colour. At one o'clock I dined in hall with the establishment, and then the coloured boys sat below the Europeans. This is justified on the plea that the Europeans pay more than the Kafirs and are entitled to a more generous fare,—which is true. The European boys would not come were they called upon to eat the coarser food which suffices for the Kafirs. But in truth neither would the Europeans frequent the schools if they were required to eat at the same table with the natives. That feeling as to eating and drinking is the same in British Kafraria as it was with Shylock in Venice. The European domestic servant will always refuse to eat with the Kafir servant. Sitting at the high table,—that is the table with the bigger of the European boys, I had a very good dinner.

At Lovedale there are altogether nearly 400 scholars, of whom about 70 are European. Of this number about 300 live on the premises and are what we call boarders. The others are European day scholars from the adjacent town of Alice who have gradually joined the establishment because the education is much better than anything else that can be had in the neighbourhood. There are among the boarders thirty European boys. The European girls were all day scholars from the neighbourhood. The coloured boarders pay £6 per annum, for which everything is supplied to them in the way of food and education. The lads are expected to supply themselves with mattresses, pillows, sheets, and towels. I was taken through the dormitories, and the beds are neat enough with their rug coverings. I did not like to search further by displacing them. The white boarders pay £40 per annum. The Kafir day scholars pay but 30s., and the European day scholars 60s. per annum. In this way £2,650 is collected. Added to this is an allowance of £2,000 per annum from the Government. These two sources comprise the certain income of the school, but the Institution owns and farms a large tract of land. It has 3,000 acres, of which 400 are cultivated, and the remainder stocked with sheep. Lovedale at present owns a flock numbering 2,000. The native lads are called upon to work two hours each afternoon. They cut dams and make roads, and take care of the garden. Added to the school are work shops in which young Kafirs are apprenticed. The carpenters department is by far the most popular, and certainly the most useful. Here they make much of the furniture used upon the place, and repair the breakages. The waggon makers come next to the carpenters in number; and then, at a long interval, the blacksmiths. Two other trades are also represented, printing namely, and bookbinding. There were in all 27 carpenters with four furniture makers, 16 waggon makers, 8 blacksmiths, 5 printers, and 2 book binders;—all of whom seemed to be making efficient way in their trades.

This direction of practical work seems to be the best which such an Institution can take. I asked what became of these apprentices and was told that many among them established themselves in their own country as master tradesmen in a small way, and could make a good living among their Kafir neighbours. But I was told also that they could not often find employment in the workshops of the country unless the employers used nothing but Kafir labour. The white man will not work along with the Kafir on equal terms. When he is placed with Kafirs he expects to be "boss," or mastery and gradually learns to think that it is his duty to look on and superintend, while it is the Kafir's duty to work under his dictation. The white bricklayer may continue to lay his bricks while they are carried for him by a black hodsman, but he will not lay a brick at one end of the wall while a Kafir is laying an equal brick at the other.

But in this matter of trades the skill when once acquired will of course make itself available to the general comfort and improvement of the Kafir world around. I was at first inclined to doubt the wisdom of the printing and bookbinding, as being premature; but the numbers engaged in these exceptional trades are not greater perhaps than Lovedale itself can use. I do not imagine that a Kafir printing press will for many years be set up by Kafir capital and conducted by Kafir enterprise. It will come probably, but the Kafir tables and chairs and the Kafir waggons should come first. At present there is a "Lovedale News," published about twice a month. "It is issued," says the Lovedale printed Report "for circulation at Lovedale and chiefly about Lovedale matters. The design of this publication was to create a taste for reading among the native pupils." It has been carried on through twelve numbers, says the report, "with a fair prospect of success and rather more than a fair share of difficulties." The difficulties I can well imagine, which generally amount to this in the establishment of a newspaper,—that the ambitious attempt so often costs more than it produces. Mr. Theal is one of the masters of Lovedale, and his History of South Africa was here printed;—but not perhaps with so good a pecuniary result as if it had been printed elsewhere. I was told by the European foreman in the printing establishment that the Kafirs learned the art of composition very readily, but that they could not be got to pull off the sheets fairly and straightly. As to the book binding, I am in possession of one specimen which is fair enough. The work is in two volumes and it was given to me at Capetown;—but unfortunately the two volumes are of different colours.

In the younger classes among the scholars the Kafirs were very efficient. None of them, I think, had reached, the dignity of Greek or Natural Philosophy, but some few had ascended to algebra and geometry. When I asked what became of all this in after life there was a doubt. Even at Lovedale it was acknowledged that after a time it "fell off,"—or in other words that much that was taught was afterwards lost. Out in the world, as I have said before, among the Europeans who regard the Kafir simply as a Savage to whom pigeon-English has to be talked, it is asserted broadly that all this education leads to no good results,—that the Kafir who has sung hymns and learned to do sums is a savage to whose natural and native savagery additional iniquities have been added by the ingenuity of the white philanthropist. To this opinion I will not accede. That such a place as Lovedale should do evil rather than good is to my thinking impossible.

To see a lot of Kafir lads and lasses at school is of course more interesting than to inspect a seminary of white pupils. It is something as though one should visit a lion tamer with a group of young lions around him. The Kafir has been regarded at home as a bitter and almost terrible enemy who, since we first became acquainted with him in South Africa, has worked us infinite woe. I remember when a Kafir was regarded as a dusky demon and there was a doubt whether he could ever be got under and made subject to British rule;—whether in fact he would not in the long run be too much for the Britons. The Kafir warrior with his assegai and his red clay, and his courageous hatred, was a terrible fellow to see. And he is still much more of a Savage than the ordinary negro to whom we have become accustomed in other parts of the world. It was very interesting to see him with a slate and pencil, wearing his coarse clothing with a jaunty happy air, and doing a sum in subtraction. I do not know whether an appearance of good humour and self-satisfaction combined does not strike the European more than any other Kafir characteristic. He never seems to assert that he is as good as a white man,—as the usual negro will do whenever the opportunity is given to him,—but that though he be inferior there is no reason why he should not be as jolly as circumstances will admit. The Kafir girl is the same when seen in the schools. Her aspect no doubt will be much altered for the worse when she follows the steps of her Kafir husband as his wife and slave.

But at Lovedale she is comparatively smart, and gay looking. Many of these pupils while still at school reach the age at which young people fall in love with each other. I was told that the young men and young women were kept strictly apart; but nevertheless, marriages between them on their leaving school are not uncommon,—nor unpopular with the authorities. It is probable that a young man who has been some years at Lovedale will treat his wife with something of Christian forbearance.

I find from the printed report of the seminary that the four following young ladies got the prizes in 1877 at Lovedale for the different virtues appended to their names. I insert the short list here not only that due honour may be given to the ladies themselves, but also that my readers may see something of Kafir female nomenclature.

GIRLS.
GENERAL PRIZES.

Bible.	*Good Conduct.*
Victoria Kwankwa.	Ntame Magazi.
Tidiness in Dress.	*For best kept room.*
Ntombenthle Njikeiana.	Sarah Ann Bobi.

Miss Kwankwa and Miss Bobi had I suppose Christian names given to them early in life. The other two are in possession of thoroughly Kafir appellations,—especially the young lady who has excelled in tidiness, and who no doubt will have become a bride before these lines are read in England.

I was taken out from King Williamstown to Peeltown to see another educational Kafir establishment. At Peeltown the Rev. Mr. Birt presides over a large Kafir congregation, and has an excellent church capable of holding 500, which has been built almost exclusively by Kafir contributions. The boys' school was empty, but I was taken to see the girls who lived together under the charge of an English lady. I wished that I might have been introduced to the presence of the girls at once, so as to find how they occupied themselves when not in school. But this was not to be. I was kept waiting for a few moments, and then was ushered into a room where I found about twenty of them sitting in a row hemming linen. They were silent, well behaved and very demure while I saw them,—and then before I left they sang a hymn.

If I had an Institution of my own to exhibit I feel sure that I should want to put my best foot forward,—and the best foot among Kafir female pupils is perhaps the singing of hymns and the hemming of linen.

CHAPTER XIII

CONDITION OF THE CAPE COLONY

LATER ON IN MY JOURNEY, when I was returning to Capetown, I came back through some of the towns I have mentioned in the last chapter or two, and also through other places belonging to the Western Province. On that occasion I took my place by coach from Bloemfontein, the capital of the little Orange Free State or Republic to Fort Elizabeth,—or to the railway station between Grahamstown and Fort Elizabeth,—and in this way passed through the Stormberg and Catberg mountains. Any traveller visiting South Africa with an eye to scenery should see these passes. For the mere sake of scenery no traveller does as yet visit South Africa, and therefore but little is thought about it. I was, however, specially cautioned by all who gave me advice on the subject, not to omit the Catberg in my journey. I may add also that this route from the Diamond Fields to Capetown is by far the easiest, and for those travelling by public conveyances is the only one that is certain as to time and not so wearisome as to cause excruciating torment. When travelling with a friend in our own conveyance I had, enjoyed our independence,—especially our breakfasts in the veld; but I had become weary of sick and dying horses, and of surrounding myself with horse provender. I was therefore glad to be able to throw all the responsibility of the road on to the shoulders of the proprietor of the coach, especially when I found that I was not to be called on to travel by night. A mail cart runs through from the Diamond Fields to Capetown, three times a week;—but it goes day and night and has no provision for meals. The journey so made is frightful, and is fit only for a very young man who is altogether regardless of his life. There is also a decent waggon;—but it runs only occasionally. Families, to whom time is not a great object, make the journey with ox-waggons, travelling perhaps 24 miles a day, sleeping in their waggons and carrying with them all that they want. Ladies who have tried it have told me that they did not look back upon the time so spent as the happiest moments of their existence. The coach was tiresome enough, taking seven days from the Diamond Fields to Fort Elizabeth. Between Bloemfontein and Grahamstown, a trip of five days, it travels about fourteen hours a day. But at night there was always ten hours for supper and rest, and the accommodation on the whole was good The beds were clean and the people along the road always civil. I was greatly taken with one little dinner which was given to us in the middle of the day at a small pretty Inn under the Catberg Mountain. The landlord, an old man, was peculiarly courteous, opening our soda water for us and handing us the brandy bottle with a grace that was all his own. Then he joined us on the coach and travelled along the road with us, and it turned out that he had been a member of the old Capetown Parliament, and had been very hot in debate in the time of the Kafir wars. He became equally hot in debate now, declaring to us that everything was going to the dogs because the Kafirs were not made to work. I liked his politics less than his leg of mutton,—which had been excellent The drive through the Stormberg is very fine;—but the mountains are without timber or water. It is the bleak wildness of the place which gives it its sublimity. Between the Stormberg and the Catberg lies Queenstown,—a picturesque little town with two or three hotels. The one at which the coach stopped was very good. It was a marvel to me that the Inns should be so good, as the traffic is small. We sat down to a table d'hôte dinner, at which the host with all his family joined us, that would have done credit to a first class Swiss hotel. I don't know that a Swiss hotel could produce such a turkey. When the landlord told his youngest child, who had modestly asked for boiled beef, that she might have turkey in spite of the number at table, I don't know whether I admired most, the kind father, the abstemious daughter, or the capacious turkey.

I think that South Africa generally is prouder of the road over the Catberg than of any other detail among its grand scenery. I had been told so often that whatever I did I must go over the Catberg! I did go over the Catberg, walking up the bleak side from the North, and travelling down in the coach, or Cape cart which we had got there, among the wooded ravines to the South. It certainly is very fine,—but not nearly so grand in my opinion as Montague Pass or Southey's Pass in the Western Province. From the foot of the Catberg we ran into Fort Beaufort, to which town I carried my reader in a previous chapter. It was over this road that I had poured into my ears the political harangue of that late member of the Legislature. He belonged to a school of politicians which is common in

South Africa, but which became very distasteful to me. The professors of it are to be found chiefly in the Eastern Province of the Cape Colony, in which I was then travelling, though the West is by no means without them. Their grand doctrine is that the Kafirs should be "ruled with a rod of iron." That phrase of the rod of iron had become odious to me before I left the country. "Thieves!" such a professor will say. "They are all thieves. Their only idea is to steal cattle." Such an one never can be made to understand that as we who are not Savages have taken the land, it is hardly unnatural that men who are Savages should think themselves entitled to help themselves to the cattle we have put on the land we have taken from them. The stealing of cattle must of course be stopped, and there are laws for the purpose; but this appealing to a "rod of iron" because men do just that which is to be expected from men so placed was always received by me as an ebullition of impotent and useless anger. A farmer who has cattle in a Kafir country, on land which has perhaps cost him 10s. or 5s., or perhaps nothing, an acre for the freehold of it, can hardly expect the same security which a tenant enjoys in England, who pays probably 20s. an acre for the mere use of his land.

As I have now finished the account of my travels in the two Provinces and am about to go on to Natal, I will say few words first as to the produce of the Cape Colony.

In the Cape Colony, as in Australia, wool has been for many years the staple of the country;—and, as in Australia the importance or seeming importance of the staple produce has been cast into the shade by the great wealth of the gold which has been found there, so in South Africa has the same been done by the finding of diamonds. Up to the present time, however, the diamond district has not in truth belonged to the Cape Colony. Soon after these pages will have been printed it will probably be annexed. But the actual political possession of the land in which the diamonds or gold have been found has had little to do with the wealth which has flowed into the different Colonies from the finding of the treasures. That in each case has come from the greatly increased consumption created by the finders. Men finding gold and diamonds eat and drink a great deal. The persons who sell such articles are enriched,—and the articles are subject to taxation, and so a public revenue is raised. It is hence that the wealth comes rather than from the gold and diamonds themselves. Had it been possible that the possession of the land round the Kimberley mines should have been left in the hands of the native tribes, there would have been but little difference in the money result. The flour, the meat, the brandy, and the imported coats and boots would still have been carried up to Kimberley from the Cape Colony.

But of the Colony itself wool has been the staple,—and among its produce the next most interesting are its wheat, vines, and its ostriches. In regard to wool I find that the number of wooled sheep in the Cape Colony has considerably increased during the last ten years. I say wooled sheep, because there is a kind of sheep in the Colony, native to the land, which bear no wool and are known by their fat tails and lob ears. As they produce only mutton I take no reckoning of them here. In 1875 there were 9,986,240 wooled sheep in the Colony producing 28,316,181 pounds of wool, whereas in 1865 there were only 8,370,179 sheep giving 18,965,936 pounds of wool. This increase in ten years would seem to imply a fair progress,—especially as it applies not only to the number of sheep in the Colony, but also to the amount of wool given by each sheep; but I regret to say that during the latter part of that period of ten years there has been a very manifest falling off. I cannot give the figures as to the Cape Colony itself, as I have done with the numbers for 1865 and 1875;—but from the ports of the Cape Colony there were exported—

In 1871, 46,279,639	pounds of wool,	value	£2,191,233
In 1872, 48,822,562	"	"	£3,275,150
In 1873, 40,393,746	"	"	£2,710,481
In 1874, 42,620,481	"	"	£2,948,571
In 1875, 40,339,674	"	"	£2,855,899
In 1876, 34,861,339	"	"	£2,278,942

These figures not only fail to shew that ratio of increase without which a colonial trade cannot be said to be in a healthy condition; but they exhibit also a very great decrease,—the falling off in the value of wool from 1872 to 1876 being no less than £1,048,208, or nearly a third of the whole. They whom I have asked as to the reason of this, have generally said that it is due to the very remunerative nature of the trade in ostrich feathers, and have intimated that farmers have gone out of wool in order that they might go into feathers. To find how far this may be a valid excuse we must enquire what has been the result of ostrich farming during the period. What was the export of ostrich feathers for each of the ten executive years, I have no means of saying. In 1865 there were but 80 tame ostriches kept by farmers in the Colony, though no doubt a large amount of feathers from wild ostriches was exported. In 1875, 21,751 ostriches were kept, and the total value of feathers exported was £306,867, the whole amount coming from ostriches thus being less by £700,000 than the falling off in the wool. Had the Colony been really progressing, a new trade might well have been developed to the amount above stated without any falling off in the staple produce of the country. The most interesting circumstance in reference to the wool and sheep of the country is the fact that the Kafirs own 1,109,346 sheep, and that they produced in 1875 2,249,000 pounds of wool.

It is certainly the case that the wools of the Cape Colony are very inferior to those of Australia. I find from the Prices Current as published by a large woolbroker in London for the year 1877, that the average prices through the year realized by what is called medium washed wool were for Australian wools,—taking all the Australian Colonies together,—something over 1s. 6d. a pound, whereas the average price for the same class of wool from the Cape Colony was only something over 1s. 1d. a pound. There has been a difference of quite 5d. a pound; or about 40. per cent. in favour of the Australian article. "There is no doubt," says my friend who furnished me with this information, "that valuable and useful as are Cape wools they are altogether distanced by the fine Australian. Breeding has to do with this. So has climate and country." For what is called Superior washed wool, the Victorian prices are fully a shilling a pound higher than those obtained by the growers of the Cape, the average prices for the best of the class being 2s. 6d. for Victorian, and is 6d. a pound for Cape Colony wool.

Perhaps the fairest standard by which to test the prosperity of a new country is its capability of producing corn,—especially wheat. It is by its richness in this respect that the United States have risen so high in the world. Australia has not prospered so quickly, and will never probably prosper so greatly, because on a large portion of her soil wheat has not been grown profitably. The first great question is whether a young country can feed herself with bread. The Cape Colony has obtained a great reputation for its wheat, and does I believe produce flour which is not to be beaten anywhere on the earth. But she is not able to feed herself. In 1875, she imported wheat and flour to the value, including the duty charged on it, of £126,654. In reaching this amount I have deducted £2,800 the value of a small amount which was exported. This is more than 10s. per annum for each white inhabitant of the country, the total white population being 236,783. The deficiency is not very large; but in a Colony the climate of which is in so many respects adapted to wheat there should be no deficiency. The truth is that it is altogether a question of artificial irrigation. If the waters from the mountains can be stored and utilized, the Cape will run over with wheat.

I find that in the whole Colony there were in 1875 about 80,000,000 acres of land in private hands;—that being the amount of land which has been partly or wholly alienated, by Government. I give the number of acres in approximate, figures because in the official return it is stated in morgen. The morgen is a Dutch measure of land and comprises a very little more, but still little more than two acres. Out of this large area only 550,000 acres or less than 1-14th are cultivated. It is interesting to know that more than a quarter of this, or 150,000 acres are in the hands of the native races and are cultivated by them;—cultivated by them as owners and not as servants. In 1875 there were 28,416 ploughs in the Cape Colony and of these 9,179, nearly a third, belonged to the Kafirs or Hottentots.

In 1855 there were 55,300,025 vines in the Colony, and in 1875 this number had increased to 69,910,215. The increase in the production of wine was about in the same proportion. The increase in the distilling of brandy was more than proportionate. The wine had risen from 3,237,428 gallons to 4,485,665, and the brandy from 430,955 to 1,067,832 gallons. I was surprised to find how very small was the exportation of brandy, the total amount sent away, and noted by the Custom House as exported, being 2,910 gallons. No doubt a comparatively large quantity is sent to the other districts of South Africa by inland carriage, so that the Custom House knows nothing abut it. But the bulk of this enormous increase in brandy has been consumed in the Colony, and must therefore have had its evil as well as its good results. Of the brandy exported by sea by far the greatest part is consumed in South Africa, the Portuguese at Delagoa Bay taking nearly half Great Britain, a country which is fond of brandy imports only 695 gallons from her own brandy-making Colony. As the Cape brandy is undoubtedly made from grapes, and as the preference for grape-made brandy is equally certain, the fact I fear tells badly for the Cape manufacture. It cannot be but that they might make their brandy better. Of wine made in the Colony 60,973 gallons were exported in 1875, or less than 1-7th of the amount produced. This is a very poor result, seeing that the Cape Colony is particularly productive in grapes and seems to indicate that the makers of wine have as yet been hardly more successful in their manufacture, than the makers of brandy. Much no doubt is due to the fact that the merchants have not as yet found it worth their while to store their wines for any lengthened period.

At the time of my visit ostrich feathers were the popular produce of the Colony. Farmers seemed to be tired of sheep,—tired at least of the constant care which sheep require, to be diffident of wheat, and down-hearted as to the present prices of wine. It seemed to me that in regard to all these articles there was room for increased energy. As to irrigation, which every one in the Colony feels to be essential to agricultural success in the greater part not only of the Colony but of South Africa generally, the first steps must I think be taken by the governments of the different districts.

The total population of the Colony is 720,984. Of these less than a third, 209,136, are represented as living on agriculture which in such a Colony should support more than half the people. The numbers given include of course men women and children. Of this latter number, less than a third again, or 60,458, are represented as being of white blood,—or Dutch and English combined. I believe about two-thirds of these to be Dutch,—though as to that I can only give an opinion. From this it would result that the residue, perhaps about 20,000 who are of English descent, consists of the farmers themselves and their families. Taking four to a family, this would give only 5,000 English occupiers of land. There is evidently no place for an English agricultural labourer in a Colony which shows such a result after seventy years of English occupation. And indeed there is much other evidence proving the same fact. Let the traveller go where he will he will see no English-born agricultural labourer in receipt of wages. The work, if not done by the farmer or his family, is with but few exceptions done by native hands. Should an Englishman be seen here or there in such a position he will be one who has fallen abnormally in the scale, and will, as an exception, only prove the rule. If a man have a little money to commence as a farmer he may thrive in the Cape Colony,—providing that he can accommodate himself to the peculiarities of the climates. As a navvy he may earn good wages on the railways, or as a miner at the copper mines. But, intending to be an agricultural labourer, he should not emigrate to South Africa. In South Africa the Natives are the labourers and they will remain so, both because they can live cheaper than the white man, and because the white man will not work along side of them on equal terms. Though an Englishman on leaving his own country might assure himself that he had no objection to such society, he would find that the ways of the Colony would be too strong for him. In Australia, in Canada, in New Zealand, or the United States, he may earn wages as an agriculturist;—but he will not do so in South Africa with content and happiness to himself. The paucity of the English population which has settled here since we owned the country is in itself sufficient proof of the truth of my assertion.

It is stated in the Blue Book of the Colony for 1876,—which no doubt may be trusted implicitly,—that the average daily hire for an agricultural labourer in the Colony is 3s. for a white man, and 2s. for a coloured man, with diet besides. But I observe also that in some of the best corn districts,—especially in Malmsbury,—no entry is made as to the wages of European agricultural labourers. Where such wages are paid, it will be found that they are paid to Dutchmen. There are no doubt instances of this sufficient in most districts to afford an average. A single instance would do so.

Taking the whole of the Colony I find that the wages of carpenters, masons, tailors, shoemakers and smiths average 9s. a day for white men and 6s. for coloured men. This is for town and country throughout. In some places wages as high as 15s. a day has been paid for white workmen and as high as 8s.-9s.—and even

10s. for coloured. The European artizan is no doubt at present more efficient than the native, and when working with the native, works as his superintendent or Boss. For tradesmen such as these,—men who know their trades and can eschew drink,—there is a fair opening in South Africa, as there is in almost all the British Colonies.

The price of living for a working man is, as well as I can make a calculation on the subject, nearly the same as in England, but with a slight turn in favour of the Colony on account of the lower price of meat. Meat is about 6d. a pound; bacon 1s. 5d. Bread is 4d. a pound; tea 3s. 10d., coffee 1s. 4d. Butter, fresh is 10d.; salt 1s. 6d. Ordinary wine per gallon,—than which a workman can drink no more wholesome liquor,—is 6s. In the parts of the Colony adjacent to Capetown it may be bought for 2s. and 3s. a gallon. The colonial beer is 5s. a gallon. Whether it be good or bad I omitted to enable myself to form an opinion. Clothing, which is imported from England, is I think cheaper than in England. This I have found to be the case in the larger Colonies generally, and I must leave those who are learned in the ways of Commerce to account for the phenomenon. I will give the list, as I found it in the Blue Book of the Cape Colony, for labourers' clothing. Shirts 30s. 5d. per dozen. Shoes 10s. per pair. Jackets 15s. each. Waistcoats 7s. each. Trowsers 11s. 6d. per pair. Hats 6d. each. In these articles so much depends on quality that it is hard to make a comparison. In South Africa I was forced to buy two hats, and I got them very much cheaper than my London hatmaker would have sold me the same articles. House-rent, taking the Colony through, is a little dearer than in England. Domestic service is dearer;—but the class of whom I am speaking would probably not be affected by this. The rate of wages for house servants as given in the Blue Book is as follows:—

Male domestic servants		European—£2 10s. a month, with board and lodging.		
"	"	Coloured—£1 8s.	"	"
Female	"	European—£1 7s.	"	"
"	"	Coloured £1 6s.	"	"

I profess the greatest possible respect for the Cape Colony Blue Book and for its compilers. I feel when trusting to it that I am standing upon a rock against which waves of statistical criticism may dash themselves in vain. Such at least is my faith as to 968 out of the 969 folio pages which the last published volume contains. But I would put it to the compilers of that valuable volume, I would put it to my particular friend Captain Mills himself, whether they, whether he, can get a European man-servant for £30 a year, or a European damsel for £16 4s! Double the money would not do it. Let them, let him, look at the book;—Section v. page 3;—and have the little error corrected, lest English families should rush out to the Cape Colony thinking that they would be nicely waited upon by white fingers at these easy but fabulous rates. The truth is that European domestic servants can hardly be had for any money.

NATAL

CHAPTER XIV

HISTORY OF THE COLONY

THE LITTLE COLONY OF NATAL has a special history of its own quite distinct from that of the Cape Colony which cannot be said to be its parent. In Australia, Queensland and Victoria were, in compliance with their own demands, separated from New South Wales. In South Africa the Transvaal Re public,—now again under British rule,—and the Orange Free State were sent into the world to shift for themselves by the Mother Country. In these cases there is something akin to the not unnatural severance of the adult son from the home and the hands of his father. But Natal did not spring into existence after this fashion and has owed nothing to the fostering care of the Cape Colony. I will quote here the commencing words of a pamphlet on the political condition of Natal published in 1869, because they convey incidentally a true statement of the causes which led to its colonization. "The motives which induced the Imperial Government to claim Natal from the Dutch. African emigrants were not merely philanthropic. The Dutch in their occupation of the country had been involved in serious struggles with the Zulus. The apprehension that these struggles might be renewed and that the wave of disturbance might be carried towards the Eastern frontier of the Cape influenced to some extent the resolution to colonize Natal. But whatever may have been the prudential considerations that entered into their counsels, the Government were deeply impressed with the wish to protect the Natives and to raise them in the scale of humanity."[1] From this the reader will learn that the British took up the country from the Dutch who had on occupying it been involved in difficulties with the Natives, and that the English had stepped in to give a government to the country, partly in defence of the Dutch against the Natives,—but partly also, and chiefly in defence of the Natives against the Dutch.

This was, in truth, the case. The difficulties which the Dutch wanderers had encountered were awful, tragic, heartrending. They had almost been annihilated. Dingaan, the then chief of the Zulus, had resolved to annihilate them, and had gone nearer to success than the Indians of Mexico or Peru had ever done with Cortez or Pizarro. But they had stood their ground,—and were not inclined to be gentle in their dealings with the Zulus,—as the congregation of tribes was called with which they had come in contact.

Natal received its name four centuries ago. In 1497 it was visited,—or at any rate seen,—by Vasco da Gama on Christmas day and was then called Terra Natalis from that cause, It is now called Na-tal, with the emphasis sharp on the last syllable. I remember when we simply translated the Latin word into plain English and called the place Port Natal in the ordinary way,—as may be remembered by the following stanza from Tom Hood's "Miss Kelmansegg":—

Into this world we come like ships,
Launched from the docks and stocks and slips,
For future fair or fatal.
And one little craft is cast away
On its very first trip to Babbicombe Bay,
While another rides safe at Port Natal.

After that no more was known of the coast for more than a hundred and fifty years. In the latter part of the eighteenth century the Dutch seem to have had a settlement there,—not the Dutch coming overland as they did afterwards, but the Dutch trading along the coast. It did not, however, come to much, and we hear no more of the country till 1823,—only fifty-five years ago,—an English officer of the name of Farewell, with a few of his country men, settled himself on the land where the town of D'Urban now stands. At that time King Chaka of the Zulus, of whom I shall speak in a following chapter, had well-nigh exterminated the natives of the coast, so that there was no one to oppose Mr. Farewell and his companions. There they remained, with more or less of trouble from Chaka's successor and from invading Zulus, till 1835, when the British of the Cape Colony took so much notice of the place as to call the settlement Durban, after Sir Benjamin D'Urban, its then Governor.

Then began the real history of Natal which like so many other parts of South Africa,—like the greater part of that South Africa which we now govern,—was first occupied by Dutchmen trekking away from the to them odious rule of British Governors, British officers, British laws,—and what seemed to them to be mawkish British philanthropy. The time is so recent that I myself have been able to hear the story told by the lips of those who were themselves among the number of indignant emigrants,—of those who had barely escaped when their brethren and friends had been killed around them by the natives. "Why did you leave your old home?" I asked one old Dutch farmer whom I found still in Natal. With the urbanity which seemed always to characterize the Dutch he would say nothing to me derogatory to the English. "He says that there was not land enough for their wants," explained the gentleman who was acting as interpreter between us. But it meant the same thing. The English were pressing on the heels of the Dutchmen.

The whole theory of life was different between the two people and remains so to the present day. The Englishman likes to have a neighbour near him; the Dutchman cannot bear to see the smoke of another man's chimney from his own front door. The Englishman would fain grow wheat; the Dutchman is fond of flocks and herds. The Englishman is of his nature democratic;—the Dutchman is patriarchal. The Englishman loves to have his finger in every pie around him. The Dutchman wishes to have his own family, his own lands, above all his own servants and dependants, altogether within his own grasp, and cares for little beyond that. There had come various laws in the Cape Colony altogether antagonistic to the feelings of the Dutch farmer, and at last in 1834, came the emancipation act which was to set free all the slaves in 1838. Although the Dutch had first explored Natal before that act came into operation,—it had perhaps more to do with the final exodus of the future Natalians than any other cause. The Dutchman of South Africa could not endure the interference with his old domestic habits which English laws were threatening and creating.

In 1834 the first Dutch party made their way from Uitenhage in the Eastern Province of the Cape Colony, by land, across the South Eastern corner of South Africa over the Drakensberg mountains to the Natal coast. Here they fraternised with the few English they found there, examined the country and seemed to have made themselves merry,—till news reached them of the Kafir wars then raging. They gallantly hurried back to their friends, postponing their idea of permanent emigration till this new trouble should be over. It was probably the feeling induced by Lord Glenelg's wonderful despatch of Dec. 1835,—in which he declared that the English and Dutch had been all wrong and the Kafirs all right in the late wars,—which at last produced the exodus. There were personal grievances to boot, all of which sprang from impatience of the Dutch to the English law; and towards the end of 1836 two hundred Dutchmen started under Hendrik Potgeiter. A more numerous party followed under Gerrit Maritz. They crossed the Orange river, to which the Cape Colony was then extended, and still travelling on, making their waggons their homes as they went, they came to the Yaal, leaving a portion of their numbers behind them in what is now the Orange

Free State. We have no written account of the mode of life of these people as they trekked on, but we can conceive it. No Dutchman in South Africa is ever without a waggon big enough to make a home for his family and to carry many of his goods, or without a span or team of oxen numerous enough to drag it. They took their flocks and horses with them, remaining here and there as water and grass would suit them. And here and there they would sow their seeds and wait for a crop, and then if the crop was good and the water pleasant and if the Natives had either not quarrelled with them or had been subdued, they would stay for another season till the waggon would at last give place to a house, and then, as others came after them, they would move on again, jealous of neighbourhood even among their own people. So they went northwards till they crossed the Vaal river and came into hostile contact with the fierce tribes of the Matabeles which then occupied the Transvaal.

What took place then belongs rather to the history of the Transvaal than to that of Natal; but the Dutch pioneers who had gone thus far were forced back over the Yaal; and though they succeeded in recovering by renewed raids many of the oxen and waggons of which they had been deprived by a great Chief of the Matabele tribe named Mazulekatze, they acknowledged that they must carry their present fortunes elsewhere,, and they remembered the pleasant valleys which some of them had seen a few years earlier on the Natal coast. With great difficulty they found a track pervious to wheels through the Drakenbergs, and made their way down to the coast. There had been disagreements among the Dutch themselves after their return back over the Yaal river, and they did not all go forth into Natal. Pieter Retief, who had now joined them from the old Colony and who had had his own reasons for quarrelling with the British authorities in the Cape, was chosen the Chief of those who made their way eastwards into Natal, and he also, on reaching the coast, fraternised with the English there who at that time acknowledged no obedience to the British Government at Capetown. It seems that Retief and the few English at Durban had some idea of a joint Republic;—but the Dutchman took the lead and finding that the natives were apparently amenable, he entertained the idea of obtaining a cession of the land from Dingaan, who had murdered and succeeded his brother Chaka as King of the Zulus.

Dingaan made his terms, which Retief executed. A quantity of cattle which another tribe had taken was to be returned to Dingaan. The cattle were obtained and given up to the Zulu Chief. In the meantime Dutchman after Dutchman swarmed into the new country with their waggons and herds through the passes which had been found. We are told that by the end of 1837 a thousand waggons had made their way into this district now called Natal and had occupied the northern portion of it. Probably not a single waggon was owned by an Englishman,—

though Natal is now especially an English and not a Dutch Colony. There was hardly a Native to be seen, the country having been desolated by the King of the Zulus. It was the very place for the Dutch,—fertile, without interference, and with space for every one.

Early in 1838 Retief with a party of picked men started for the head quarters of Dingaan, the Zulu King, with the recovered cattle which he was to give up as the price of the wide lands assigned to him. Then there was a festival and rejoicings among the Zulus in which the Dutchmen joined. A deed of cession was signed, of which Dingaan, the King, understood probably but little. But he did understand that these were white men coming to take away his land and at the moment in which the ceremonies were being completed,—he contrived to murder them all. That was the end of Pieter Retief, whose name in conjunction with that of his friend and colleague Gerrit Maritz still lives in the singular appellation found for the capital of Natal,—Pieter Maritzburg.

Then Dingaan, with a spirit which I cannot reprobate as I find it reprobated by other writers, determined to sally forth and drive the Dutch out of the land. It seems to me of all things the most natural for a king of Natives to do,—unless the contemplation of such a feat were beyond his intelligence or its attempt beyond his courage. It may be acknowledged that it is the business of us Europeans first to subjugate and then to civilize the savage races—but that the Savage shall object to be subjugated is surely natural. To abuse a Savage for being treacherous and cruel is to abuse him for being a Savage, which is irrational. Dingaan failed neither in intelligence or courage, and went forth to annihilate the Dutch in those northern portions of the present Colony which are now called Klip-River and Wienen. The latter word is Dutch for wailing and arose from the sufferings which Dingaan then inflicted. He first came across a party of women and children at the Blue Krans river,—in the district now called Wienen,—and killed them all. Various separated parties were destroyed in the same way, till at last an entrenchment of waggons was formed,—a "laager" as it is called in Dutch,—and from thence a battle was fought as from a besieged city against the besiegers. The old man who told me that he had trekked because land in the Colony was insufficient had been one of the besieged, and his old wife, who sat by and added a word now and then to the tale, had been inside the laager with him and had held her baby with one hand while she supplied ammunition to her husband with the other. It was thus that the Dutch always defended themselves, linking their huge waggons together into a circle within which were collected their wives and children, while their cattle were brought into a circle on the outside. It must be remembered that they, few in number, were armed with rifles while the Savages around were attacking them with their pointed spears which they call assegais.

By far the greater number of Dutch who had thus made their way over into Natal were killed,—but a remnant remained sufficient to establish itself. In these contests the white man always comes off as conqueror at last. Dingaan, however, carried on the battle for a long time, and though driven out of Natal was never thoroughly worsted on his own Zulu territory. Both Dutch and English attacked him in his own stronghold, but of those who went over the Buffalo or Tugela river in Dingaan's time with hostile intentions but few lived to return and tell the tale. There was one raid across the river in which it is said that 3,000 Zulus were killed, and that Dingaan was obliged to burn his head kraal or capital, and fly; but even in this last of their attacks on Zulu land the Dutch were at first nearly destroyed.

At last these battles with Dingaan were brought to an end by a quarrel which the emigrants fostered between Dingaan and his brother Panda,—who was also his heir. I should hardly interest my readers if I were to go into the details of this family feud. It seems however that in spite of the excessive superstitious reverence felt by these Savages for their acknowledged Chief, they were unable to endure the prolonged cruelties of their tyrant. Panda himself was not a warrior, having been kept by Dingaan in the back-ground in order that he might not become the leader of an insurrection against him; but he was put forward as the new king; and the new king's party having allied themselves with the Europeans, Dingaan was driven into banishment and seems to have been murdered by those among whom he fell. That was the end of Dingaan and has really been the end, up to this time, of all fighting between the Zulus and the white occupiers of Natal. From the death of Dingaan the ascendancy of the white man seems to have been acknowledged in the districts south and west of the Tugela and Buffalo rivers.

The next phase in the history of Natal is that which has reference to the quarrels between the Dutch and the English. There is I think no doubt that during the first occupation of the land by the Dutch the English Government refused to have anything to do with the territory. It was then the same as it has been since when we gave up first the Transvaal, and afterward the Orange Free State, or "Sovereignty" as it used to be called. A people foreign to us in habits and language, which had become subject to us, would not endure our rule,—would go further and still further away when our rule followed them. It was manifest that we could not stop them without the grossest tyranny;—but were we bound to go after them and take care of them? The question has been answered in the negative even when it has been asked as to wandering Englishmen who have settled themselves on strange shores,—but though answered in the negative it has always turned out that when the Englishmen have reached a number too great to be ignored the establishment of a new Colony has been inevitable. Was it necessary that

Downing Street should run after the Dutch? Downing Street declared that she would do nothing of the kind. Lord Glenelg had disclaimed "any intention on the part of Her Majesty's Government to assert any authority over any part of this territory." But Downing Street was impotent to resist. The Queen's subjects had settled themselves in a new country, and after some shilly-shallying on the part of the Cape authorities, after the coming and going of a small body of troops, these subjects declared their intention of establishing themselves as a Republic—and begged Her Majesty to acknowledge their independent existence. This was in January 1841, when Sir George Napier was Governor. In the meantime the Dutch had had further contests with remaining natives,—contests in which they had been the tyrants and in which they shewed a strong intention of driving the black tribes altogether away from any lands which they might want themselves. This, and probably a conviction that there were not sufficient elements of rule among the Dutch farmers to form a government,—a conviction for which the doings of the young Volksraad of Natalia gave ample reason,—at last caused our Colonial Office to decide that Natal was still British territory. Sir George Napier on 2nd Dec. 1841 issued a proclamation stating, "That whereas the Council of emigrant farmers now residing at Port Natal and the territory adjacent thereto had informed His Excellency that they had ceased to be British subjects," &c. &c.; the whole proclamation is not necessary here;—"his Excellency announced his intention of resuming military occupation of Port Natal by sending thither without delay a detachment of Her Majesty's forces." And so the war was declared.[2]

The war at first went very much in favour of the Dutch. A small detachment of British troops,—about 300 men,—was marched overland to Durban, and two little vessels of war were sent round with provisions and ammunition. The proceedings of this force were so unfortunate that a part of it was taken and marched up to prison at Pieter Maritzburg and the remainder besieged in its own camp where it was nearly starved to death. The story of the whole affair is made romantic by the remarkable ride made by one Mr. King, during six days and nights, along the coast and through the Kafir country, into the Cape Colony, bearing the sad news and demanding assistance. As Great Britain had now begun the campaign, Great Britain was of course obliged to end it successfully. A larger force with better appurtenances was sent, and on 5th July, 1842, a deed of submission was signed on behalf of the Dutch owning the sovereignty of Queen Victoria. That is the date on which in fact Natal did first become a British possession. But a contest was still carried on for more than a twelvemonth longer through which the Dutch farmers strove to regain their independence, and it was not till the 8th of August, 1843, that the twenty-four members of the still existing Volksraad declared Her Majesty's Government to be supreme in Port Natal.

But the Dutchmen could hardly even yet be said to be beaten. They certainly were not contented to remain as British subjects. Very many of them passed again back over the Drakenberg mountains determined to free themselves from the British yoke, and located themselves in the districts either to the North or South of the Vaal river,—although they did so far away from the ocean which is the only high-way for bringing to them stores from other countries, and although they were leaving good low-lying fertile lands for a high arid veld the most of which was only fit for pastoral purposes. But they would there be, if not free from British rule,—for the Republics were not yet established,—far at any rate from British interference. If any people ever fought and bled for a land, they had fought and bled for Natal. But when they found they could not do what they liked with it, they "trekked" back and left it. And yet this people have shewn themselves to be generally ill-adapted for self government,—as I shall endeavour to shew when I come to speak of the Transvaal Republic,—and altogether in want of some external force to manage for them their public affairs. Nothing perhaps is harder than to set a new Government successfully afloat, and the Dutch certainly have shewn no aptitude for the task either in Natal or in the Transvaal.

It is not to be supposed that all the Dutch went, or that they went all at once. In some parts of the Colony they are still to be found prospering on their lands,—and some of the old names remain. But the country strikes the stranger as being peculiarly English, in opposition to much of the Cape Colony which is peculiarly Dutch. In one district of Natal I came across a congregation of Germans, with a German minister and a German church service, and German farmers around, an emigration from Hanover having been made to the spot. But I heard of no exclusively Dutch district. The traveller feels certain that he will not require the Dutch language as he moves about, and he recognises the Dutchman as a foreigner in the land when he encounters him. In the Transvaal, in the Orange Free State, and in many parts of the Western districts of the Cape Colony, even in Capetown itself,—he feels himself to be among a Dutch people. He knows as a fact that the Dutch in South Africa are more numerous than the English. But in Natal he is on English soil, among English people,—with no more savour of Holland than he has in London when he chances to meet a Dutchman there. And yet over the whole South African continent there is no portion of the land for which the Dutchman has fought and bled and dared and suffered as he has done for Natal. As one reads the story one is tempted to wish that he had been allowed to found his Natalia, down by the sea shore, in pleasant lands, where he would not have been severed by distance and difficulties of carriage from the comforts of life,—from timber for instance with which to floor his rooms, and wood to burn his bricks, and iron with which to make his ploughs.

But the Dutch who went did not go at once, nor did the English who came come at once. It is impossible not to confess that what with the Home Government in Downing Street and what with the Governors who succeeded each other at the Cape there was shilly-shallying as to adopting the new Colony. The province was taken up in the manner described in 1843, but no Governor was appointed till 1845. Major Smith, who as Captain Smith had suffered so much with his little army, was the military commander during the interval, and the Dutch Volksraad continued to sit. Questions as to the tenure of land naturally occupied the minds of all who remained. If a Boer chose to stay would he or would he not be allowed to occupy permanently the farm, probably of 6,000 acres which he had assumed to himself? And then, during this time, the tribes who had fled in fear of the Dutch or who had been scattered by the Zulu King, flocked in vast hordes into the country when they had been taught to feel that they would be safe under British protection. It is said that in 1843 there were not above 3,000 natives in all Natal, but that within three or four years 80,000 had crowded in. Now the numbers amount to 320,000. Of course they spread themselves over the lands which the Dutch had called their own, and the Dutch were unable to stop them. In December 1845 Mr. West was appointed the first Governor of Natal, and attempts were made to arrange matters between the remaining Boers and the Zulus. A commission was appointed to settle claims, but it could do but little,—or nothing. Native locations were arranged;—that is large tracts of land were given over to the Natives. But this to the Boers was poison. To them the Natives were as wild beasts,—and wild beasts whom they with their blood and energy had succeeded in expelling. Now the wild beasts were to be brought back under the auspices of the British Government!

In 1847 Andrias Pretorius was the dominant leader of the Natal Boers and he went on a pilgrimage to Sir Henry Pottenger who was then Governor in the Cape Colony. Sir Henry Pottenger would not see him,—required him to put down what he had to say in writing, which is perhaps the most heartbreaking thing which any official man can do to an applicant. What if our Cabinet Ministers were to desire deputations to put down their complaints in writing? Pretorius, who afterwards became a great rebel against British authority and the first President of the Transvaal Republic, returned furious to Pieter Maritzburg,—having however first put down "what he had to say" in very strong writing. Sir Henry was then leaving the Colony and answered by referring the matter to his successor. Pretorius flew to the public press and endeavoured to instigate his fellow subjects to mutiny by the indignant vehemence of his language. When the news of his failure with Sir Henry Pottenger reached the Boers in Natal, they determined upon a further wholesale and new expatriation. They would all "trek" and they did trek, on this occasion into the district between the Orange and the Vaal,—where we shall have to follow them in speaking of the origin of the two Dutch Republics. In this way Natal was nearly cleared of Dutchmen in the year 1848.

It all happened so short a time ago that many of the actors in those early days of Natal are still alive, and some of my readers will probably remember dimly something of the incidents as they passed;—how Sir Harry Smith, who succeeded Sir Henry Pottenger as Governor of the Cape, became a South African hero, and somewhat tarnished his heroism by the absurdity of his words. The story of Retief hardly became known to us in England with all its tragic horrors, but I myself can well remember how unwilling we were to have Natal, and how at last it was borne in upon us that Natal had to be taken up by us,—perhaps as a fourth rate Colony, with many regrets, much as the Fiji islands have been taken up since. The Transvaal, inferior as it is in advantages and good gifts, has just now been accepted with very much greater favour. The salary awarded to a Governor may perhaps best attest the importance of a new Colony. The Transvaal has begun with £3,000 a year. A poor £2,500 is even still considered sufficient for the much older Colony of Natal.

Since 1848 Natal has had its history, but not one that has peculiarly endeared it to the Mother Country. In 1849 a body of English emigrants went out there who have certainly been successful as farmers, and who came chiefly 1 think from the County of York. I do not know that there has since that been any one peculiar influx of English, though of course from time to time Englishmen have settled there,—some as farmers, more probably as traders, small or large. In 1850 Mr. Pine succeeded Mr. West as second Governor,—a gentleman who has again been Governor of the same Colony as Sir Benjamin Pine, and who has had to encounter,—somewhat unfairly, as I think,—the opprobrium incident to the irrational sympathy of a certain class at home in the little understood matter of Langalibalele. Langalibalele has, however, been so interesting a South African personage that I must dedicate a separate chapter to his history. In 1853 Dr. Colenso was appointed Bishop of Natal, and by the peculiarity of his religious opinions has given more notoriety to the Colony,—has caused the Colony to be more talked about,—than any of its Governors or even than any of its romantic incidents. Into religious opinion I certainly shall not stray in these pages. In my days I have written something about clergymen but never a word about religion. No doubt shall be thrown by me either upon the miracles or upon Colenso. But when he expressed his unusual opinions he became a noted man, and Natal was heard of for the first time by many people. He came to England in those days, and I remember being asked to dinner by a gushing friend. "We have secured Colenso," said my gushing friend, as though she was asking me to meet a royal duke or a Japanese ambassador. But I had never met the Bishop till I arrived in his own see, where it was allowed me to come in contact with that clear intellect, the gift of which has always been allowed to him. He is still Bishop of Natal, and will probably remain so till he dies. He is not the man to abandon any position of which he is proud. But there is another bishop—of Maritzburg—whose tenets are perhaps more in accord with those generally held by the Church of England. The confusion has no doubt been unfortunate,—and is still unfortunate, as has been almost everything connected with Natal. And yet it is a smiling pretty land, blessed with numerous advantages; and if it were my fate to live in South Africa I should certainly choose Natal for my residence. Fair Natal, but unfortunate Natal! Its worldly affairs have hitherto not gone smoothly.

In 1856 the Colony, which had hitherto been but a sub-Colony under the Cape was made independent, and a Legislative Council was appointed, at first of twelve elected and of four official member;—but this has since been altered. From that day to this there seems to have always been alive in Natal questions of altering the constitution, with a desire on the part of many of the English to draw nearer to, if not to adopt a system of government by parliamentary majorities,—and with a feeling on the part of a few that a further departure and a wider severance from such form of government would be expedient.

In 1873 came the Langalibalele affair to which I will only refer here for the purpose of saying that it led to the sending out of Sir Garnet Wolseley as a temporary governor or political head mediciner to set things right which were supposed at home to be wrong. There can be no doubt that the coming of a picked man, as was Sir Garnet, had the effect of subordinating the will of the people of the Colony to the judgment of the Colonial Office at home. Such effects will always be caused by such selections. A Cabinet Minister will persuade with words which from an Under Secretary would be inoperative. A known man will be successful with arguments which would be received with no respect from the mouth of one unknown. Sir Garnet Wolseley enjoyed an African reputation and was recognised as a great man when he landed in South Africa. The effect of his greatness was seen in his ability to induce the Legislative Council to add eight nominated members to their own House and thus to clip their own wings. Before his coming there were 15 elected members, and 5 official members—who were the Governor's Council and who received a salary. Now there are 13 nominated members, of whom eight are chosen by the Governor but who receive no salaries. The consequence is that the Government can command a majority in almost all cases, and that Natal is therefore, in truth, a Crown Colony. I know that the word will be received with scorn and denial in Natal. A Legislative Council with a majority of freely elected members will claim that it has the dominant power and that it can do as it pleases. But in truth a Chamber so constituted as is that now at Natal has but little power of persistent operation.

It was stated in the House of Commons, in the debate on the South African Permissive Bill in the summer of 1877, that Natal contained a population of 17,000 white and 280,000 Natives. I am assured that the former number is somewhat understated, and I have spoken therefore of 20,000 white people. The Natives are certainly much more numerous than was supposed. I have taken them as 320,000; but judging from the hut tax I think they must be at least 10,000 more. Many probably evade the hut tax and some live without huts. Let us take the numbers as 20,000 and 320,000. With such a population can it be well to draw even near to a system of government by parliamentary majorities? We cannot exclude the black voter by his colour. To do so would be to institute a class legislation which would be opposed to all our feelings. Nor can any one say who is black or who white. But we all know how impossible it is that any number of whites, however small, should be ruled by any number of blacks, however great. In dealing with such a population we are bound to think of Ceylon or British Guiana, or of India,—and not of Canada, Australia, or New Zealand. At present the franchise in Natal is only given to such Natives as have lived for seven years in conformity with European laws and customs,—having exempted themselves in that time from native law,—and who shall have obtained from the Governor of the Colony permission to vote on these grounds. At present the Native is in this way altogether excluded. But the embargo is of its nature too arbitrary;—and, nevertheless, would not be strong enough for safety were there adventurous white politicians in the Colony striving to acquire a parliamentary majority and parliamentary power by bringing the Zulus to the poll.

I think that the nature of the population of South Africa, and the difficulties which must in coming years arise from that population, were hardly sufficiently considered when government by parliamentary majorities was forced upon the Cape Colony and carried through its Legislative Houses by narrow majorities. That action has, I fear, rendered the Cape unfit to confederate with the other Provinces; and especially unfit to confederate with Natal, where the circumstances of the population demand direct government from the Crown. I trust that the experiment of parliamentary government may not be tried in Natal, where the circumstances of the population are very much more against it than they were in the Cape Colony.

1."The form of Constitutional Government existing in the Colony of Natal considered," by John Bird. Mr. Bird's object is to shew that Natal is not in a condition to be benefitted by a parliamentary form of government, and his arguments are well worthy of the attention of gentlemen in Downing Street. He thoroughly understands his subject, and, as I think, proves his conclusion. Mr. Bird is now Colonial Treasurer in Natal.

2. My narrative of the facts of this period is based chiefly on the story as told in Judge Cloete's five lectures on the Emigration of the Dutch farmers into Natal.

CHAPTER XV

Condition of the Colony

PART ONE

I reached Durban, the only seaport in the Colony of Natal, about the end of August,—that is, at the beginning of spring in that part of the world. It was just too warm to walk about pleasantly in the middle of the day and cool enough at night for a blanket. Durban has a reputation for heat, and I had heard so much of musquitoes on the coast that I feared them even at this time of the year. I did kill one in my bedroom at the club, but no more came to me. In winter, or at the season at which I visited the place, Durban is a pleasant town, clean, attractive and with beautiful scenery near it;—but about midsummer, and indeed for the three months of December, January and February, it can be very hot, and, to the ordinary Englishman unaccustomed to the tropics, very unpleasant on that account.

I was taken over the bar on entering the harbour very graciously in the mail tug which as a rule passengers are not allowed to enter, and was safely landed at the quay about two miles from the town. I mention my safety as a peculiar incident because the bar at Durban has a very bad character indeed. South African harbours are not good and among those which are bad Durban is one of the worst. They are crossed by shifting bars of sand which prevent the entrance of vessels. At a public dinner in the Colony I heard The Bar given as a toast. The Attorney General arose to return thanks, but another gentleman was on his legs in a moment protesting against drinking the health of the one great obstacle to commercial and social success by which the Colony was oppressed. The Attorney General was a popular man, and the lawyers were popular; but in a moment they were obliterated by the general indignation of the guests at the evil done to their beautiful land by this ill natured freak of Nature. A vast sum of money has been spent at Durban in making a breakwater, all of which has,—so say the people of Durban and Maritzburg,—been thrown away. Now Sir John Coote has been out to visit the bar, and all the Colony was waiting for his report when I was there. Sir John is the great emendator of South African harbours,—full trust being put in his capability to stop the encroachments of sand, and to scour away such deposits when in spite of his precautions they have asserted themselves. At the period of my visit nothing was being done, but Natal was waiting, graciously if not patiently, for Sir John's report. Very much depends on it. Up in the very interior of Africa, in the Orange Free State and at the Diamond Fields it is constantly asserted that goods can only be had through the Cape Colony because of the bar across the mouth of the river at Durban;—and in the Transvaal the bar is given as one of the chief reasons for making a railway down to Delagoa Bay instead of connecting the now two British Colonies together. I heard constantly that so many, or such a number of vessels, were lying out in the roads and that goods could not be landed because of the bar! The legal profession is peculiarly well represented in the Colony; but I am inclined to agree with the gentleman who thought that "The Bar" in Natal was the bar across the mouth of the river.

I was carried over it in safety and was driven up to the club. There is a railway from the port to the town, but its hours of running did not exactly suit the mails, to which I was permitted to attach myself. This railway is the beginning of a system which will soon be extended to Pieter Maritzburg, the capital, is already opened some few miles northward into the sugar district, and which is being made along the coast through the sugar growing country of Victoria to its chief town, Verulum. There is extant an ambitious scheme for carrying on the line from Pieter Maritzburg to Ladismith, a town on the direct route to the Transvaal, and from thence across the mountains to Harrismith in the Orange Free State, with an extension from Ladismith to the coal district of Newcastle in the extreme north of the Colony. But the money for these larger purposes has not yet been raised, and I may perhaps be justified in saying that I doubt their speedy accomplishment. The lines to the capital and to Verulum will no doubt be open in a year or two. I should perhaps explain that Ladismith and Harrismith are peculiar names given to towns in honour of Sir Harry Smith, who was at one time a popular Governor in the Cape Colony. There is a project also for extending the Verulum line to the extreme northern boundary of the Colony so as to serve the whole sugar producing district. This probably will be effected at no very distant time as sugar will become the staple produce of the coast, if not of the entire Colony. There is a belt of land lying between the hills and the sea which is peculiarly fertile and admirably adapted for the growth of sugar, on which very large sums of money have been already expended. It is often sad to look back upon the beginnings of commercial enterprises which ultimately lead to the fortunes not perhaps of individuals but of countries. Along this rich strip of coast-land large sums of money have been wasted, no doubt to the ruin of persons of whom, as they are ruined, the world will hear nothing. But their enterprise has led to the success of others of whom the world will hear. Coffee was grown here, and capital was expended on growing it upon a large scale. But Natal as a coffee-growing country has failed. As far as I could learn the seasons have not been sufficiently sure and settled for the growth of coffee. And now, already, in the new Colony, on which white men had hardly trodden half a century ago, there are wastes of deserted coffee bushes,—as there came to be in Jamaica after the emancipation of the slaves,—telling piteous tales of lost money and of broken hopes. The idea of growing coffee in Natal seems now to be almost abandoned.

But new ground is being devoted to the sugar cane every day, and new machinery is being continually brought into the Colony. The cultivation was first introduced into Natal by Mr. Morewood in 1849, and has progressed since with various vicissitudes. The sugar has progressed; but, as is the nature of such enterprises, the vicissitudes have been the lot of the sugar growers. There has been much success, and there has also been much failure. Men have gone beyond their capital, and the banks with their high rates of interest have too often swallowed up the profits. But the result to the Colony has been success. The plantations are there, increasing every day, and are occupied if not by owners then by managers. Labourers are employed, and public Revenue is raised. A commerce with life in it has been established so that no one travelling through the sugar districts can doubt but that money is being made, into whatever pocket the money may go.

Various accounts of the produce were given to me. I was assured by one or two sugar growers that four ton to the acre was not uncommon,—whereas I knew by old experience in other sugar countries that four ton to the acre per annum would be a very heavy crop indeed. But sugar, unlike almost all other produce, can not be measured by the year's work. The canes are not cut yearly, at a special period, as wheat is reaped or apples are picked. The first crop in Natal is generally the growth of nearly or perhaps quite two years, and the second crop, being the crop from the first ratoons, is the produce of 15 months. The average yield per annum is, I believe, about 1½ tons per acre of canes,—which is still high.

It used to be the practice for a grower of canes to have as a matter of course a plant for making sugar,—and probably rum. It seemed to be the necessity of the business of cane-growing that the planter should also be a manufacturer,—as though a grower of hemp was bound to make ropes or a grower of wheat to make bread. Thus it came to pass that it required a man with considerable capital to grow canes, and the small farmer was shut out from the occupation. In Cuba and Demerara and Barbados the cane grower is, I think, still almost always a manufacturer. In Queensland I found farmers growing canes which they sold to manufacturers who made the sugar. This plan is now being largely adopted in Natal and central mills are being established by companies who can of course command better machinery than individuals with small capitals. But even in this arrangement there is much difficulty,—the mill owners finding it sometimes impossible to get cane as they want it, and the cane growers being equally hard set to obtain the miller's services just as their canes are fit for crushing. It becomes necessary that special agreements shall be made beforehand as to periods and quantities, which special agreements it is not always easy to keep. The payment for the service done is generally made in kind, the miller retaining a portion of the sugar produced, half or two thirds, as he or the grower may have performed the very onerous work of carrying the canes from the ground to the mill. The latter operation is another great difficulty in the way of central mills. When the sugar grower had his own machinery in the centre of his own cane fields he was able to take care that a minimum amount of carriage should be required;—but with large central manufactories the growing cane is necessarily thrown back to a distance from the mill and a heavy cost for carriage is added. The amount of cane to make a ton of sugar is so bulky that a distance is easily reached beyond which the plants cannot be carried without a cost which would make any profit impossible.

In spite of all these difficulties,—and they are very great,—the stranger cannot pass through the sugar districts of Natal without becoming conscious of Colonial success. I have heard it argued that sugar was doing no good to Natal because the profits reached England in the shape of dividends on bank shares which were owned and spent in the mother country. I can never admit the correctness of this argument, for it is based on the assumption that in large commercial enterprises the gain, or loss, realized by the capitalist is the one chief point of interest;—that if he makes money all is well, and that if he loses it all is ill. It may be so to him. But the real effect of his operations is to be found in the wages and salaries he pays and the amount of expenditure which his works occasion. I have heard of a firm which carried on a large business without any thought of profit, merely for political purposes. The motive I think was bad;—but not the less beneficial to the population was the money spent in wages. Even though all the profits from sugar grown in Natal were spent in England,—which is by no means the case,—the English shareholders cannot get at their dividends without paying workmen of all classes to earn them,—from the black man who hoes the canes up to the Superintendent who rides about on his horse and acts the part of master.

There is a side to the sugar question in Natal which to me is less satisfactory than the arrangements made in regard to Capital. As I have repeated, and I fear shall repeat too often,—there are 320,000 Natives in Natal; Kafirs and Zulus, strong men as one would wish to see; and yet the work of the estates is done by Coolies from India. I ought not to have been astonished by this for I had known twenty years ago that sugar was grown or at any rate manufactured by Coolie labour in Demerara and Trinidad, and had then been surprised at the apathy of the people of Jamaica in that they had not introduced Coolies into that island. There were stalwart negroes without stint in these sugar colonies,—who had been themselves slaves, or were the children of slaves; but these negroes would only work so fitfully that the planters had been forced to introduce regular labour from a distance. The same thing, and nothing more, had taken place in Natal. But yet I was astonished. It seemed to be so sad that with all their idle strength standing close by, requiring labour, for its own salvation,—with so large a population which labour only can civilize, we who have taken upon ourselves to be their masters should send all the way to India for men to do that which it ought to be their privilege to perform. But so it is. There are now over 10,000 Coolies domiciled in Natal, all of whom have been brought there with the primary object of making sugar.

The Coolies are brought into the Colony by the Government under an enactment of the Legislature. They agree to serve for a period of 10 years, after which they are, if they please, taken back. The total cost to the Government is in excess of £20 per man. Among the items of expenditure in 1875 £20,000 was voted for the immigration of Coolies, of which a portion was reimbursed during that year, and further portions from year to year. The Coolie on his arrival is allotted to a planter,—or to any other fitting applicant,—and the employer for 5 years pays £4 per annum to the Government for the man's services. He also pays the man 12s. a month, and clothes him. He feeds the Coolie also, at an additional average cost of 12s. a month, and with some other small expenses for medical attendance and lodging pays about £20 per annum for the man's services. As I shall state more at length in the next volume, there are twelve thousand Kafirs at the Diamond Fields earning 10s. a week and their diet;—and as I have already stated there are in British Kafraria many Kafirs earning very much higher wages than that! But in Natal a Zulu, who generally in respect to strength and intelligence is superior to the ordinary Kafir, is found not to be worth £20 a year.

The Coolie after his five years of compulsory service may seek a master where he pleases,—or may live without a master if he has the means. His term of enforced apprenticeship is over and he is supposed to have earned back on behalf of the Colony the money which the Colony spent on bringing him thither. Of course he is worth increased wages, having learned his business, and if he pleases to remain at the work he makes his own bargain. Not unfrequently he sets up for himself as a small farmer or market gardener, and will pay as much as 30s. an acre rent for land on which he will live comfortably. I passed through a village of Coolies where the men had their wives and children and were living each under his own fig tree. Not unfrequently they hire Kafirs to do for them the heavy work, assuming quite as much mastery over the Kafir as the white man does. Many of them will go into service,—and are greatly prized as domestic servants. They are indeed a most popular portion of the community, and much respected,—whereas the white man does I fear in his heart generally despise and dislike the Native.

I have said that the ordinary Kafir is found by the sugar grower not to be worth £20 a year. The sugar grower will put the matter in a different way and will declare that the Kafir will not work for £20 a year,—will not work as a man should work for any consideration that can be offered to him. I have no doubt that sugar can for the present be best made by Coolie labour,—and that of course is all in all with the manufacturer of sugar. It cannot be otherwise. But it is impossible not to see that under it all there is an aversion to the Kafir,—or Zulu as I had perhaps better call him now,—because he cannot be controlled, because his labour cannot be made compulsory. The Zulu is not an idle man,—not so idle I think as were the negroes in the West Indies who after the emancipation were able to squat on the deserted grounds and live on yams. But he loves to be independent. I heard of one man who on being offered work at certain wages, answered the European by offering him work at higher wages. This he would do,—if the story be true,—with perfect good humour and a thorough appreciation of the joke. But the European in Natal, and, indeed, the European throughout South Africa, cannot rid himself of the feeling that the man having thews and sinews, and being a Savage in want of training, should be made to work,—say nine hours a day for six days a week,—should be made to do as much as a poor Englishman who can barely feed himself and his wife and children. But the Zulu is a gentleman and will only work as it suits him.

This angers the European. The Coolie has been brought into the land under a contract and must work. The Coolie is himself conscious of this and does not strive to rebel. He is as closely bound as is the English labourer himself who would have to encounter at once all the awful horrors of the Board of Guardians, if it were to enter into his poor head to say that he intended to be idle for a week. The Zulu has his hut and his stack of Kafir corn, and can kill an animal out in the veld, and does not care a straw for any Board of Guardians. He is under no contract by which he can be brought before a magistrate. Therefore the sugar planter hates him and loves the Coolie.

I was once interrogating a young and intelligent superintendent of machinery in the Colony as to the labour he employed and asked him at last whether he had any Kafirs about the place. He almost flew at me in his wrath,—not against me but against the Kafirs. He would not, he said, admit one under the same roof with him. All work was impossible if a Kafir were allowed even to come near it. They were in his opinion a set of human wretches whom it was a clear mistake to have upon the earth. His work was all done by Coolies, and if he could not get Coolies the work would not be worth doing at all by him. His was not a sugar mill, but he was in the sugar country, and he was simply expressing unguardedly,—with too little reserve,—the feelings of those around him.

I have no doubt that before long the Zulus will make sugar, and will make it on terms cheaper to the Colony at large than those paid for the Coolies. But the Indian Coolie has been for a long time in the world's workshop, whereas the Zulu has been introduced to it only quite of late.

The drive from the railway station at Ungeni, about four miles from Durban, through the sugar district to Verulum is very pretty. Some of the rapid pitches into little valleys, and steep rapid rises put me in mind of Devonshire. And, as in Devonshire, the hills fall here and there in a small chaos of broken twisted ridges which is to me always agree able and picturesque. After a few turns the traveller, ignorant of the locality, hardly knows which way he his going, and when he is shewn some object which he is to approach cannot tell how he will get there. And then the growth of the sugar cane is always in some degıee green, even in the driest weather. I had hardly seen anything that was not brown in the Cape Colony, so long and severe had been the drought. In Natal there was still no rain, but there was a green growth around which was grateful to the eyes. Altogether I was much pleased with what I saw of the sugar district of Natal, although I should have been better satisfied could I have seen Natives at work instead of imported Coolies.

Immediately west of the town as you make the first ascent up from the sea level towards the interior there is the hill called the Berea on and about which the more wealthy inhabitants of Durban have built their villas. Some few of them are certainly among the best houses in South Africa, and command views down upon the town and sea which would be very precious to many an opulent suburb in England. Durban is proud of its Berea and the visitor is taken to see it as the first among the sights of the place. And as he goes he is called upon to notice the road on which he is riding. It is no doubt a very good road,—as good as an ordinary road leading out of an ordinary town in England, and therefore does not at first attract the attention of the ordinary English traveller. But roads in young countries are a difficulty and sometimes a subject of soreness;—and the roads close to the towns and even in the towns are often so imperfect that it is felt to be almost rude to allude to them specially. In a new town very much has to be done before the roads can be macadamized. I was driven along one road into Durban in company with the Mayor which was certainly not all that a road ought to be. But this road which we were on now was, when I came to observe it, a very good road indeed. "And so it ought," said my companion. "It cost the Colony," I forget what he said it cost. £30,000, I think, for three or four miles. There had been some blundering, probably some speculation, and thus the money of the young community had been squandered. Then, at the other side of Durban, £100,000 had been thrown into the sea in a vain attempt to keep out the sand. These are the heartrending struggles which new countries have to make. It is not only that they must spend their hard-earned money, but that they are so often compelled to throw it away because in their infancy they have not as yet learned how to spend it profitably.

Natal has had many hardships to endure and Durban perhaps more than its share. But there it is now, a prosperous and pleasant seaport town with a beautiful country round it and thriving merchants in its streets. It has a park in the middle of it,—not very well kept. I may suggest that it was not improved in general appearance when I saw it by having a couple of old horses tethered on its bare grass. Perhaps the grass is not bare now and perhaps the horses have been taken away. The combination when I was there suggested poverty on the part of the municipality and starvation on the part of the horses. There is also a botanical garden a little way up the hill very rich in plants but not altogether well kept. The wonder is how so much is done in these places, rather than why so little;—that efforts so great should be made by young and therefore poor municipalities to do something for the recreation and for the relief of the inhabitants! I think that there is not a town in South Africa,—so to be called,—which has not its hospital and its public garden. The struggles for these institutions have to come from men who are making a dash for fortune, generally under hard circumstances in which every energy is required; and the money has to be collected from pockets which at first are never very full. But a colonial town is ashamed of itself if it has not its garden, its hospital, its public library, and its two or three churches, even in its early days.

I can say nothing of the hotels at Durban because I was allowed to live at the club,—which is so peculiarly a colonial institution. Somebody puts your name down beforehand and then you drive up to the door and ask for your bed room. Breakfast, lunch, and dinner are provided at stated hours. At Durban two lunches were provided in separate rooms, a hot lunch and a cold lunch,—an arrangement which I did not see elsewhere. I imagine that the hot lunch is intended as a dinner to those who like to dine early. But, if I am not mistaken, I have seen the same faces coming out of the hot lunch and going in to the hot dinner. I should imagine that these clubs cannot be regarded with much favour by the Innkeepers as they take away a large proportion of the male travellers.

The population of Durban is a little in excess of that of the capital of the Colony, the one town running the other very close. They each have something above 4,000 white inhabitants, and something above half that number of coloured people. In regard to the latter there must I think be much uncertainty as they fluctuate greatly and live, many of them, nobody quite knows where. They are in fact beyond the power of accurate counting, and can only be computed. In Durban, as in Pieter Maritzburg, every thing is done by the Zulus,—or by other coloured people;—and when anything has to be done there is always a Zulu boy to do it. Nothing of manual work seems ever to be done by an European. The stranger would thus be led to believe that the coloured population is greater than the white. But Durban is a sea port town requiring many clerks and having no manufactures. Clerks are generally white, as are also the attendants in the shops. It is not till the traveller gets further up the country that he finds a Hottentot selling him a pocket handkerchief. I am bound to say that on leaving Durban I felt that I had visited a place at which the settlers had done the very utmost for themselves and had fought bravely and successfully with the difficulties which always beset new comers into strange lands. I wish the town and the sugar growers of its neighbourhood every success,—merely suggesting to them that in a few years' time a Zulu may become quite as handy at making sugar as a Coolie.

Pieter Maritzburg is about 55 miles from Durban, and there are two public conveyances running daily. The mail cart starts in the morning, and what is called a Cobb's coach follows at noon. I chose the latter as it travels somewhat faster than the other and reaches its destination in time for dinner. The troubles of the long road before me,—from Durban through Natal and the Transvaal to Pretoria, the Diamond Fields. Bloemfontein—the capital of the Orange Free State,—and thence back through the Cape Colony to Capetown were already beginning to lie heavy on my mind. But I had no cause for immediate action at Durban. Whatever I might do, whatever resolution I might finally take, must be done and taken at Pieter Maritzburg. I could therefore make this little journey without doubt, though my mind misgave me as to the other wanderings before me.

I found the Cobb's coach,—which however was not a Cobb's coach at all,—to be a very well horsed and well arranged Institution. We travelled when we were going at about ten miles an hour and were very well driven indeed by one of those coloured half-bred Cape boys, as they are called, whose parents came into the Cape Colony from St. Helena. Almost all the driving of coaches and mail carts of South Africa has fallen into their hands, and very good coachmen they are. I sometimes flatter myself that I know something about the driving of ill-sorted teams, having had much to do for many years with the transmission of mails at home, and I do not know that I ever saw a more skilful man with awkward horses than was this Cape driver. As well as I could learn he was called Apollo. I hope that if he has a son he will not neglect to instruct him in his father's art as did the other charioteer of that name. At home, in the old coaching days, we entertained a most exaggerated idea of the skill of the red-faced, heavy, old fashioned jarveys who used to succeed in hammering their horses along a road as smooth as a bowling green, and who would generally be altogether at their wits' end if there came any sudden lack of those appurtenances to which they were accustomed. It was not till I had visited the United States, and Australia, and now South Africa that I saw what really might be done in the way of driving four, six, or even eight horses. The animals confided to Apollo's care were generally good; but, as is always the case in such establishments, one or two of them were new to the work,—and one or two were old stagers who had a will of their own. And the road was by no means a bowling-green all the way. I was much taken with the manner in which Apollo got the better of four jibbing brutes, who, taking the evil fashion one from another, refused for twenty minutes to make any progress with the vehicle to which they had just been harnessed. He suddenly twisted them round and they started full gallop as though they were going back to Durban. The animals knew that they were wanted to go the other way and were willing to do anything in opposition to the supposed will of their master. They were flying to Durban. But when he had got them warm to the harness he succeeded in turning them on the veld, keeping them still at a gallop, till they had passed the stage at which they had been harnessed to the coach.

As much of the driving in such a country has to be done with the brake as with the reins and whip, and this man, while his hands and arms were hard at work, had to manage the brake with his feet. Our old English coachman could not have moved himself quick enough for the making of such exertions. And Apollo sat with a passenger on each side, terribly cramped for room. He was hemmed in with mail bags. My luggage so obliterated the foot-board that he had to sit with one leg cocked up in the air and the other loose upon the brake. Every now and again new indignities were heaped upon him in the shape of parcels and coats which he stuffed under him as best he could. And yet he managed to keep the mastery of his reins and whip. It was very hot and he drank lemonade all the way. What English coachman of the old days could have rivalled him there? At the end of the journey he asked for nothing but took the half-crown offered to him with easy nonchalance. He was certainly much more like a gentleman than the old English coachman,—whose greedy eye who does not remember that can remember at all those old days?

We were apparently quite full but heard at starting that there was still a place vacant which had been booked by a gentleman who was to get up along the road. The back carriage, which was of the waggonette fashion, uncovered, with seats at each side, seemed to be so full that the gentleman would find a difficulty in placing himself, but as I was on the box the idea did not disconcert me. At last, about half way, at one of the stages, the gentleman appeared. There was a lady inside with her husband, with five or six others, who at once began to squeeze themselves. But when the gentleman came it was not a gentleman only, but a gentleman with the biggest fish in his arms that I ever saw, short of a Dolphin. I was told afterwards that it weighed 45 pounds. The fish was luggage, he said, and must be carried. He had booked his place. That we knew to be true. When asked he declared he had booked a place for the fish also. That we believed to be untrue. He came round to the front and essayed to put it on the foot-board. When I assured him that any such attempt must be vain and that the fish would be at once extruded if placed there, he threatened to pull me off the box. He was very angry, and frantic in his efforts. The fish, he said, was worth £5, and must go to Maritzburg that day. Here Apollo shewed, I think, a little inferiority to an English coachman. The English coachman would have grown very red in the face, would have cursed horribly, and would have persistently refused all contact with the fish. Apollo jumped on his box, seized the reins, flogged the horses, and endeavoured to run away both from the fish and the gentleman.

But the man, with more than colonial alacrity, and with a courage worthy of a better cause, made a successful rush, and catching the back of the vehicle with one hand got on to the step behind, while he held on to the fish with his other hand and his teeth. There were many exclamations from the folks behind. The savour of the fish was unpleasant in their nostrils. It must have been very unpleasant as it reached us uncomfortably up on the box. Gradually the man got in,—and the fish followed him! Labor omnia vincit improbus. By his pertinacity the company seemed to become reconciled to the abomination. On looking round when we were yet many miles from Pieter Maritzburg I saw the gentleman sitting with his feet dangling back over the end of the car; his neighbour and vis-à-vis, who at first had been very loud against the fish, was sitting in the same wretched position; while the fish itself was placed upright in the place of honour against the door, where the legs of the two passengers ought to have been. Before we reached our journey's end I respected the gentleman with the fish,—who nevertheless had perpetrated a great injustice; but I thought very little of the good-natured man who had allowed the fish to occupy the space intended for a part of his own body.

I never afterwards learned what became of the fish. If all Maritzburg was called together to eat it I was not asked to join the party.

I must not complete my record of the journey without saying that we dined at Pinetown, half way, and that I never saw a better coach dinner put upon a table.

The scenery throughout from Durban to Pieter Maritzburg is interesting and in some places is very beautiful. The road passes over the ridge of hills which guards the interior from the sea, and in many places from its altitude allows the traveller to look down on the tops of smaller hills grouped fantastically below, lying as though they had been crumbled down from a giant's hand. And every now and then are seen those flat-topped mountains,—such as is the Table mountain over Capetown,—which from so remarkable a feature in South African scenery, and occur so often as to indicate some peculiar cause for their formation.

Altogether what with the scenery, the dinner, Apollo, and the fish, the journey was very interesting.

CHAPTER XVI

Condition of the Colony

PART TWO

On arriving at Pieter Maritzburg I put up for a day or two at the Royal Hotel which I found to be comfortable enough. I had been told that the Club was a good club but that it had not accommodation for sleeping. I arrived late on Saturday evening, and on the Sunday morning I went, of course, to hear Bishop Colonso preach. Whatever might be the Bishop's doctrine, so much at any rate was due to his fame. The most innocent and the most trusting young believer in every letter of the Old Testament would have heard nothing on that occasion to disturb a cherished conviction or to shock a devotional feeling. The church itself was all that a church ought to be, pretty, sufficiently large and comfortable. It was, perhaps, not crowded, but was by no means deserted. I had expected that either nobody would have been there, or else that it would have been filled to inconvenience,—because of the Bishop's alleged heresies. A stranger who had never heard of Bishop Colenso would have imagined that he had entered a simple church in which the service was pleasantly performed,—all completed including the sermon within an hour and a half,—and would have had his special attention only called to the two facts that one of the clergymen wore lawn sleeves, and that the other was so singularly like Charles Dickens as to make him expect to hear the tones of that wonderful voice when ever a verse of the Bible was commenced.

Pieter Maritzburg is a town covering a large area of ground but is nevertheless sufficiently built up and perfected to prevent that look of scattered failure which is so common to colonial embryo cities. I do not know that it contains anything that can be called a handsome building;—but the edifices whether public or private are neat, appropriate, and sufficient. The town is surrounded by hills, and is therefore, necessarily, pretty. The roadways of the street are good, and the shops have a look of established business. The first idea of Pieter Maritzburg on the mind of a visitor is that of success, and this idea remains with him to the last. It contains only a little more than 4,000 white inhabitants, whereas it would seem from the appearance of the place, and the breadth and length of the streets, and the size of the shops, and the number of churches of different denominations, to require more than double that number of persons to inhabit it. Observation in the streets, however, will show that the deficiency is made up by natives, who in fact do all the manual and domestic work of the place. Their number is given as 2,500; but I am disposed to think that a very large number come in from the country for their daily occupations in the town. The Zulu adherents to Pieter Maritzburg are so remarkable that I must speak separately of them in a separate chapter. The white man in the capital as in Durban is not the working man, but the master, or boss, who looks after the working man.

I liked Pieter Maritzburg very much,—perhaps the best of all South African towns. But whenever I would express such an opinion to a Pieter Maritzburger he would never quite agree with me. It is difficult to get a Colonist, to assent to any opinion as to his own Colony. If you find fault, he is injured and almost insulted. The traveller soon learns that he had better abstain from all spoken criticism, even when that often repeated, that dreadful question is put to him,—which I was called upon to answer sometimes four or five times a day,—"Well, Mr. Trollope, what do you think of—,"—let us say for the moment, "South Africa?" But even praise is not accepted with contradiction, and the peculiar hardships of a Colonist's life are insisted upon almost with indignation when colonial blessings' are spoken of with admiration. The Government at home is doing everything that is cruel, and the Government in the Colony is doing everything that is foolish. With whatever interest the gentleman himself is concerned, that peculiar interest is peculiarly ill-managed by the existing powers. But for some fatuous maddening law he himself could make his own fortune and almost that of the Colony. In Pieter Maritzburg everybody seemed to me very comfortable, but everybody was ill-used. There was no labour,—though the streets were full of Zulus, who would do anything for a shilling and half anything for sixpence. There was no emigration from England provided for by the country. There were not half soldiers enough in Natal,—though Natal has luckily had no real use for soldiers since the Dutch went away. But perhaps the most popular source of complaint was that everything was so dear that nobody could afford to live. Nevertheless I did not hear that any great number of the inhabitants of the town were encumbered by debt, and everybody seemed to live comfortably enough.

"You must begin," said one lady to me, "by computing that £400 a year in England means £200 a year here." To this I demurred before the lady,—with very little effect, as of course she had the better of me in the argument. But I demur again here, with better chance of success, as I have not the lady by me to contradict me.

The point is one, on which it is very difficult to come to a direct and positive conclusion. The lady began by appealing to wages, rent, the price of tea and all such articles as must be imported, the price of clothes, the material of which must at least be imported, the price of butter and vegetables, the price of schooling, of medical assistance and of law, which must be regulated in accordance with the price of the articles which the schoolmaster, doctors, and lawyers consume,—and the price of washing. In all such arguments the price of washing is brought forward as a matter in which the Colonist suffers great hardships. It must be acknowledged that the washing is dear,—and bad, atrociously bad;—so bad that the coming home of one's linen is a season for tears and wailing. Bread and meat she gave up to me. Bread might be about the same as in Europe, and meat no doubt in Pieter Maritzburg was to be had at about half the London prices. She defied me to name another article of consumption which was not cheaper at home than in the Colony.

I did not care to go through the list with her, though I think that a London butler costs more than a Zulu boy. I found the matter of wages paid to native servants to be so inexplicable as to defy my enquiries. A boy,—that is a Zulu man—would run almost anywhere for a shilling with a portmanteau on his head. I often heard of 7s. a month as the amount of wages paid by a farmer,—with a diet exclusively of mealies or of Kafir corn. And yet housekeepers have told me that they paid £5 and £6 a month wages for a man, and that they considered his diet to cost them 15s. a week. In the heat of argument exceptional circumstances are often taken to prove general statements; you will be assured that the Swiss are the tallest people in Europe because a Swiss has been found seven feet high. A man will teach himself to think that he pays a shilling each for the apples he eats, because he once gave a shilling for an apple in Covent Garden. The abnormally dear Zulu servants of whom I have heard have been I think like the giant Swiss and the shilling apple. Taking it all round I feel sure that Zulu service in Natal is very much cheaper than English service in England,—that it does not cost the half. I have no doubt that it is less regular,—but then it is more good humoured, and what it lacks in comfort is made up in freedom.

But I would not compare items with my friend; nor do I think that any true result can be reached by such comparison. Comfort in living depends not so much on the amount of good things which a man can afford to consume, but on the amount of good things which those with whom he lives will think that he ought to consume. It may be true,—nay, it certainly is true,—that for every square foot of house room which a householder enjoys he pays more in Pieter Maritzburg than a householder of the same rank and standing pays in London for the same space. But a professional man, a lawyer let us say, can afford to live, without being supposed to derogate from his position, in a much smaller house in Natal than he can in England. It may cost sixpence to wash a shirt in Natal, and only threepence in England; but if an Englishman be required by the exacting fastidiousness of his neighbours to put on a clean white shirt every day, whereas the Natalian can wear a flannel shirt for three days running, it will be found, I think, that the Natalian will wash his shirts a penny a day cheaper than the Englishman. A man with a family, living on £400 a year, cannot entertain his friends very often either in London or in Pieter Maritzburg;—but, of the two, hospitality is more within the reach of the latter because the Colonist who dines out expects much less than the Englishman. We clothe ourselves in broadcloth instead of fustian because we are afraid of our neighbours, but the obligation on us is imperative. In a country where it is less so, money spent in clothing will of course go further. I do not hesitate to say that a gentleman living with a wife and children on any income between £400 and £1,000 would feel less of the inconveniences of poverty in Natal than in England. That he would experience many drawbacks,—especially in regard to the education of his children,—is incidental to all colonial life.

I find the following given in a list of prices prevailing at Pieter Maritzburg in March 1876, and I quote from it as I have seen no list so general of later date. Meat 6d. per pound. Wheat 13s. per cwt. Turkeys from 8s. upwards. Fowls 2s. 4d. each. Ham 1s. 1d. per lb. Bacon 8d. Butter, fresh, 1s. 2d. to 1s. 6d. This is an article which often becomes very much dearer, and is always too bad to be eaten. Coals £3 6s. 8d. per ton. Good coal could not be bought for this; but coal is never used in houses. Little fuel is needed except for cooking, and for that wood is used—quoted at 1s. 4d. per cwt. Potatoes 4s. to 6s. per cwt. Onions 16s. per cwt. A horse can be kept at livery at 17s. 6d. a week. The same clothes would be dearer in Pieter Maritzburg than in London, but, the same clothes are not worn. I pay £2 2s. for a pair of trowsers in London. Before I left South Africa I found myself wearing garments that a liberal tradesman in the Orange Free State, six hundred miles away from the sea, had sold me for 16s.—although they had been brought ready made all the way from England. This purchase had not taken place when I was discussing the matter with the lady, or perhaps I might have been able to convince her. I bought a hat at the Diamond Fields cheaper than my friend Scott would sell it me at the corner of Bond Street.

While in Pieter Maritzburg a public dinner was given to which I had the honour of receiving an invitation. After dinner, as is usual on such occasions, a great many speeches were made,—which differed very much from such speeches as are usually spoken at public dinners in England, by being all worth hearing. I do not know that I ever heard so many good speeches made before on a so-called festive occasion. I think I may say that at home the two or three hours after the health of Her Majesty has been drunk are generally two or three hours of misery,—sometimes intensified to such a degree as to induce the unfortunate one to fly for support to the wine which is set before him. I have sometimes fancied that this has come, not so much from the inability of the speakers to make good speeches,—because as a rule able men are called upon on such occasions,—as from a feeling of shame on the part of the orators. They do not like to seem to wish to shine on an occasion so trivial. The "Nil admirari" school of sentiment prevails. To be in earnest about anything, except on a very rare occasion, would almost be to be ridiculous. Consequently man after man gets up and in a voice almost inaudible mumbles out a set of platitudes, which simply has the effect of preventing conversation. Here, at Pieter Maritzburg, I will not say that every speaker spoke his best. I do not know to what pitch of excellence they might have risen. But they spoke so that it was a pleasure to hear them. The health of the Chief Justice was given, and it is a pity that every word which he used in describing the manner in which he had endeavoured to do his duty to the public and the bar, and the pleasure which had pervaded his life because the public had been law-abiding, and the bar amenable, should not have been repeated in print. Judges at home have not so much to say about their offices. There was a tradesman called to his legs with reference to the commerce of Natal who poured forth such a flood of words about the trade of the Colony as to make me feel that he ought not to be a tradesman at all. Probably, however, he has made his fortune, which he might not have done had he become a member of Parliament. It was here that the gentleman protested against drinking the health of The Bar at Durban, to the infinite delight of his hearers. Napier Brome, who was known to many of us in London, is now Colonial Secretary at Natal. I don't remember that he ever startled us by his eloquence at home; but on this occasion he made a speech which if made after a London public dinner would be a great relief. Everybody had something to say, and nobody was ashamed to say it.

I found 1,200 British soldiers in Pieter Maritzburg, for the due ordering of whom there was assembled there the rather large number of eight or nine Field Officers. But in Natal military matters have had a stir given to them by the necessity of marching troops up to Pretoria,—at a terrible cost, and now an additional stir by Zulu ambition. An Englishman in these parts, when he remembers the almost insuperable difficulty of getting a sufficient number of men in England to act as soldiers, when he tells himself what these soldiers cost by the time they reach their distant billets, and reminds himself that they are supported by taxes levied on a people who, man for man, are very much poorer than the

Colonists themselves, that they are maintained in great part out of the beer and tobacco of rural labourers who cannot earn near as much as many a Kafir,—the Englishman as he thinks of all this is apt to question the propriety of their being there. He will say to himself that at any rate the Colony should pay for them. A part of the cost is paid for by the Colony, but only a small part. In 1876 £4,596 9s. 11d, was so expended, and in 1877 £2,318 2s. 7d.

Other countries, Spain most notoriously and Holland also, have held the idea that they should use their Colonies as a source of direct wealth to themselves,—that a portion of the Colonist earnings, or findings, should periodically be sent home to enrich the mother country. England has disavowed that idea and has thought that the Colonies should be for the Colonists. She has been contented with the advantage to her own trade which might come from the creating of new markets for her goods, and from the increase which accrued to her honour from the spreading of her language, her laws and her customs about the world. Up to a certain point she has had to manage the Colonies herself as a mother manages her child; and while this was going on she had imposed on her the necessary task of spending Colonial funds, and might spend them on soldiers or what not as seemed best to her. But when the Colonies have declared themselves able to manage themselves and have demanded the privilege of spending their own moneys, then she has withdrawing her soldiers. It has seemed monstrous to her to have to send those luxuries,—which of all luxuries are in England the most difficult to be had,—to Colonies which assume to be able to take care of themselves with their own funds. But the act of withdrawing them has been very unpopular. New South Wales has not yet quite forgiven it, nor Tasmania. For a time there was a question whether it might not drive New Zealand into rebellion. But the soldiers have been withdrawn, from all parliamentary Colonies, I think, except the Cape. Natal is not a parliamentary Colony in the proper sense, and cannot therefore in this matter be put on quite the same footing as the Cape Colony. But she spends her own revenues and according to the theory which prevails on the subject, she should provide for her own defence.

Australia wants no soldiers, nor does New Zealand in spite of the unsubdued Maoris who are still resident within her borders. They fear no evil from aboriginal races against which their own strength will not suffice for them. At the Cape and in Natal it is very different. It has to be acknowledged, at any rate as to Natal, that an armed European force in addition to any that the Colony can supply for itself, has to be maintained for its protection against the black races. But who should pay the bill? I will not say that assuredly the Colony should do so,—or else not have the soldiers. What is absolutely necessary in the way of soldiers must be supplied, whoever pays for them. England will not let her Colonies be overcome by enemies, black or white, even though she herself must pay the bill. But it seems to me that a Colony should either pay its bill or else be ruled from home. I cannot admit that a Colony is in a position to levy, collect, and spend its own taxes, till it is in a position to pay for whatever it wants with those taxes. Were there many Colonies situated as are those of South Africa it would be impossible for England to continue to send her soldiers for their protection. In the mean time it is right to say that the Colony keeps a colonial force of 150 mounted police who are stationed at three different places in the Colony,—the Capital, Eastcourt, and Greyton. In these places there are barracks and stables, and the force as far as it goes is very serviceable.

The Colony is governed by a Lieutenant-Governor,—who however is not in truth Lieutenant to any one but simply bears that sobriquet, and an Executive Council consisting I think of an uncertain number. There is a Colonial Secretary, a Secretary for Native Affairs, a Treasurer, and an Attorney-General. The Commandant of the Forces is I think also called to the Council, and the Superintendent of Public Works. The Governor is impowered also to invite two members of the Legislative Council. They meet as often as is found necessary and in fact govern the Colony. Laws are of course passed by the Legislative Council of twenty-eight members, of which, as I have stated before, fifteen are elected and thirteen nominated. New laws are I think always initiated by the Government, and the action of the Council, if hostile to the Government, is confined to repudiating propositions made by the Government. But the essential difference between such a government as that of Natal, and parliamentary government such as prevails in Canada, the Australias, New Zealand and in the Cape Colony, consists in this—that the Prime Minister in these self-governing Colonies is the responsible head of affairs and goes in and out in accordance with a parliamentary majority, as do our Ministers at home; whereas in Natal the Ministers remain in,—or go out if they do go out,—at the dictation of the Crown. Though the fifteen elective members in Natal were to remain hostile to the Government on every point year after year, there would be no constitutional necessity to change a single Minister of the Colony. The Crown,—or Governor,—would still govern in accordance with its or his prevailing ideas. There might be a deadlock about money. There might be much that would be disagreeable. But the Governor would be responsible for the government, and no one would necessarily come in or go out. Such a state of things, however, is very improbable in a Colony in which the Crown nominates so great a minority as thirteen members out of a Chamber of twenty-eight. It is not probable that the fifteen elected members will combine themselves together to create a difficulty.

In 1876 the Revenue of the Colony was £265,551. In 1846 it was only £3,095. In 1876 the expenditure was £261,933. What was the expenditure in 1846 I do not know, but certainly more than the Revenue,—as has often been the case since. The Colony owes an old funded debt of £331,700, and it has now borrowed or is in the act of borrowing £1,200,000 for its railways. The borrowed money will no doubt all be expended on public works. When a country has but one harbour, and that harbour has such a sandbank as the bar at Durban, it has to spend a considerable sum of money before it can open the way for its commerce. Upon the whole it may be said that the financial affairs of the Colony are now in a good condition.

When I had been a day or two in the place the Governor was kind enough to ask me to his house and extended his hospitality by inviting me to join him in an excursion which he was about to make through that portion of his province which lies to the immediate North of Pieter Maritzburg, and thence, eastward, down the coast through the sugar districts to Durban. It was a matter of regret to me that my arrangements were too far fixed to enable me to do all that he suggested; but I had a few days at my disposal and I was very glad to take the opportunity of seeing, under such auspices, as much as those few days would allow. An active Colonial Governor will be so often on the move as to see the whole of the territory confided to his care and to place himself in this way within the reach of almost every Colonist who may wish to pay his respects or may have ought of which to complain. This is so general that Governors are very often away from home, making semi-regal tours through their dominions, not always very much to their own comfort, but greatly to the satisfaction of the male Colonist who always likes to see the Governor,—very much indeed to the satisfaction of the lady Colonist who likes the Governor to call upon her.

Upon such occasions everything needed upon the road has to be carried, as, except in towns, no accommodation can be found for the Governor and his suite. In Natal for instance I imagine that Durban alone would be able to put the Governor up with all his followers. He lives as he goes under canvas, and about a dozen tents are necessary. Such at least was the case on this trip. Cooks, tent pitchers, butlers, guards, aides-de-camp, and private secretary are all necessary. The progress was commenced by the despatch of many waggons with innumerable oxen. Then there followed a mule waggon in which those men were supposed to sit who did not care to remain long on horseback. While I remained the mule waggon was I think presided over by the butler, and tenanted by his satellites, the higher persons preferring the more animated life of the saddle. I had been provided with a remarkably strong little nag, named Toby Tub, who seemed to think nothing of sixteen stone for six or seven hours daily and who would canter along for ever if not pressed beyond eight miles an hour. The mode of our progress was thus;—as the slow oxen made their journeys of twelve or fourteen miles a day the Governor deviated hither and thither to the right and the left, to this village or to that church, or to pay a visit to some considerable farmer; and thus we would arrive at the end of our day's journey by the time the tents were pitched,—or generally before. There was one young officer who used to shoot ahead about three in the afternoon, and it seemed that everything in the way of comfort depended on him. My own debt of gratitude to him was very great, as he let me have his own peculiar indiarubber tub every morning before he used it himself! Tubbing on such occasions is one of the difficulties, as the tents cannot be pitched quite close to the spruits, or streams, and the tubs have to be carried to the water instead of the water to the tubs. Bathing would be convenient, were it not that the bather is apt to get out of a South African spruit much more dirty than he went into it. I bathed in various rivers during my journey, but I did not generally find it satisfactory.

We rode up to many farms at which we were of course received with the welcome due to the Governor, and where in the course of the interview most of the material facts as to the farmer's enterprise,—whether on the whole he had been successful or the reverse, and to what cause his success or failure had been owing,—would come out in conversation. An English farmer at home would at once resent the questionings which to a Colonial farmer are a matter of course. The latter is conscious that he has been trying an experiment and that any new comer will be anxious to know the result. He has no rent to pay and does not feel that his condition ought to remain a secret between him and his landlord alone. One man whom we saw had come from the East Riding of Yorkshire more than twenty years ago, and was now the owner of 1,200 acres,—which however in Natal is not a large farm. But he was well located as to land, and could have cultivated nearly the whole had labour been abundant enough, and cheap enough. He was living comfortably with a pleasant wife and well-to do children, and regaled us with tea and custard. His house was comfortable, and everything no doubt was plentiful with him. But he complained of the state of things and would not admit himself to be well off. O fortunati nimium sua si bona norint Agricolæ. He had no rent to pay. That was true. But there were taxes,—abominable taxes. This was said with a side look at the Governor. And as for labour,—there was no making a Zulu labour. Now you could get a job done, and now you couldn't. How was a man to grow wheat in such a state of things, and that, too, with the rust so prevalent? Yes;—he had English neighbours and a school for the children only a mile and a half off. And the land was not to say bad. But what with the taxes and what with the Zulus, there were troubles more than enough. The Governor asked, as I thought at the moment indiscreetly, but the result more than justified the question,—whether he had any special complaint to make. He had paid the dog tax on his dogs,—5s. a dog, I think it was;—whereas some of his neighbours had escaped the imposition! There was nothing more. And in the midst of all this the man's prosperity and comfort were leaking out at every corner. The handsome grown-up daughter was telling me of the dancing parties around to which she went, and there were the pies and custards all prepared for the family use and brought out at a moment's notice. There were the dining room and drawing room, well furnished and scrupulously clean,—and lived in, which is almost more to the purpose. There could be no doubt that our Yorkshire friend had done well with himself in spite of the Zulus and the dog tax.

An Englishman, especially an English farmer, will always complain, where a Dutchman or a German will express nothing but content. And yet the Englishman will probably have done much more to secure his comfort than any of his neighbours of another nationality. An English farmer in Natal almost always has a deal flooring to his living rooms; while a Dutchman will put up with the earth beneath his feet. The one is as sure to be the case as the other. But the Dutchman rarely grumbles,—or if he grumbles it is not at his farm. He only wants to be left alone, to live as he likes on his earthen floor as his fathers lived before him, and not to be interfered with or have advice given to him by any one.

In the course of our travels we came to a German village,—altogether German, and were taken by the Lutheran parson to see the Lutheran church and Lutheran school. They were both large and betokened a numerous congregation. That such a church should have been built and a clergyman supported was evidence of the possession of considerable district funds. I am not sure but that I myself was more impressed by the excellence of the Lutheran oranges, grown on the spot. It was very hot and the pastor gave us oranges just picked from his own garden to refresh us on our journey. I never ate better oranges. But an orange to be worth eating should always be just picked from the tree.

Afterwards as we went on we came to Hollanders, Germans, Dutchmen, and Englishmen, all of whom were doing well, though most of them complained that they could not grow corn as they would wish to do because the natives would not work. The Hollander and the Dutchman in South Africa are quite distinct persons. The Hollander is a newly arrived emigrant from Holland, and has none of the Boer peculiarities, of which I shall have to speak when I come to the Transvaal and the Free State. The Dutchman is the descendant of the old Dutch Colonist, and when living on his farm is called a Boer,—the word having the same signification as husbandman with us. It flavours altogether of the country and country pursuits, but would never be applied to any one who worked for wages. They are rare in the part of the country we were then visiting, having taken themselves off, as I have before explained, to avoid English rule. There is however a settlement of them still left in the northern part of the Colony, about the Klip River and in Weenen.

One Hollander whom we visited was very proud indeed of what he had done in the way of agriculture and gave us, not only his own home-grown oranges, but also his own home-grown cigars. I had abandoned smoking, perhaps in prophetical anticipation of some such treat as this. Others of the party took the cigars,—which, however, were not as good as the oranges. This man had planted many trees, and had done marvels with the land round his house. But the house itself was deficient,—especially in the article of flooring.

Then we came to a German farmer who had planted a large grove about his place, having put down some thousands of young trees. Nothing can be done more serviceable to the country at large than the planting of trees. Though there is coal in the Colony it is not yet accessible,—nor can be for many years because of the difficulty of transport. The land is not a forest-land,—like Australia. It is only on the courses of the streams that trees grow naturally and even then the growth is hardly more than that of shrubs. Firewood is consequently very dear, and all the timber used in building is imported. But young trees when planted almost always thrive. It has seemed to me that the Governments of South Africa should take the matter in hand,—as do the Governments of the Swiss Cantons and of the German Duchies, which are careful that timber shall be reproduced as it is cut down. In Natal it should be produced; and Nature, though she has not given the country trees, has manifestly given it the power of producing them. The German gentleman was full of the merits of the country, freely admitting his own success, and mitigating in some degree the general expressions against the offending Native. He could get Zulus to work—for a consideration. But he was of opinion that pastoral pursuits paid better than agriculture.

We came to another household of mixed Germans and Dutch where we received exactly the same answers to our enquiries. Farming answered very well,—but cattle or sheep were the articles which paid. A man should only grow what corn he wanted for himself and his stock. A farmer with 6,000 acres, which is the ordinary size of a farm, should not plough at the most above 40 acres,—just the patches of land round his house. For simply agricultural purposes 6,000 acres would of course be unavailable. The farming capitalists in England who single-handed plough 6,000 acres might probably be counted on the ten fingers. In Natal,—and in South Africa generally,—when a farm is spoken of an area is signified large enough for pastoral purposes. This may be all very well for the individual farmer, but it is not good far a new country, such as are the greater number of our Colonies. In Australia the new coming small farmer can purchase land over the heads of the pastoral Squatters who are only tenants of the land under Government. But in South Africa the fee of the land has unfortunately been given away.

On many of these farms we found that Zulus had "locations." A small number,—perhaps four or five families,—had been allowed to make a kraal,—or native village,—on condition that the men would work for wages. The arrangement is not kept in any very strict way, but is felt to be convenient by farmers who have not an antipathy to the Zulus. The men will work, unless they are particularly anxious just then to be idle;—which is, I think, as much as can be expected from them just at present. Throughout this country there are other "locations,"—very much larger in extent of land and numerously inhabited,—on which the Natives reside by their own right, the use of the soil having been given to them by the Government.

At Greyton the capital of the district I met an English farmer, a gentleman living at a little distance whose residence and station I did not see, and found him boiling over with grievances. He found me walking about the little town at dawn, and took out of his pocket a long letter of complaint, addressed to some one in authority, which he insisted on reading to me. It was a general accusation against the Zulus and all those who had the management of the Zulus. He was able to do nothing because of the injuries which the vagabond Natives inflicted upon him. He would not have had a Zulu near him if he could have helped it. I could not but wish that he might be deserted by Zulus altogether for a year,—so that he might have to catch his own horse, and kill his own sheep, and clean his own top boots—in which he was dressed when he walked about the streets of Greyton that early morning reading to my unwilling ears his long letter of complaint.

At his camp in the neighbourhood of Greyton I bade adieu to the Governor and his companions and went back to Pieter Maritzburg by the mail cart. I had quite convinced myself that the people whom I had seen during my little tour had done well in settling themselves in Natal, and had prospered as Colonists, in spite of the dog tax and the wickedness of the Zulus to the unfortunate owner of the top boots.

CHAPTER XVII

THE ZULUS

UPON ENTERING NATAL WE EXCHANGE the Kafir for the Zulu,—who conceives himself to be a very superior sort of man—not as being equal to the white man whom he reverences, but as being greatly above the other black races around him. And yet he is not a man of ancient blood, or of long established supremacy. In the early part of this century,—beyond which I take it Zulu history goeth not,—there was a certain chief of the Zulus whom we have spoken of as King Chaka. To spell the name aright there should be a T before the C, and an accent to mark the peculiar sound in the Kafir language which is called a click. To the uninstructed English ear Chaka will be intelligible and sufficient. He was King of the Zulus, but the tribe was not mighty before his time. He was a great warrior and was brave enough and gradually strong enough to "eat up" all the tribes around him; and then, according to Kafir fashion, the tribes so eaten amalgamated themselves with the eaters, and the Zulus became a great people. But Chaka was a bloody tyrant and if the stories told be true was nearly as great an eater of his own people as of his enemies. In his early days the territory which we now call Natal was not inhabited by Zulus but by tribes which fell under his wrath, and which he either exterminated or assimilated,—which at any rate he "ate up." Then the Zulus flocked into the land, and hence the native population became a Zulu people. But Zulu-land proper, with which we Britons have no concern and where the Zulus live under an independent king of their own, is to the North of Natal, lying between the Colony and the Portuguese possession called Delagoa Bay.

It may be as well to say here a few words about the Zulus on their own land. I did not visit their country and am not therefore entitled to say much, but from what I learned I have no doubt that had I visited the nation I should have been received with all courtesy at the Court of his dreaded Majesty King Cetywayo,—who at this moment, January, 1878, is I fear our enemy. The spelling of this name has become settled, but Cetch-way-o is the pronunciation which shews the speaker to be well up in his Zulu. King Chaka, who made all the conquests, was murdered by his brother Dingaan[1] who then reigned in his stead. Dingaan did not add much territory to the territories of his tribe as Chaka had done, but he made himself known and probably respected among his Zulu subjects by those horrible butcheries of the Dutch pioneers of which I have spoken in my chapter on the early history of the Colony. The name of Dingaan then became dreadful through the land. It was not only that he butchered the Dutch, but that he maintained his authority and the dread of his name by the indiscriminate slaughter of his own people. If the stories told be true, he was of all South African Savages the most powerful and the most savage. But as far as I can learn English missionaries were safe in Zulu-land even in Dingaan's time.

Then Dingaan was murdered and his brother Panda became Chief. Neither Chaka or Dingaan left sons, and there is extant a horrible story to the effect that they had their children killed as soon as born, thinking that a living son would be the most natural enemy to a reigning father. Panda was allowed to live and reign, and seems to have been a fat do-nothing good-natured sort of King,—for a Zulu. He died some years since,—in his bed if he had one,—and now his son Cetywayo reigns in his stead.

Cetywayo has certainly a bad reputation generally, though he was till quite lately supposed to be favourable to the English as opposed to the Dutch. When dealing with the troubles of the Transvaal I shall have to say something of him in that respect. He has probably been the indirect cause of the annexation of that country. In Natal there are two opinions about the Zulu monarch. As the white man generally dislikes the black races by whom he is surrounded and troubled in South Africa,—not averse by any means to the individual with whom he comes in immediate contact, but despising and almost hating the people,—Cetywayo and his subjects are as a rule evil spoken of among the Europeans of the adjacent Colony. He is accused of murdering his people right and left according to his caprices. That is the charge brought against him. But it is acknowledged that he does not murder white people, and I am not at all sure that there is any conclusive evidence of his cruelty to the blacks. He has his white friends as I have said, and although they probably go a little too far in whitewashing him, I am inclined to believe them when they assert that the spirit of European clemency and abhorrence from bloodshed has worked its way even into the Zulu Court and produced a respect for life which was unknown in the days of Chaka and Dingaan. It is no doubt the case that some of the missionaries who had been settled in Zulu-land have in the year that is last past,—1877,—left the country as though in a panic. I presume that the missionaries have gone because two or three of their converts were murdered. Two or three certainly have been murdered, but I doubt whether it was done by order of the Chief. The converts have as a rule been safe,—as have the missionaries,—not from any love borne to them by Cetywayo, but because Cetywayo has thought them to be protected by English influence. Cetywayo has hitherto been quite alive to the expediency of maintaining peace with his white neighbours in Natal, though he could afford to despise his Dutch neighbours in the Transvaal. It has yet to be seen whether we shall be able to settle questions as to a line of demarcation between himself and us in the Transvaal without an appeal to force.

When I was at Pieter Maritzburg a young lady who was much interested in the welfare of the Zulus and who had perhaps a stronger belief in the virtues of the black people than in the justice of the white, read to me a diary which had just been made by a Zulu who had travelled from Natal into Zulu-land to see Cetywayo, and had returned not only in safety but with glowing accounts of the King's good conduct to him. The diary was in the Zulu language and my young friend, if I may call her so, shewed her perfect mastery over that and her mother tongue by the way in which she translated it for me. That the diary was an excellent literary production, and that it was written by the Zulu in an extremely good running hand, containing the narrative of his journey from day to day in a manner quite as interesting as many published English journals, are certainly facts. How far it was true may be a matter of doubt. The lady and her family believed it entirely,—and they knew the man well. The bulk of the white inhabitants of Pieter Maritzburg would probably not have believed a word of it. I believed most of it, every now and then arousing the gentle wrath of the fair reader by casting a doubt upon certain details. The writer of the journal was present, however, answering questions as they were asked; and, as he understood and spoke English, my doubts could only be expressed when he was out of the room. "There is a touch of romance there," I would say when he had left us alone. "Wasn't that put in specially for you and your father?" I asked as to another passage. But she was strong in support of her Zulu, and made me feel that I should like to have such an advocate if ever suspected myself.

The personal adventures of the narrator and the literary skill displayed were perhaps the most interesting features of the narrative;—but the purport was to defend the character of Cetywayo. The man had been told that being a Christian and an emissary from Natal he would probably be murdered if he went on to the Chief's Kraal; but he had persevered and had been brought face to face with the King. Then he had made his speech. "I have come, O King, to tell you that your friend Langalibalele is safe." For it was supposed in Zulu-land that Langalibalele, who shall have the next chapter of this volume devoted to him, had been made away with by the English. At this the King expressed his joy and declared his readiness to receive his friend into his kingdom, if the Queen of England would so permit. "But, O King," continued the audacious herald, "why have you sent away the missionaries, and why have you murdered the converts? Tell me this, O King, because we in Natal are very unhappy at the evil things which are said of you." Then the King, with great forbearance and a more than British absence of personal tyranny, explained his whole conduct. He had not sent the missionaries away. They were stupid people, not of much use to any one as he thought, who had got into a fright and had gone. He had always been good to them;—but they had now run away without even the common civility of saying good-bye. He seemed to be very bitter because they had "trekked" without even the ceremony of leaving a P.P.C. card. He had certainly not sent them away; but as they had left his dominions after that fashion they had better come back again. As for the murders he had had nothing to do with them. There was a certain difficulty in ruling his subjects, and there would be bad men and violent men in his kingdom,—as in others. Two converts and two only had been murdered and he was very sorry for it. As for making his people Christians he thought it would be just as well that the missionaries should make the soldiers in Pieter Maritzburg Christians before they came to try their hand upon the Zulus.

I own I thought that the highly polished black traveller who was sitting before me must have heard the last little sarcasm among his white friends in Natal and had put the sharp words into the King's mouth for effect. "I think," said my fair friend, "that Cetywayo had us there," intending in her turn to express an opinion that the poor British soldier who makes his way out to the Colony is not always all that he should be. I would not stop to explain that the civilization of the white and black men may go on together, and that Cetywayo need not remain a Savage because a soldier is fond of his beer.

Such was the gist of the diary,—which might probably be worth publishing as showing something of the manners of the Zulus, and something also of the feeling of these people towards the English Zulu-land is one of the problems which have next to be answered. Let my reader look at his map. Natal is a British Colony;—so is now the Transvaal. The territory which he will see marked as Basuto Land has been annexed to the Cape Colony. Kafraria, which still nominally belongs to the natives, is almost annexed. The Kafrarian problem will soon be solved in spite of Kreli. But Zulu-land, surrounded as it is by British Colonies and the Portuguese settlement at Delagoa Bay, is still a native country,—in which the king or chief can live by his own laws and do as his soul lusts. I am very far from recommending an extension of British interference; but if I know anything of British manners and British ways, there will be British interference in Zulu-land before long.

In the meantime our own Colony of Natal is peopled with Zulus whom we rule, not very regularly, but on the whole with success. They are, to my thinking, singularly amenable; and though I imagine they would vote us out of the country if a plebiscite were possible, they are individually docile and well-mannered, and as Savages are not uncomfortable neighbours. That their condition as a people has been improved by the coming of the white man there can be no doubt. I will put out of consideration for a moment the peculiar benefits of Christianity which have not probably reached very many of them, and will speak only of the material advantages belonging to this world. The Zulu himself says of himself that he can now sleep with both eyes shut and both ears, whereas, under tribal rule, it was necessary that he should ever have one eye open and one ear, ready for escape. He can earn wages if he pleases. He is fed regularly, whereas it was his former fate,—as it is of all Savages and wild beasts,—to vacillate between famine and a gorge. He can occupy land and know it for his own, so that no Chief shall take away his produce. If he have cattle he can own them in safety. He cannot be "smelt out" by the witch-finder and condemned, so that his wealth be confiscated. He is subjected no doubt to thraldom, but not to tyranny. To the savage subject there is nothing so terrible as the irresponsible power of a savage ruler. A Dingaan is the same as a Nero,—a ruler whose heart becomes impregnated by power with a lust for blood. "No emperor before me," said Nero, "has known what an emperor could do." And so said Dingaan. Cetywayo would probably have said the same and done the same had he not been checked by English influences. The Zulu of Natal knows well what it is to have escaped from such tyranny.

He is a thrall, and must remain so probably for many a year to come. I call a man a thrall when he has to be bound by laws in the making of which he has no voice and is subject to legislators whom he does not himself choose. But the thraldom though often irrational and sometimes fantastic is hardly ever cruel. The white British ruler who is always imperious,—and who is often irrational and sometimes fantastic,—has almost always at his heart an intention to do good. He has a conscience in the matter—with rare exceptions, and though he may be imperious and fantastic, is not tyrannical. He rules the Zulu after a fashion which to a philanthropist or to a stickler for the rights of man, is abominable. He means to be master, and knowing the nature of the Zulu, he stretches his power. He cannot stand upon scruples or strain at gnats. If a blow will do when a word has not served he gives the blow, the blow will probably be illegal. There are certain things which he is entitled to demand, certain privileges which he is entitled to exact; but he cannot stop himself for a small trifle. There are twenty thousand whites to be protected amidst three hundred thousand blacks, with other hundreds of thousands crowding around without number, and he has to make the Zulu know that he is master. And he quite understands that he has to keep the philanthropist and Exeter Hall,—perhaps even Downing Street and Printing House Square,—a little in the dark as to the way he does it. But he is not wilfully cruel to the Zulu, and not often really unkind.

I was riding, when in Natal, over a mountain with a gentleman high in authority when we met a Zulu with his assegai and knobkirrie.[2] It is still the custom of a Zulu to carry with him his assegai and knobkirrie, though the assegai is unlawful wherever he may be, and the knobkirrie is forbidden in the towns. My companion did not know the Zulu, but found it necessary, for some official reason, to require the man's presence on the following morning at the place from which we had ridden, which was then about ten miles distant. The purport of the required attendance I now forget,—if I ever knew it,—but it had some reference to the convenience of the party of which I made one. The order was given and the Zulu, assenting, was passing on. But a sudden thought struck my companion. He spoke a word in the native tongue desiring that the assegai and knobkirrie might be given up to him. With a rueful look the weapons were at once surrendered and the unarmed Zulu passed on. "He knows that I do not know him," said my companion, "and would not come unless I had a hold upon him;"—meaning that the Zulu would surely come to redeem his assegai and knobkirrie.

Then I enquired into this practice, and perhaps expostulated a little. "What would you have done," I asked, "if the man had refused to give up his property?" "Such a thing has never yet occurred to me," said the gentleman in authority. "When it does I will tell you." But again I remonstrated. "The things were his own, and why should they have been taken away from him?" The gentleman in authority smiled, but another of our party remarked that the weapons were illegal, and that the confiscation of them was decidedly proper. But the knobkirrie on the mountain side was not illegal, and even the assegai was to be restored when the man shewed himself at the appointed place. They were not taken because they were illegal, but as surety for the man's return. I did not press the question, but I fear that I was held to have enquired too curiously on a matter which did not concern me. I thought that it concerned me much, for it told me plainer than could any spoken description how a savage race is ruled by white men.

The reader is not to suppose that I think that the assegai and knobkirrie should not have been taken from the man. On the other hand I think that my companion knew very well what he was about, and that the Zulu generally is lucky to have such men in the land. I say again that we must have resort to such practices, or that we must leave the country. But I have told the tale because it exemplifies what I say as to the manner in which savage races are ruled by us. We were all shocked the other day because an Indian servant was struck by a white master, and died from the effects of the blow. The man's death was an unfortunate accident which probably caused extreme anguish to the striker, but cannot be said to have increased at all the criminality of his act. The question is how far a white master is justified in striking a native servant. The idea of so doing is to us at home abominable;—but I fear that we must believe that it is too common in India to create disgust. It is much the same in Zulu-land. Something is done occasionally which should not be done, but the rule generally is beneficent.

Of all the towns in South Africa Pieter Maritzburg is the one in which the native element is the most predominant. It is not only that the stranger there sees more black men and women in the streets than elsewhere, but that the black men and women whom he sees are more noticeable. While I was writing of "The Colony," as the Cape Colony is usually called in South Africa, I spoke of Kafirs. Now I am speaking of Zulus,—a comparatively modern race of savages as I have already said. I have seen a pedigree of Chaka their king, but his acknowledged ancestors do not go back far. Chaka became a great man, and the Zulus swallowed all the remainder of the conquered tribes, and became so dominant that they have given their name to the natives of this part of the continent.

The Zulus as seen in Maritzburg are certainly a peculiar people, and very picturesque. I have said of the Kafir that he is always dressed when seen in town, but that he is dressed like an Irish beggar. I should have added, however, that he always wears his rags with a grace. The Zulu rags are perhaps about equal to the Kafir rags in raggedness, but the Zulu grace is much more excellent than the Kafir grace. Whatever it be that the Zulu wears, he always looks as though he had chosen that peculiar costume, quite regardless of expense, as being the one mode of dress most suitable to his own figure and complexion. The rags are there, but it seems as though the rags have been chosen with as much solicitude as any dandy in Europe gives to the fit and colour of his raiment. When you see him you are inclined to think, not that his clothes are tattered, but "curiously cut,"—like Catherine's gown. One fellow will walk erect with an old soldier's red coat on him and nothing else, another will have a pair of knee breeches and a flannel shirt hanging over it. A very popular costume is an ordinary sack, inverted, with a big hole for the head, and smaller holes for the arms, and which comes down below the wearer's knees. This is serviceable and decent, and has an air of fashion about it too as long as it is fairly clean. Old grey great coats with brass buttons, wherever they may come from, are in request, and though common always seem to confer dignity. A shirt and trowsers worn threadbare, so ragged as to seem to defy any wearer to find his way into them, will assume a peculiar look of easy comfort on the back and legs of a Zulu. An ordinary flannel shirt, with nothing else, is quite sufficient to make you feel that the black boy who is attending you, is as fit to be brought into any company as a powdered footman. And then it is so cheap a livery! and over and above their dress they always wear ornaments. The ornaments are peculiar, and might be called poor, but they never seem amiss. We all know, at home the detestable appearance of the vulgar cad who makes himself odious with chains and pins,—the Tittlebat Titmarch from the counter. But when you see a Zulu with his ornaments you confess to yourself that he has a right to them. As with a pretty woman at home, whose attire might be called fantastic were it not fashionable, of whom we feel that as she was born to be beautiful, graceful, and idle, she has a right to be a butterfly,—and that she becomes and justifies the quaint trappings which she selects, so of the Zulu do we acknowledge that he is warranted by the condition of his existence in adorning his person as he pleases. Load him with bangle, armlet, ear-ring and head-dress to any extent, and he never looks like a hog in armour. He inserts into the lobes of his ears trinkets of all sorts,—boxes for the conveyance of his snuff and little delights, and other pendants as though his ears had been given to him for purposes of carriage. Round his limbs he wears round shining ornaments of various material, brass, ivory, wood and beads. I once took from off a man's arm a section of an elephant's tooth which he had hollowed, and the remaining rim of which was an inch and a half thick. This he wore, loosely slipping up and down and was apparently in no way inconvenienced by it. Round their heads they tie ribbons and bandelets. They curl their crisp hair into wonderful shapes. I have seen many as to whom I would at first have sworn that they had supplied themselves with miraculous wigs made by miraculous barbers. They stick quills and bones and bits of wood into their hair, always having an eye to some peculiar effect. They will fasten feathers to their back hair which go waving in the wind. I have seen a man trundling a barrow with a beautiful green wreath on his brow, and have been convinced at once that for the proper trundling of a barrow a man ought to wear a green wreath. A Zulu will get an old hat,—what at home we call a slouch hat,—some hat probably which came from the corner of Bond Street and Piccadilly three or four years ago, and will knead it into such shapes that all the establishments of all the Christys could not have done the like. The Zulu is often slow, often idle, sometimes perhaps hopelessly useless, but he is never awkward. The wonderfully pummelled hat sits upon him like a helmet upon Minerva or a furred pork pie upon a darling in Hyde Park in January. But the Zulu at home in his own country always wears on his head the "isicoco," or head ring, a shining black coronet made hard with beaten earth and pigments,—earth taken from the singular ant hills of the country, which is the mark of his rank and virility and to remove which would be a stain.

I liked the Zulu of the Natal capital very thoroughly. You have no cabs there,—and once when in green ignorance I had myself carried from one end of the town to another in a vehicle, I had to pay 10s. 6d. for the accommodation. But the Zulu, ornamented and graceful as he is, will carry your portmanteau on his head all the way for sixpence. Hitherto money has not become common in Natal as in British Kafraria, and the Zulu is cheap. He will hold your horse for you for an hour, and not express a sense of injury if he gets nothing;—but for a silver threepence he will grin at you with heartfelt gratitude. Copper I believe he will not take,—but copper is so thoroughly despised in the Colony that no one dares to shew it. At Maritzburg I found that I could always catch a Zulu at a moment's notice to do anything. At the hotel or the club, or your friend's house you signify to some one that you want a boy, and the boy is there at once. If you desired him to go a journey of 200 miles to the very boundary of the Colony, he would go instantly, and be not a whit surprised. He will travel 30 or 40 miles in the twenty-four hours for a shilling a day, and will assuredly do the business confided to him. Maritzburg is 55 miles from Durban and an acquaintance told me that he had sent down a very large wedding cake by a boy in 24 hours. "But if he had eaten it?" I asked. "His Chief would very soon have eaten him," was the reply.

But there is a drawback to all these virtues. A Zulu will sometimes cross your path with so strong an injury to your nose as almost to make you ill. I have been made absolutely sick by the entrance of a good-natured Zulu into my bedroom of a morning, when he has come near me in his anxiety about my boots or my hot water. In this respect he is more potent than any of his brethren of the negro race who have come in my way. Why is or whence I am unable to say, or how it comes to pass that now and again there is one who will almost knock you down, while a dozen others shall cross you leaving no more than a mere flavour of Zuluism on your nasal organs. I do not think that dirt has anything to do with it. They are a specially clean people, washing themselves often and using soap with a bountiful liberality unknown among many white men. As the fox who leaves to the hounds the best scent is always the fox in the strongest health, so I fancy is it with the Zulu,—whereas dirt is always unhealthy. But there is the fact; and any coming visitor to Natal had better remember it, and be on his guard.

Almost all domestic service is done by the Zulu or Kafir race in Natal. Here and there may be found a European servant,—a head waiter at an hotel, or a nurse in a lady's family, or a butler in the establishment of some great man. But all menial work is as a rule done by the natives and is done with fidelity. I cannot say that they are good servants at all points. They are slow, often forgetful, and not often impressed with any sense of awe as to their master, who cannot eat them up or kill them as a black master might do. But they are good-humoured, anxious to oblige, offended at nothing, and extremely honest. Their honesty is so remarkable that the white man falls unconsciously into the habit of regarding them in reference to theft as he would a dog. A dog, unless very well mannered, would take a bit of meat, and a Zulu boy might help himself to your brandy if it was left open within his reach. But your money, your rings, your silver forks, and your wife's jewels,—if you have a wife and she have jewels,—are as safe with a Zulu servant as with a dog. The feeling that it is so comes even to the stranger, after a short sojourn in the land. I was travelling through the country by a mail cart, and had to stay at a miserable wayside hut which called itself an hotel, with eight or ten other passengers. Close at hand, not a hundred yards from the door, were pitched the tents of a detachment of soldiers, who were being marched up to the border between Natal and the Transvaal. Everybody immediately began to warn his neighbour as to his property because of the contiguity of the British soldier. But no one ever warns you to beware of a Zulu thief though the Zulus swarm round the places at which you stop. I found myself getting into a habit of trusting a Zulu just as I would trust a dog.

I have already said something of Zulu labour when speaking of the sugar districts round Durban. It is the question upon which the prosperity of South Africa and the civilization of the black races much depend. If a man can be taught to want, really to desire and to covet the good things of the world, then he will work for them and by working he will be civilized. If, when they are presented to his notice, he still despises them,—if when clothes and houses and regular meals and education come in his way, he will still go naked, and sleep beneath the sky, and eat grass or garbage and then starve, and remain in his ignorance though the schoolmaster be abroad, then he will be a Savage to the end of the chapter. It is often very hard to find out whether the good things have been properly proffered to the Savage, and whether the man's neglect of them has come from his own intellectual inability to appreciate them or from the ill manner in which they have been tendered to him. The aboriginal of Australia has utterly rejected them, as I fear we must say the North American Indian has done also,—either from his own fault or from ours. The Maori of New Zealand seemed to be in the way of accepting them when it was found out that the reception of them was killing him. He is certainly dying whether from that or other causes. The Chinaman and the Indian Coolie are fully alive to the advantages of earning money, and are consequently not to be clasped among Savages. The South Sea Islander has as yet had but few chances of working; but when he is employed he works well and saves his wages. With the Negro as imported into the West Indies the good things of the world have, I fear, made but little way. He despises work and has not even yet learned to value the advantages which work will procure for him. The Negro in the United States, who in spite of his prolonged slavery has been brought up in a better school, gives more promise; but even with him the result to be desired,—the consciousness that by work only can he raise himself to an equality with the white man,—seems to be far distant. I cannot say that it is near with the Kafir or the Zulu;—but to the Kafir and the Zulu the money market has been opened comparatively but for a short time. They certainly do not die out under the yoke, and they are not indifferent to the material comforts of life. Therefore I think there is a fair hope that they will become a laborious and an educated people.

At present no doubt throughout Natal there is a cry from the farmer that the Zulu will not work. The farmer cannot plough his land and reap it because the Zulu will not come to him just when work is required. It seems hard to the farmer that, with 300,000 of a labouring class around, the 20,000 white capitalists,—capitalists in a small way,—should be short of labour. That is the way in which the Natal farmer looks at it, when he swears that the Zulu is trash, and that it would be well if he were swept from the face of the earth. It seems never to occur to a Natal farmer that if a Zulu has enough to live on without working he should be as free to enjoy himself in idleness as an English lord. The business of the Natal farmer is to teach the Zulu that he has not enough to live on, and that there are enjoyments to be obtained by working of which the idle man knows nothing.

But the Zulu does work, though not so regularly as might be desirable. I was astonished to find at how much cheaper a rate he works than does the Kafir in British Kafraria or in the Cape Colony generally. The wages paid by the Natal farmer run from 10s. down to 5s. a month, and about 3 lbs. of mealies or Indian corn a day for diet. I found that on road parties,—where the labour is I am sorry to say compulsory, the men working under constraint from their Chiefs,—the rate is 5s. a month, or 4d. a day for single days. The farmer who complains of course expects to get his work cheap, and thinks that he is injuring not only himself but the community at large if he offers more than the price which has been fixed in his mind as proper. But in truth there is much of Zulu agricultural work done at a low rate of wages, and the custom of such work is increasing.

As to other work, work in towns, work among stores, domestic work, carrying, carting, driving, cleaning horses, tending pigs, roadmaking, running messages, scavengering, hod bearing and the like, the stranger is not long in Natal before he finds, not only that all such work is done by Natives, but that there are hands to do it more ready and easy to find than in any other country that he has visited.

1. He was murdered either by Dingaan or by another brother named Umolangaan who was then murdered by Dingaan. Diagaan at any rate became Chief of the tribe.
2. A knobkirrie is a peculiar bludgeon with a thin stick and a large knob which in the hands of an expert might be very deadly. An assegai, as my reader probably knows, is a short spear with a sharp iron head.

CHAPTER XVIII

LANGALIBALELE

THE STORY OF LANGALIBALELE IS one which I must decline to tell with any pretence of accuracy, and as to the fate of the old Zulu,—whether he has been treated wrongly or rightly I certainly am not competent to give an opinion with that decision which a printed statement should always convey. But in writing of the Colony of Natal it is impossible to pass Langalibalele without mention. It is not too much to say that the doings of Langalibalele have altered the Constitution of the Colony; and it is probable that as years run on they will greatly affect the whole treatment of the Natives in South Africa. And yet Langalibalele was never a great man among the Zulus and must often have been surprised at his own importance.

Those who were concerned with the story are still alive and many of them still sore with the feeling of unmerited defeat. And to no one in the whole matter has there been anything of the triumph of success. The friends of Langalibalele, and his enemies, seem equally to think that wrong has been done,—or no better than imperfect justice. And the case is one the origin and end of which can hardly now be discovered, so densely are they enveloped in Zulu customs and past Zulu events. Whether a gentleman twenty years ago when firing a pistol intended to wound or only frighten? Such, and such like, are the points which the teller of the story would have to settle if he intended to decide upon the rights and wrongs of the question. Is it not probable that a man having been called on for sudden action, in a great emergency, may himself be in the dark as to his own intention at so distant a period,—knowing only that he was anxious to carry out the purpose for which he was sent, that purpose having been the establishment of British authority? And then this matter was one in which the slightest possible error of judgment, the smallest deviation from legal conduct where no law was written, might be efficacious to set everything in a blaze. The natives of South Africa, but especially the natives of Natal, have to be ruled by a mixture of English law and Zulu customs, which mixture, I have been frequently told, exists in its entirety only in the bosom of one living man. It is at any rate unwritten,—as yet unwritten though there now exists a parliamentary order that this mixture shall be codified by a certain fixed day. It is necessarily irrational,—as for instance when a Zulu is told that he is a British subject but yet is allowed to break the British law in various ways, as in the matter of polygamy. It must be altogether unintelligible to the subject race to whom the rules made by their white masters, opposed as they are to their own customs, must seem to be arbitrary and tyrannical,—as when told that they must not carry about with them the peculiar stick or knobkirrie which has been familiar to their hands from infancy. It is opposed to the ideas of justice which prevail in the intercourse between one white man and another, as when the Zulu, whom the white man will not call a slave, is compelled through the influence of his Chief to do the work which the white man requires from him;—as an instance of which I may refer to those who are employed on the roads, who are paid wages, indeed, but who work not by their own will, but under restraint from their Chiefs. It must I think be admitted that when a people have to be governed by such laws mistakes are to be expected,—and that the best possible intentions, I may almost say the best possible practice, may be made matter of most indignant reproach from outraged philanthropists.

The white man who has to rule natives soon teaches himself that he can do no good if he is overscrupulous. They must be taught to think him powerful or they will not obey him in anything. He soon feels that his own authority, and with his authority the security of all those around him, is a matter of "prestige." Prestige in a highly civilized community may be created by virtue,—and is often created by virtue and rank combined. The Archbishop of Canterbury is a very great man to an ordinary clergyman. But, with the native races of South Africa, prestige has to be created by power though it may no doubt be supported and confirmed by justice. Thus the white ruler of the black man knows that he must sometimes be rough. There must be a sharp word, possibly a blow. There must be a clear indication that his will, whatsoever it may be, has to be done,—that the doing of his will has to be the great result let the opposition to it be what it may. He cannot strain at a gnat in the shape of a little legal point. If he did so the Zulus would cease to respect him, and would never imagine that their ruler had been turned from his way by a pang of conscience. The Savage, till he has quite ceased to be savage, expects to be coerced, and will no more go straight along the road without coercion, than will the horse if you ride him without reins. And with a horse a whip and spurs are necessary,—till he has become altogether tamed.

The white ruler of the black man feels all this, and knows that without some spur or whip he cannot do his work at all. His is a service, probably, of much danger, and he has to work with a frown on his brow in order that his life may be fairly safe in his hand. In this way he is driven to the daily practice of little deeds of tyranny which abstract justice would condemn. Then, on occasion, arises some petty mutiny,—some petty mutiny almost justified by injustice but which must be put down with a strong hand or the white man's position will become untenable. In nineteen cases the strong hand is successful and the matter goes by without any feeling of wrong on either side. The white man expects to be obeyed, and the black man expects to be coerced, and the general work goes on prosperously in spite of a small flaw. Then comes the twentieth case in which the one little speck of original injustice is aggravated till a great flame is burning. The outraged philanthropist has seen the oppression of his black brother, and evokes Downing Street, Exeter Hall, Printing House Square and all the Gospels. The savage races from the East to the West of the Continent, from the mouth of the Zambesi to the Gold Coast, all receive something of assured protection from the effort;—but, probably, a great injustice is done to the one white ruler who began it all, and who, perhaps, was but a little ruler doing his best in a small way. I am inclined to think that the philanthropist at home when he rises in his wrath against some white ruler of whose harshness to the blacks he has heard the story forgets that the very civilization which he is anxious to carry among the savage races cannot be promulgated without something of tyranny,—some touch of apparent injustice. Nothing will sanctify tyranny or justify injustice, says the philanthropist in his wrath. Let us so decide and so act;—but let us understand the result. In that case we must leave the Zulus and other races to their barbarities and native savagery.

In what I have now said I have not described the origin of the Langalibalele misfortune, having avoided all direct allusion to any of its incidents,—except that of the firing of a pistol twenty years ago. But I have endeavoured to make intelligible the way in which untoward circumstances may too probably rise in the performance of such a work as the gradual civilization of black men with much fault on either side. And my readers may probably understand how, in such a matter as that of Langalibalele, it would be impossible for me as a traveller to unravel all its mysteries, and how unjust I might be were I to attempt to prove that either on this side or on that side wrong had been done. The doers of the wrong, if wrong there was, are still alive; and the avengers of the wrong,—whether a real or a fancied wrong,—are still keen. In what I say about Langalibalele I will avoid the name of any white man,—and as far as possible I will impute no blame. That the intentions on both sides have been good and altogether friendly to the black man I have no doubt whatsoever.

Langalibalele was sent for and did not come. That was the beginning of the whole. Now it is undoubted good Kafir law in Natal,—very well established though unwritten,—that any Kafir or Zulu is to come when sent for by a white man in authority. The white man who holds chief authority in such matters is the Minister for Native Affairs, who is one of the Executive Council under the Governor, and probably the man of greatest weight in the whole Colony. He speaks the Zulu language, which the Governor probably has not time to learn during his period of governorship. He is a permanent officer,—as the Ministry does not go in and out in Natal. And he is in a great measure irresponsible because the other white men in office do not understand as he does that mixture of law and custom by which he rules the subject race, and there is therefore no one to judge him or control him. In Natal the Minister for Native Affairs is much more of a Governor than his Excellency himself for he has over three hundred thousand natives altogether under his hand, while his Excellency has under him twenty thousand white men who are by no means tacitly obedient. Such is the authority of the Minister for Native Affairs in Natal, and among other undoubted powers and privileges is that of sending for any Chief among the Zulu races inhabiting the Colony, and communicating his orders personally. Naturally, probably necessarily, this power is frequently delegated to others as the Minister cannot himself see every little Chief to whom instructions are to be given. As the Secretary of State at home has Under Secretaries, so has the Minister for Native Affairs under Ministers. In 1873 Langalibalele was sent for but Langalibalele would not come.

He had in years long previous been a mutinous Chief in Zulu-land,—where he was known as a "rain-maker," and much valued for his efficacy in that profession;—but he had quarrelled with Panda who was then King of Zulu-land and had run away from Panda into Natal. There he had since lived as the Chief of the Hlubi tribe, a clan numbering about 10,000 people, a proportion of whom had come with him across the borders from Zulu-land. For it appears that these tribes dissolve themselves and reunite with other tribes, a tribe frequently not lasting as a tribe under one great name for many years. Even the great tribe of the Zulus was not powerful till the time of their Chief Chaka, who was uncle of the present King or Chief Cetywayo. Thus Langalibalele who had been rainmaker to King Panda, Cetywayo's father, became head of the Hlubi tribe in Natal, and lived under the mixture of British law of which I have spoken. But he became mutinous and would not come when he was sent for.

When a Savage,—the only word I know by which to speak of such a man as a Zulu Chief so that my reader shall understand me; but in using it of I do not wish to ascribe to him any specially savage qualities;—when a Savage has become subject to British rule and will not obey the authority which he understands,—it is necessary to reduce him to obedience at almost any cost. There are three hundred and twenty thousand Natives in Natal, with hundreds of thousands over the borders on each side of the little Colony, and it is essential that all these should believe Great Britain to be indomitable. If Langalibalele had been allowed to be successful in his controversy every Native in and around Natal would have known it;—and in knowing it every Native would have believed that Great Britain had been so far conquered. It was therefore quite essential that Langalibalele should be made to come. And he did more than refuse to obey the order. A messenger who was sent for him,—a native messenger,—was insulted by him. The man's clothes were stripped from him,—or at any rate the official great coat with which he had been invested and which probably formed the substantial part of his raiment. It has been the peculiarity of this case that whole books have been written about its smallest incidents. The Langalibalele literature hitherto written,—which is not I fear as yet completed,—would form a small library. This stripping of the great coat, or jazy[1] as it is called,—the word ijazi having been established as good Zulu for such an article,—has become a celebrated incident. Langalibalele afterwards pleaded that he suspected that weapons had been concealed, and that he had therefore searched the Queen's messenger. And he justified his suspicion by telling how a pistol had been concealed and had been fired sixteen years before. And then that old case was ripped up, and thirty or forty native messengers were examined about it. But Langalibalele after taking off the Queen's messenger's jazy turned and fled, and it was found to be necessary that the Queen's soldiers should pursue him. He was pursued,—with terrible consequences. He turned and fought and British blood was shed. Of course the blood of the Hlubi tribe had to flow, and did flow too freely. It was very bad that it should be so;—but had it not been so all Zululand, all Kafirland, all the tribes of Natal and the Transvaal would have thought that Langalibalele had gained a great victory, and our handful of whites would have been unable to live in their Colony.

Then Langalibalele was caught. As to matters that had been done up to that time I am not aware that official fault of very grave nature has been found with those who were concerned; but the trial of Langalibalele was supposed to have been conducted on unjust principles and before judges who should not have sat on the judgment seat. He was tried and was condemned to very grave punishment, and his tribes and his family were broken up. He was to be confined for his life, without the presence of any of his friends, in Robben Island, which, as my reader may remember, lies just off Capetown, a thousand miles away from Natal,—and to be reached by a sea journey which to all Zulus is a thing of great terror. The sentence was carried out and Langalibalele was shipped away to Robben Island.

It may be remembered how the news of Langalibalele's rebellion, trial and punishment gradually reached England, how at first we feared that a great rebel had arisen, to conquer whom would require us to put out all our powers, and then how we were moved by the outraged philanthropist to think that a grievous injustice had been done. I cannot but say that in both matters we allowed ourselves to be swayed by exaggerated reports and unwarranted fears and sympathies. Langalibalele did rebel and had to be punished. His trial was no doubt informal and overformal. Too much was made of it. The fault throughout has been that too much has been made of the whole affair. Partisans arose on behalf of the now notorious and very troublesome old Pagan, and philanthropy was outraged. Then came the necessity of doing something to set right an acknowledged wrong. It might be that Langalibalele had had cause for suspicion when he stripped the Queen's Messenger. It might be that the running away was the natural effect of fear, and that the subsequent tragedies had been simply unfortunate. The trial was adjudged to have been conducted pith overstrained rigour and the punishment to have been too severe. Therefore it was decided in England that he should be sent back to the mainland from the island, that he should be located in the neighbourhood of Capetown,—and that his tribe should be allowed to join him.

That was promising too much. It was found to be inconvenient to settle a whole tribe of a new race in the Cape Colony. Nor was it apparent that the tribe would wish to move after its Chieftain. Then it was decided that instead of the tribe the Chieftain's family should follow him with any of his immediate friends who might wish to be transported from Natal. Now Langalibalele had seventy wives and a proportionate offspring. And it soon became apparent that whoever were sent after him must be maintained at the expense of Government. Moreover it could hardly be that Exeter Hall and the philanthropists should desire to encourage polygamy by sending such a flock of wives after the favoured prisoner. Complaint was made to me that only two wives and one man were sent. With them Langalibalele was established in a small house on the sea shore near to Capetown, and there he is now living at an expense of £500 per annum to the Government.

But this unfortunately is not the end. He has still friends in Natal, white friends, who think that not nearly enough has been done for him. A great many more wives ought to be allowed to join him, or the promise made to him will not have been kept. He is languishing for his wives, and all should be sent who would be willing to go. I saw one of them very ill,—dying I was told because of her troubles, and half a dozen others, all of them provided with food gratis, but in great tribulation,—so it was said,—because of this cruel separation. The Government surely should send him three or four more wives, seeing that to a man who has had seventy less than half a dozen must be almost worse than none. But his friends are not content with asking for this further grace, but think also that the time has come for forgiveness and that Langalibalele should be restored to his own country. He has still fame as a rain-maker and Cetywayo the Zulu King would be delighted to have him in Zulu-land. The prayer is much the same as that which is continually being put forward for the pardon of the Fenians. I myself in such matters am loyal, but, I fear, hard-hearted. I should prefer that Langalibalele should be left to his punishment, thinking that would-be rebels, whether Zulu or Irish, will be best kept quiet by rigid adherence to a legal sentence. Such is the story of Langalibalele as I heard it.

On my return to Capetown I visited the captured Chieftain at his farm house on the flats five or six miles from the city, having obtained an order to that effect from the office of the Secretary for Native Affairs. I found a stalwart man, represented to be 65 years of age, but looking much younger, in whose appearance one was able to recognise something of the Chieftain. He had with him three wives, a grown-up son, and a nephew; besides a child who has been born to him since he has been in the Cape Colony. The nephew could talk a little English, and acted as interpreter between us.

The prisoner himself was very silent, hardly saying a word in answer to the questions put to him,—except that he should like to see his children in Natal. The two young men were talkative enough, and did not scruple to ask for sixpence each when we departed. I and a friend who was with me extended our liberality to half a crown a piece,—with which they expressed themselves much delighted.

1. I have seen it asserted that this word comes from "jersey"—a flannel under shirt; but I seem to remember the very sound as signifying an old great coat in Ireland, and think that it was so used long before the word "jersey" was introduced into our language.

CHAPTER XIX

Pieter Maritzburg to Newcastle

When starting from Pieter Maritzburg to Pretoria I have to own that I was not quite at ease as to the work before me. From the moment in which I had first determined to visit the Transvaal, I had been warned as to the hard work of the task. Friends who had been there, one or two in number,—friends who had been in South Africa but not quite as far as the capital of the late Republic, perhaps half a dozen,—and friends very much more numerous who had only heard of the difficulties, combined either in telling me or in letting me understand that they thought that I was,—well—-much too old for the journey. And I thought so myself. But then I knew that I could never do it younger. And having once suggested to myself that it would be desirable, I did not like to be frightened out of the undertaking. As far as Pieter Maritzburg all had been easy enough. Journeys by sea are to me very easy,—so easy that a fortnight on the ocean is a fortnight at any rate free from care. And my inland journeys had not as yet been long enough to occasion any inconvenience. But the journey now before me, from the capital of Natal to the capital of the Transvaal and thence round by Kimberley, the capital of the Diamond Fields, to Bloemfontein, the capital of the Orange Free State, and back thence across the Cape Colony to Capetown, exceeding 1,500 miles in length, all of which had to be made overland under very rough circumstances, was awful to me. Mail conveyances ran the whole way, but they ran very roughly, some of them very slowly, generally travelling as I was told, day and night, and not unfrequently ceasing to travel altogether in consequence of rivers which would become unpassable, of mud which would be nearly so, of dying horses,—and sometimes of dying passengers! A terrible picture had been painted. As I got nearer to the scene the features of the picture became more and more visible to me.

One gentleman on board the ship which took me out seemed to think it very doubtful whether I should get on at all, but hospitably recommended me to pass by his house, that I might be sure at least of one quiet night. At Capetown where I first landed a shower of advice fell upon me. And it was here that the awful nature of the enterprise before me first struck my very soul with dismay. There were two schools of advisers, each of which was sternly strenuous in the lessons which it inculcated. The first bade me stick obdurately to the public conveyances. There was no doubt very much against them. The fatigue would be awful, and quite unfitted for a man of my age. I should get no sleep on the journey, and be so jolted that not a bone would be left to me. And I could carry almost no luggage It must be reduced to a minimum,—by which a toothbrush and a clean shirt were meant. And these conveyances went but once a week, and it might often be the case that I might not be able to secure a place. But the post conveyances always did go, and I should at any rate be able to make my way on;—if I could live and endure the fatigue.

The other school recommended a special conveyance. The post carts would certainly kill me. They generally did kill any passengers, even in the prime of life, who stuck to them so long as I would have to do. If I really intended to encounter the horrors of the journey in question I must buy a cart and four horses, and must engage a coloured driver, and start off round the world of South Africa under his protection. But among and within this school of advisers there was a division which complicated the matter still further. Should they be horses or should they be mules;—or, indeed, should they be a train of oxen as one friend proposed to me? Mules would be slow but more hardy than horses. Oxen would be the most hardy, but would be very slow indeed. Horses would be more pleasant but very subject in this country to diseases and death upon the roads. And then where should I buy the equipage,—and at what price,—and how should I manage to sell it again,—say at half price? For my friends on the mail cart side of the question had not failed to point out to me that the carriage-and-horses business would be expensive,—entailing an outlay of certainly not less than £250, with the probable necessity of buying many subsidiary horses along the road, and the too probable impossibility of getting anything for my property when my need for its use was at an end.

One friend, very experienced in such matters, assured me that my only plan was to buy the cart in Capetown and carry it with me by ship round the coast to Durban, and to remain there till I could fit myself with horses. And I think that I should have done thus under his instructions, had I not given way to the temptations of procrastination. By going on without a cart I could always leave the ultimate decision between the private and the public conveyance a little longer in abeyance. Thus when I reached Durban I had no idea what I should do in the matter. But finding an excellent public conveyance from Durban to Pieter Maritzburg, I took advantage of that, and arrived in the capital of Natal, embarrassed as yet with no purchased animals and impeded by no property, but still with my heart very low as to the doubts and perils and fatigue before me.

At East London I had made the acquaintance of a gentleman of about a third of my own age, who had been sent out by a great agricultural-implement-making firm with the object of spreading the use of ploughs and reaping machines through South Africa, and thus of carrying civilization into the country in the surest and most direct manner. He too was going to Pretoria, and to the Diamond Fields,—and to the Orange Free State. He was to carry ploughs with him,—that is to say ploughs in the imagination, ploughs in catalogues, ploughs upon paper, and ploughs on his eloquent and facile tongue; whereas it was my object to find out what ploughs had done, and perhaps might do, in the new country. He, too, thought that the public conveyance would be a nuisance, that his luggage would not get itself carried, and that from the mail conveyances he would not be able to shoot any of the game with which the country abounds. When we had travelled together as far as Pieter Maritzburg we put our heads together,—and our purses, and determined upon a venture among the dealers in carts, horses, and harness.

I left the matter very much to him, merely requiring that I should see the horses before they were absolutely purchased. A dealer had turned up with all the articles wanted,—just as though Providence had sent him,—with a Cape cart running on two wheels and capable of holding three persons beside the driver, the four horses needed,—and the harness. The proposed vendor had indeed just come off a long journey himself, and was therefore able to say that everything was fit for the road. £200 was to be the price. But when we looked at the horses, their merits, which undoubtedly were great, seemed to consist in the work which they had done rather than in that which they could immediately do again. In this emergency I went to a friendly British major in the town engaged in the commissariat department, and consulted him. Would he look at the horses? He not only did so, but brought a military veterinary surgeon with him, who confined his advice to three words, which, however, he repeated thrice, "Physical energy deficient!" The words were oracular, and the horses were of course rejected.

I was then about to start from Pieter Maritzburg on a visit of inspection with the Governor and was obliged to leave my young friend to look out for four other horses on his own responsibility,—without the advice of the laconic vet whom he could hardly ask to concern himself a second time in our business. And I must own that while I was away I was again down at heart. For he was to start during my absence, leaving me to follow in the post cart as far as Newcastle, the frontier town of Natal. This was arranged in order that three or four days might be saved, and that the horses might not be hurried over their early journey. When I got back to Pieter Maritzburg I found that he had gone, as arranged, with four other horses;—but of the nature of the horses no one could tell me anything.

The mail cart from the capital to Newcastle took two and a half days on the journey, and was on the whole comfortable enough. One moment of discord there was between myself and the sable driver, which did not, however, lead to serious results. On leaving Pieter Maritzburg I found that the vehicle was full. There were seven passengers, two on the box and five behind,—the sixth seat being crowded with luggage. There was luggage indeed everywhere, above below and around us,—but still we had all of us our seats, with fair room for our legs. Then came the question of the mails. The cart to Newcastle goes but once a week; and though subsidiary mails are carried by Zulu runners twice a week over the whole distance,—175 miles,—and carried as quickly as by the cart, the heavier bulk, such as newspapers, books, &c., are kept for the mail conveyance. The bags therefore are, in such a vehicle, somewhat heavy. When I saw a large box covered with canvas brought out I was alarmed, and I made some enquiry. It was, said the complaisant postmaster's assistant who had come out into the street, a book-post parcel; somewhat large as he acknowledged, and not strictly open at the ends as required by law. It was, he confessed, a tin box and he believed that it contained bonnets. But it was going up to Pretoria, nearly 400 miles, at book-parcel rate of postage,—the total cost of it being, I think he said, 8s. 6d. Now passengers' luggage to Pretoria is charged. 4s. a pound, and the injustice of the tin box full of bonnets struck my official mind with horror. There was a rumour for a moment that it was to be put in among us, and I prepared myself for battle. But the day was fine, and the tin box was fastened on behind with all the mails,—merely preventing any one from getting in or out of the cart without climbing over them. That was nothing, and we went away very happily, and during the first day I became indifferent to the wrong which was being done.

But when we arrived for breakfast on the second morning the clouds began to threaten, and it is known to all in those parts that when it rains in Natal it does rain. The driver at once declared that the bags must be put inside and that we must all sit with our legs and feet in each other's lap. Then we looked at each other, and I remembered the tin box. I asked the conscientious mail-man what he would do with the bag which contained the box, and he immediately replied that it must come behind himself, inside the cart, exactly in the place where my legs were then placed. I had felt the tin box and had found that the corners of it were almost as sharp as the point of a carving knife. "It can't come here," said

I “It must,” said the driver surlily. “But it won’t,” said I decidedly. “But it will,” said the driver angrily. I bethought myself a moment and then declared my purpose of not leaving the vehicle, though I knew that breakfast was prepared within. “May I trouble you to bring a cup of tea to me here,” I said to one of my fellow victims. “I shall remain and not allow the tin box to enter the cart.” “Not allow!” said the custodian of the mails. “Certainly not,” said I, with what authority I could command. “It is illegal.” The man paused for a moment awed by the word and then entered upon a compromise “Would I permit the mail bags to be put inside, if the tin box were kept outside?” To this I assented, and so the cart was packed. I am happy to say that the clouds passed away, and that the bonnets were uninjured as long as I remained in their company. I fear from what I afterwards heard that they must have encountered hard usage on their way from Newcastle to Pretoria.

The mail cart to Newcastle was, I have said, fairly comfortable, but this incident and other little trifles of the same kind made me glad that I had decided on being independent. Three of my fellow passengers were going on to Pretoria and I found that they looked forward with great dread to their journey,—not even then expecting such hardships as did eventually befall them.

The country from Pieter Maritzhurg to Newcastle is very hilly,—with hills which are almost mountains on every side, and it would be picturesque but for the sad want of trees. The farm homesteads were few and far between, and very little cultivation was to be seen. The land is almost entirely sold,—being, that is, in private possession, having been parted with by the governing authorities of the Colony. I saw cattle, and as I got further from Maritzburg small flocks of sheep. The land rises all the way, and as we get on to the colder altitudes is capable of bearing wheat. As I went along I heard from every mouth the same story. A farmer cannot grow wheat because he has no market and no labour. The little towns are too distant and the roads too bad for carriage;—and though there be 300,000 natives in the Colony, labour cannot be procured. I must remark that through this entire district the Kafirs or Zulus are scarce,—from a complication of causes. No doubt it was inhabited at one time; but the Dutch came who were cruel tyrants to the natives,—which is not surprising, as they had been most disastrously handled by them. And Chaka too had driven from this country the tribes who inhabited it before his time. In other lands, nearer to the sea or great rivers, and thus lying lower, the receding population has been supplied by new comers; but the Zulus from the warmer regions further north seem to have found the high ground too cold for them. At any rate in these districts neither Kafirs or Zulus are now numerous,—though there are probably enough for the work to be done if they would do it.

At Howick, twelve miles from Maritzburg, are the higher falls on the Umgeni,—about a dozen miles from other falls on the same river which I had seen on my way to Greyton. Here they fall precipitously about 300 feet, and are good enough to make the fortune of a small hotel, if they were anywhere in England. At Estcourt, where we stopped the first night, we found a comfortable Inn. After that the accommodation along the road was neither plenteous nor clean. The second night was passed under very adverse circumstances. Ten of us had to sleep in a little hovel with three rooms including that in which we were fed, and as one of us was a lady who required one chamber exclusively to herself, we were somewhat pressed. I was almost tempted to think that if ladies will travel under such circumstances they should not be so particular. As I was recognized to be travelling as a stranger, I was allowed to enjoy the other bedroom with only three associates, while the other five laid about on the table and under the table, as best they could, in the feeding room.

Immediately opposite to this little hovel there was on that night a detachment of the 80th going up to join its regiment at Newcastle. The soldiers were in tents, ten men in a tent, and when I left them in the evening seemed to be happy enough. It poured during the whole night and on the next morning the poor wretches were very miserable. The rain had got into their tents and they were wet through in their shirts. I saw some of them afterwards as they got into Newcastle, and more miserable creatures I never beheld. They had had three days of unceasing rain,—and, as they said, no food for two days. This probably was an exaggeration;—but something had gone wrong with the commissariat and there had been no bread where bread was expected. When they reached Newcastle there was a river between them and their camping ground. In fine weather the ford is nearly dry; but now the water had risen up to a man's middle, and the poor fellows went through with their great coats on, too far gone in their misery to care for further troubles.

All along the road the little Inns and stores at which we stopped were kept by English people;—nor till I had passed Newcastle into the Transvaal did I encounter a Dutch Boer; but I learned that the farms around were chiefly held by them, and that the country generally is a Dutch country. Newcastle is a little town with streets and squares laid out, though the streets and squares are not yet built. But there is a decent Inn, at which a visitor gets a bedroom to himself and a tub in the morning;—at least such was my fate. And there is a billiard room and a table d'hote, and a regular bar. In the town there is a post office, and there are stores, and a Court House. There is a Dutch church and a Dutch minister,—and a clergyman of the Church of England, who however has no church, but performs service in the Court House.

Newcastle is the frontier town of the Natal Colony, and is nearly half-way between Pieter Maritzburg and Pretoria, the capital of the Transvaal. It is now being made a military station,—with the double purpose of overawing the Dutch Boers who have been annexed, and the Zulus who have not. The Zulus I think will prove to be the more troublesome of the two. A fort is being planned and bar racks are being built, but as yet the army is living under canvas. When we were there 250 men constituted the army; but the number was about to be increased. The poor fellows whom I had seen so wet through on the road were on their way to fill up deficiencies. We had hardly been an hour in the place before one of the officers rode down to call and to signify to us,—after the manner of British officers,—at what hour tiffin went on up at the mess, and at what hour dinner. There was breakfast also if we could cross the river and get up on the hill early enough. And, for the matter of that, there was a tent also, ready furnished, if we chose to occupy it. And there were saddle horses for us whenever we wanted them. The tiffins and the dinners and the saddle horses we took without stint. Everything was excellent; but that on which the mess prided itself most was the possession of Bass's bitter beer. An Englishman in outlandish places, when far removed from the luxuries to which he has probably been accustomed, sticks to his Bass more constantly than to any other home comfort. A photograph of his mother and sister,—or perhaps some other lady,—and his Bass, suffice to reconcile him to many grievances.

We stayed at Newcastle over a Sunday and went up to service in the camp. The army had its chaplain, and 150 men collected themselves under a marquee to say their prayers and hear a short sermon in which they were told to remember their friends at home, and to write faithfully to their mothers. I do not know whether soldiers in London and in other great towns are fond of going to church, but a church service such as that we heard is a great comfort to men when everything around them is desolate, and when the life which they lead is necessarily hard. We were only three nights at Newcastle, but when we went away we, seemed to be leaving old friends under the tents up on the hill.

I had come to the place on the mail cart, and on my arrival was very anxious to know what my travelling companion had done in the way of horse-buying. All my comfort for the next six weeks, and perhaps more than my comfort, depended on the manner in which he had executed his commission. It seemed now as though the rainy season had begun in very truth, for the waters for which everybody had been praying since I had landed in South Africa came down as though they would never cease to pour. On the day after our arrival I had got up to see the departure of the mail cart for Pretoria, and a more melancholy attempt at a public vehicle I had never beheld. Prophecies were rife that the horses would not be able to travel and that the miseries to be surmounted by the passengers before they reached their destination would be almost unendurable. When I saw the equipage I felt that the school of friends who had warned me against a journey to Pretoria in the mail carts had been right. I was extremely happy, therefore, when all the quidnuncs about the place, the butcher who had been travelling about the Colony in search of cattle for the last dozen years, the hotel-keeper who was himself in want of horses to take him over the same road, the commissariat employés, and all the loafers about the place, congratulated me on the team of which I was now the joint proprietor. There was a cart and four horses,—one of which however was a wicked kicker,—and complete harness, with a locker full of provisions to eke out the slender food to be found on the road,—all of which had cost £220. And there was a coloured driver, one George, whom everybody seemed to know, and who was able, as everybody said to drive us anywhere over Africa. George was to have £5 a month, his passage paid back home, his keep on the road, and a douceur on parting, if we parted as friends.

Remembering what I might have had to suffer,—what I might have been suffering at that very moment,—I expressed my opinion that the affair was very cheap. But my young friend indulged in grander financial views than my own. "It will be cheap," said he, "if we can sell it at the end of the journey, for £150." That was a contingency which I altogether refused to entertain. It had become cheap to me without any idea of a resale, as soon as I found what was the nature of the mail cart from Newcastle to Pretoria,—and what was the nature of the mail cart horses.

Before leaving the Colony of Natal I must say that at this Newcastle,—as at other Newcastles,—coal is to be found in abundance. I was taken down to the river side where I could see it myself. There can be no doubt but that when the country is opened up coal will be one of its most valuable products. At present it is all but useless. It cannot be carried because the distances are so great and the roads so bad; and it cannot be worked because labour has not been organised.

END OF VOLUME ONE

Index

P

Q

R

S

T

U

V

W

Y

Z

ALSO AVAILABLE FROM NONSUCH PUBLISHING

Anthony Trollope toured South Africa in 1877 and provides a fascinating account of his travels around a still untamed land at a time when British rule was being challenged by the native peoples. *South Africa* is an unrivalled account of the land and its people by a master writer. This second volume covers Trollope's travels in the Transvaal, Griqualand West, the Orange Free State and the Native Territories.

£10.00
ISBN 1-84588-048-X
224 pages

In 1795 Mungo Park set off at the tender age of 23 into the wilds of Africa with only local guides for company. *Travels* charts the course of his momentous attempt to chart the course of the River Niger, and records the perils and wonders he experienced on his travels. The book ends with an account of Park's second expedition from which he never returned.

£14.00
ISBN: 1-84588-068-4
288 pages, 10 illustrations

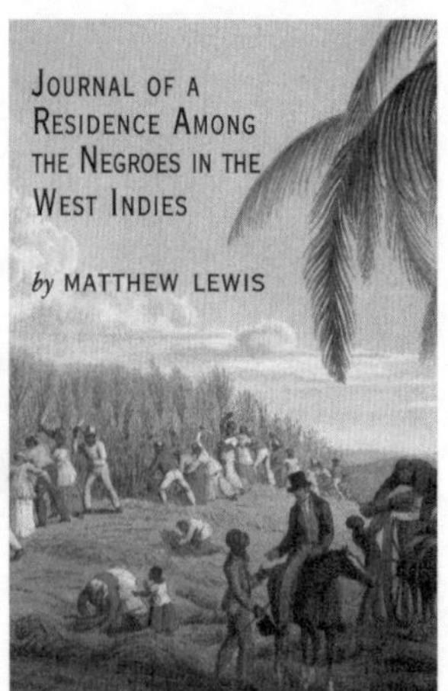

Journal of a Residence describes the author's visits to his estate on the island in 1815-1816 and 1817, after the abolition of the slave trade but before emancipation. Written in an engaging and witty style, Lewis' journal provides a fascinating account of life on a Jamaican sugar plantation during the period when the abolition of slavery in the British Empire was an important political issue.

£12.00
ISBN: 1-84588-037-4
192 pages

For sales information please see our website:
www.nonsuch-publishing.com